THE ALTERNATIVE

THE ALTERNATIVE

Towards a New Progressive Politics

Edited by Lisa Nandy MP, Caroline Lucas MP and Chris Bowers

Biteback Publishing

First published in Great Britain in 2016 by
Biteback Publishing Ltd
Westminster Tower
3 Albert Embankment
London SE1 7SP
Editorial and selection apparatus copyright © Lisa Nandy, Caroline Lucas
and Chris Bowers 2016

Copyright in the individual essays resides with the named authors.

Lisa Nandy, Caroline Lucas and Chris Bowers have asserted their
rights under the Copyright, Designs and Patents Act 1988 to

BRENT LIBRARIES	
EAL	
91120000321862	
Askews & Holts	31-Mar-2017
320.941	£12.99

...ced,
...any
....

This bool... e or otherwise,
be lent, re... prior consent in
any form o... without a similar
condit... purchaser.

Eve... of material
r... looked
the publishers would be glad to hear from them.

ISBN 978-1-78590-049-5

10 9 8 7 6 5 4 3 2 1

A CIP catalogue record for this book is available from the British Library.

Set in Bulmer by Adrian McLaughlin

Printed and bound in Great Britain by
CPI Group (UK) Ltd, Croydon CR0 4YY

CONTENTS

PREFACE

This book is the result of nine months of research, negotiation and compilation from late September 2015 to late June 2016. In the referendum held on 23 June, Britain voted to leave the European Union.

This book went to press exactly a week after the result was declared. We were able to make a few late alterations to allow for Britain's imminent exit from the EU, but with the political situation changing dramatically on a daily basis that week, no safe assumptions could be made about how the political situation might continue to evolve before the book was published. For example, we have worked on the basis of the next general election being in May 2020, as dictated by the Fixed Term Parliaments Act, but at time of going to press there was considerable speculation about an election taking place well before then.

We therefore ask the reader to bear in mind the shifting political sands against which we sent this book to press, and reiterate our belief that this new context only serves to underline its urgency and timeliness.

LN/CL/CB
29 June 2016

ACKNOWLEDGEMENTS

We would like to thank everyone who has inspired us to write this book and who have made contributions to it, some of them long-suffering victims caught between ultra-busy MPs and ultra-voracious book compilers. They are too numerous for us to mention them all, but they include, in alphabetical order: Paul Butters, Fiona Hall, Carl Harris, Magnus Haslebo, Julian Huppert, Ben Louvre, Rob Parsons and Ben Williams, plus Andrew Simms and David Boyle of the New Weather Institute and Neal Lawson of Compass.

We are also greatly indebted to the Joseph Rowntree Reform Trust, without whose support this book would not have been possible.

LN/CL/CB

EDITORS' INTRODUCTION

Lisa Nandy, Caroline Lucas & Chris Bowers

Many an inspiring initiative comes from a place of great darkness. Sometimes it's the very darkness that makes certain things that seemed fanciful or just a nice idea suddenly seem plausible, or at least worth a try. Other times the darkness creates the blank canvas on which new approaches and ideas find expression. The old adage about the darkest hour being just before dawn may not be astronomically accurate, but as a metaphor it's often true.

The 2015 general election was a very dark moment for those who believe in a more compassionate and participative approach to government in the UK. This was supposed to be the election in which the incumbent government was on a hiding to nothing. In the run-up to the 2010 election, the Governor of the Bank of England, Mervyn King, said that whichever party formed the government would have to take so many unpopular measures in the aftermath of the 'credit crunch' of 2007–08 that 'it would be out of power for a generation'. And yet the Conservatives won, Labour did badly, and the Liberal Democrats, who had presented themselves as a brake on the extremism of the Conservatives in government, were hammered.

Against this background, it would be easy to assume that an initiative by a Labour MP, a Green MP and a moderately prominent Liberal Democrat to form a new force among the progressives of British politics would be one of desperation. That would be wrong. True, many progressives did wonder why policies on the economy, immigration and welfare that promoted a kinder Britain did not convince enough of the public to vote for them. And many progressives did suffer from a form of despondency and desperation for something better amidst the wreckage of their 2015 electoral fortunes, coupled with a fear that the Conservatives will win again next time round.

But no. This book is not motivated by any sense of despair. We are not proposing cooperation among the progressives because we have to, but because we want to. Quite simply, we believe that political pluralism delivers better answers and better government; and that a progressive alliance, speaking to different constituencies about a shared agenda of social, environmental and democratic reform, united in a commitment to create a fairer, more sustainable Britain, to rebuild our democracy and safeguard our public sector, would have an attractive force and political reach that no one party alone could have today.

We can happily talk of two broad movements – the progressives and the conservatives – but in an era where people have a choice of at least half a dozen realistic parties, we either seek consensus across party lines where there is broad philosophical agreement, or we ignore the views of many committed citizens and, as a result, face the chilling prospect of Tory rule for a generation, with all the social and environmental destruction that would accompany it.

There is nothing inevitable about social progress, as the rise of the right across Europe grimly demonstrates. The gloom of the 2015 election and 2016 referendum results gives us both the space to explore this – and the urgency to address it.

The first-past-the-post electoral system, based around two dominant political parties, simply does not deliver results that serve the UK in the twenty-first century. In the middle of the last century this arrangement was still relatively functional – there were two parties, largely representing the two classes of British society, and 95 per cent of the votes went to either Labour or the Conservatives. In fact, in the 1955 election, 96.1 per cent of the votes were cast for one of these two parties, which shared 622 of the then 630 seats between them. British society is much more fluid these days, yet we still run our elections according to this system that over-represents the two biggest parties and dramatically under-represents the smaller ones, and the effect of this on our political debate is to shrink a conversation when there is a growing clamour to expand it.

We are in a different place now. In economic terms, those with purchasing power have vastly more choice than they did in the 1940s and 1950s, when post-war austerity limited the availability of goods, and people's ability to buy them. As a result, we have come to expect greater choice and control. In politics, affiliation has become much more fluid, with voters increasingly likely to switch between parties at elections, and with new technology offering many more citizens the ability to be heard in the political debate. We live in a networked society, and a world that is infinitely more complex and nuanced than it was in 1955.

But politics has not responded. In recent decades, nation states have been at times unable, and too often unwilling, to shape the forces of globalisation, technology and individualisation in our shared interest. The dominance of global capital has changed the face of our high streets – enabling astonishing rates of poverty to co-exist with extraordinary levels of wealth in one of the world's richest countries – and has done little to deal with intractable problems facing many young people: unemployment, high housing costs and debt. New forms of technology have proven themselves a force for both good and ill. A new financial crash is threatened, and the realities of climate change, the dwindling of scarce resources and the challenges associated with movement of people are ever more apparent.

And yet these concerns are not effectively addressed by, or represented in, our politics. If we can imagine tourism in space, why not a change to our economic and political order here on earth?

It doesn't have to be like this. We believe the growing discontent with the current political settlement offers not just a threat but an opportunity. New technology has brought with it new challenges, with its downsides of personal bullying, misogyny and far-reaching state surveillance, as well as the prospect of people losing paid work because of advances in technology. But, at its best, it has sparked political and social change across the world, offering millions more people a meaningful voice. With that voice comes the chance to bring into being the structure and tools of a society based on compassion and equality, as well as dealing with resentments caused by social developments that certainly look unfair and often are. But vested interests in politics, the media and the business world stand in the way of this society, and will be remarkably hard to dislodge.

The scale of that challenge was laid bare by the 2015 general election result. The Conservatives won an overall majority of twelve seats in the House of Commons on the basis of just 24.4 per cent of eligible voters. And they look set to use that power not to make the 2020 general election fairer, but to enact a redrawing of constituency boundaries that will make it easier for the Tories to strengthen their parliamentary representation. One estimate suggests Labour would need to win back more than 100 seats in order to form a majority government.

This was the most disproportionate result in British election history. Votes for the two largest parties came to just 67.3 per cent of the total votes cast. The Greens and UKIP won nearly 5 million votes but received just two seats between them. Labour saw their vote share increase while their number of seats collapsed. The Conservatives won an overall majority on a minority of the vote, while, despite winning 8 per cent of the vote, the Liberal Democrats lost nearly all their seats. The SNP won 50 per cent of the Scottish vote share, but 95 per cent of Scottish seats.

Increasingly, people are being denied a voice by the political system, a situation that is neither just nor sustainable. There is an urgent need for cooperation between progressives, whether only for the 2020 election or in an ongoing arrangement. A striking feature of the 2015 election was how many people were left with a Conservative MP they didn't want because the progressive vote was split. At times, the difference between progressive candidates is profound, but often the differences between many Labour, Lib Dem and Green candidates are far smaller than the differences between figures who are at home in the Conservative Party. If people like Ken Clarke and Iain Duncan Smith can co-exist in the same party, then for Labour, Lib Dems and Greens to be fighting each other creates at best an uneven playing field between progressives and Conservatives, and at worst is political sabotage. Progressives have to be smarter about the way we do politics.

This is why the central theme of this book is how the progressives can work together. We do not pretend it will be easy, but it's vital that any new politics is based on putting power back in the hands of people. For that reason we are advocating electoral reform to give us all a genuine voice in the political system, not just the floating voters in the marginal constituencies, while recognising that all electoral systems have pros and cons. Crucially, reform must not happen at the cost of more power landing in the committee rooms of party elites. That's why Katie Ghose's essay on electoral reform (page 273) looks at all possible systems of electing the Westminster Parliament and tests them against various criteria, one of which is whether they genuinely do give power to the people, rather than the parties. Significantly, there are signs that within Labour the debate about electoral reform is back on the table, with an increasing number of Labour MPs from all sides of the party backing proportional representation.

But we are looking to do more than just ensure people are genuinely represented by the electoral system. We want to build a bridge between the growing number of people who are politically active without being members of a political party, and the political system. Whether it's online campaigns like 38 Degrees, Avaaz and Change.org, or direct forms of protest to save hospitals, housing or jobs, our ambition is to enlist their help in confronting the difficult choices politics often presents, and to ensure that they are heard and represented from the town hall to Westminster. And we want to learn from recent ways in which people who have felt alienated by the political system have been enabled and inspired to reconnect, like the campaigners in the 2014 Scottish referendum who reached out to people at job centres, and the charities that are helping people with literacy and income barriers to breach the digital divide. A new form of politics is needed if the disconnect between everyday reality and how we are governed is not to grow. This is explored in Indra Adnan's essay on what future there is for political parties (page 253) and Zoe Williams's ideas on creating the space for change (page 290).

There is a surge of optimistic political movements afoot. Podemos in Spain and The Alternative in Denmark are among the most prominent, but there are similar elements in movements in Italy, Greece, Iceland and even aspects of American politics. Out of the despair that traditional politics is failing, new movements are emerging that rekindle people's imagination. We're delighted to have Uffe Elbæk, the leader of The Alternative, among our contributors (page 237) and particularly value his reflections about the conditions that enabled his new party to break into Danish politics so dramatically.

Unfortunately, while some of these movements may influence their government, they will have difficulty making up the government themselves. This is why we are exploring cross-party cooperation among the progressives in the hope of creating a force that can genuinely bring imaginative, sustainable and socially equitable policies to fruition. But for that to happen, there will need to be a change of thinking. There is no point people talking about a realignment in politics if there is not first a deeper realignment of minds.

THE TERM 'PROGRESSIVE'

As the word 'progressive' is a central part of this book, we feel we need to set out what we mean by this and, by extension, who the progressives actually are.

Traditionally, political activity has been defined in terms of left, right and centre, with right denoting the state playing a minimalist role in society and the economy, left denoting the state playing a much bigger role, and centre being a compromise. In those terms, we are talking about those who would classify themselves as 'centre', 'centre-left' or 'left'. But such terms are also inadequate in today's complex world. Where does the 'radical' who wants change 'from the roots' fit in with a linear categorisation of politics? Where are the environmentally aware who believe in building a sustainable future but who may differ among themselves over whether to rely more on markets and pricing instruments, or more on state regulation? And where does the 'left/right' scale leave people who believe passionately that the state should *ensure* the provision of various services but aren't convinced the state should necessarily *provide* those services?

This is why we are keen to group those seeking fairer, more sustainable outcomes with a term that encapsulates that better society. Of all the terms on offer, 'progressive' seems the most appropriate.

The word is not without problems. Few people would say they were against progress, but we wish to see progress in a bigger context. There has been a lot of progress over the past century, notably on race, gender and working conditions. This should be celebrated, but we still have chronic and entrenched problems, and even where we have made progress there have been side effects we should not simply accept. Despite medical advances, air pollution is still killing thousands of people prematurely each year and the power of food multinationals means we stuff our bodies with junk. We create equal opportunities for women but still find forty years later that more than 1,000 women are killed or injured annually by male domestic violence, and glass ceilings persist that limit women's potential for promotion. And while basic educational standards in the UK's schools have clearly improved, that progress is undermined when large numbers of teenagers leave school with little prospect of a secure job, and the gap between minimum and maximum incomes yawns ever wider. The word 'progressive' has to mean progress overall, and not a way of swapping one problem for a different one.

A number of thinkers have tried to define 'progressive', and many are covered in the essay by the chess-champion-turned-philosopher Jonathan Rowson (page 157). To us, if 'progressive' is to mean anything, it has to empower and trust citizens, not to the point where some can run riot at other people's expense and not to the point where the state cannot defend itself from terrorist threats or play its part in international defence forces, but where everyone has much greater control both over their own destiny and in shaping the society in which they live. To this end we offer this three-paragraph definition:

> Progressives want to move beyond the current system and create a better one. We continue in the tradition of those who ended slavery, won votes for women, built our welfare state, and fought for the protection of our environment. Progressives believe in cooperation. We want a supportive and responsive state that brings the best out of people's instinct to share success and support each other in hard times, and which offers genuine equality to all citizens, together with social justice, civil liberties, human rights and responsibilities, without discrimination on grounds of gender, age, physical ability, race or sexual orientation.
>
> •
>
> Progressives are, by definition, radicals. We reimagine the way our society and our economy works from the bottom up. We wish to reform the socially isolating and environmentally degrading mainstream economics that has dominated our political discourse for several decades. While wealth

creation is important, we need fairer and more effective ways of distributing the fruits of that wealth so that everyone benefits. We therefore want power and wealth redistributed, and corporations regulated, in order to empower citizens to work together to build fair and resilient communities for generations to come.

•

Progressives come from many ideological positions – including socialists, liberals, feminists, ecologists – and none. We share a rejection of the politics of fear and division, and wish to move towards a more inclusive society in which every citizen not only has the opportunity to develop themselves to their full potential but has as much control as possible over their own destiny and the chance to shape the society in which they live. This way we believe we will build a society that both empowers people and allows us to live within environmental limits.

•

We are not claiming this as the ultimate definition of 'progressive'; and certainly fighting over what 'progressive' means won't improve the lot of the jobless single parent who relies on food banks, or take us any closer to keeping temperature rises within limits that will tackle climate change. It is simply that, if we use the word as the core term of this book and seek to build a new cooperation among progressives to offer a better chance of imaginative ideas being put into practice at government level, we have to have a definition. It was also important to have a definition of 'progressive' to enable John Curtice to write his essay – our in-house reality check (page 186) – on how much the British public will vote for the ideas we believe in.

Of course, once we have a definition, people will question who falls into it, and whether they can work together. These too are difficult issues.

There are plenty of people in the Labour, Liberal Democrat and Green Parties who baulk at the idea of working with people in the other two. Many Lib Dems and Greens question whether Labour is a progressive party, and wonder whether it simply represents a different form of conservatism to the Tories. Plenty of Labour people feel the same way about the Scottish Nationalists. Many Labour people have spent their lives fighting the Lib Dems, and wouldn't even want to be in the same lifeboat as them; years of frustration with the Lib Dems and Greens for what many in Labour perceive as too little attention paid to material deprivation and inequality, and an unwillingness to confront the difficult choices of government, do not disappear overnight. Many Greens feel Labour has not been radical enough on tackling inequality and poverty, and mistrust Labour's commitment to the environment after Labour's years of viewing 'green' issues as a luxury, middle-class pursuit. Many Lib Dems insist they are not liberals as a form of anti-Toryism but are radicals who are neither red nor blue; some of these are 'economic liberals' whose apparent comfort and ease in working with the Conservatives while in coalition has raised questions among many progressives about the extent to which they share the same progressive values. And many in Labour do not share the Lib Dems' and Greens' enthusiasm for electoral reform, which for the Lib Dems and Greens is a holy grail. Suffice to say, there is plenty of historical tribalism in progressives' ranks yet to be overcome.

For these reasons and more, we are not suggesting mergers between the progressive parties, or even a coalition. Just because socially and environmentally aware Tories can exist under the same roof as

Eurosceptic, no-state-interference right-wingers – although the tensions in that arrangement are becoming ever more plain to see – it doesn't mean the centre-left and left-wing parties need to be under their own single roof. But, in order to compete on roughly equal terms, they do need to focus on what unites them as well as what divides them, and on when and how they can cooperate in their common interest.

No one party can hope to have a monopoly on the progressive vote. Moreover, building a new political culture based on cooperation, where parties have core values in common, goes beyond electoral interest. We believe that the process of challenging and learning from each other can itself lead to better outcomes. And if our aim is a better society, this society cannot be built on foundations that allow some voices to be heard and not others. A progressive future will be one negotiated with others, not imposed by one group. This will mean being willing to listen to voices that say things we don't want to hear. As progressives, we are entitled to dislike or even despise what parties like UKIP espouse, and to disagree with their proposed policy solutions, but as progressives we also need to understand the anger and frustration that often drives people to vote for them. Indeed, we should see it as a sign of our collective failure and recognise that it provides yet another impetus for working together to better convince the public that there is a credible alternative to the politics of divisiveness and hate.

WORKING TOGETHER WON'T BE EASY

The three of us came together four months after the 2015 election. The seed of this book was sown in the small hours of 8 May, when two of us, Chris Bowers and Caroline Lucas, sat in the Brighton

Centre awaiting the count of the Brighton Pavilion constituency. We were two like-minded progressive candidates who were fighting each other, a particularly futile exercise in retrospect given that we disagreed on relatively little, certainly environmentally and socially. But even with the Greens' impending victory, the sense of gloom was palpable when we spoke to each other at about 6 a.m. and agreed that the overall result we were mourning would happen again and again if the progressives didn't work together.

The third member of our editing trio, Lisa Nandy, had just defended her Wigan seat as a mother of eight days' standing. She had become frustrated at being defined by who she disagreed with rather than by what she stood for. She became convinced that finding common ground across party boundaries was an essential component of good decision-making, and that different parties representing largely the same philosophy but with differences of emphasis presented a challenge that should make overall outcomes better, not a reason to beat each other to a political pulp.

Four months later the three of us sat round a table at Westminster and drew up the concept for this book. We wanted to work out an optimistic vision for Britain, one that has at its core both an abhorrence of the level of poverty and material inequality in one of the richest countries in the world, and an urgent need to live within our environmental means. In some parts of the country, half of all children grow up without enough food to eat or decent clothes to wear. For too many of us, work no longer pays enough to live on. The post-war contract – that if you work hard and do your bit you'll be rewarded – is broken. In 2016, it is still the case that the circumstances of our parents' lives are the biggest determinant of our own. This situation is neither acceptable nor sustainable. We know that most progressive thinkers share these views, so we wanted to nurture the vision and give all progressives – regardless of which party they are in – a stake in bringing it to fruition.

The cooperation across party lines that is such a staple of the European Parliament is a foreign language in the British political system. That has to change. So, while the three of us don't agree on everything (including certain compromises we had to make to get this chapter and the final one of this book written), we do believe in working together on those issues where there is sufficient consensus to get things done, and towards a new progressive politics that empowers people and presents a compelling vision of Britain post-2020. That's why the idea of some form of cooperation among the progressives is a fundamentally optimistic one, regardless of this book being born out of the disappointment of the 2015 election result.

And party politics is far from dead. Even for his most ardent critics, the phenomenon of Jeremy Corbyn's leadership campaign in the summer of 2015 cannot be underestimated. Corbyn stood in the Labour leadership election hoping to broaden the policy debate. As a rank outsider, he attracted the required number of nominations to make the ballot paper with only seconds to spare. And yet his campaign tapped into a rich seam of latent political interest, particularly among younger people who felt alienated from the political system, and he romped to an emphatic victory in the first round of voting. In the four months following the 2015 general election, Labour recruited an astonishing 400,000 new members. Regardless of political leanings and individual judgements about his leadership qualities, the surge of interest Corbyn created is a force that has to be harnessed by those seeking a more compassionate Britain. At the very least, the questions Corbyn raised in his campaign have to be at the heart of progressive thinking. One of those questions concerned what public ownership of common assets and resources should mean in a globalised world, and we are pleased to have a Labour MP and a Lib Dem MP, Steve Reed and Norman Lamb, cooperating to write the essay on a new approach to public services (page 44).

The Liberal Democrats may have a long period of wound-licking ahead of them after the drubbing they took, but there is some light at the end of their tunnel. They increased their membership by 20,000 in the four months after May 2015, they are still strong in local government, which is frequently the foundation on which success in parliamentary elections is built, and they are the clear challenger to the Conservatives in a number of Westminster seats. The Greens increased their membership by 40,000 in the months after May 2015, and with the environmental imperative becoming ever more urgent, their support – if not their representation – continues to grow.

We are keen to explore the experiences in Scotland and Wales, especially in light of the Scottish National Party's remarkable performance in the 2015 election, built on the back of a phenomenal surge in people joining the SNP that saw the party's membership expand fivefold in less than a year. Regardless of one's stance on independence for Scotland or Wales, there are lessons in how to inspire people to develop a confidence in politics that stem from the 2014 Scottish independence referendum, which are set out with eloquence and passion by Mhairi Black and Chris Law (page 141). The essay by the Plaid MP Jonathan Edwards (page 63) makes the case for an end to a one-size-fits-all approach to regeneration, arguing that a government that sets the framework for an imaginative and creative regeneration programme based on specific local attributes would be making a profound and tangible contribution to narrowing the gap between the poorest and the rest.

IT CAN BE DONE!

The differences between the progressive parties will be easy to highlight. This is why Section One of the book is devoted to essays on the values, ideas and policies that we believe have the potential to unite progressives in all parties. We have a wide range of contributors representing a broad range of opinions, and the opinions of one writer do not necessarily represent the views of other writers, nor the views of the three co-editors. Indeed, some writers had to overcome a certain resistance to being featured in the same book as others. But that's part of the project – we need to seek common ground in order to define ourselves not just by who we disagree with but by what we believe in (even though this may be a harder sell to the electorate).

There will be some deep-seated disagreements to overcome. And even after exploring the policies and values that have broad support across the progressives, the crucial question remains: can practical cooperation actually happen? This is why the main focus of this book is Section Two on how the progressives can work together. It includes an essay by Duncan Brack (page 202) on what lessons can be learned from past cooperation, one from Andrew George (page 301) that sets out different potential mechanisms for cooperation, and one from Carys Afoko (page 318) on how we need to rethink the ways we communicate our vision to a sceptical and often detached public. There will be difficult questions to answer, some of which we explore in our concluding chapter. There are no right or wrong answers, but on one thing we are all united: whatever form cooperation takes, it must be built on the contribution of grass roots members and must not continue to concentrate power in the hands of party elites.

It can be done! We are not talking about a new party – we respect the traditional parties. But neither are we assuming everyone in the Labour, Lib Dem and Green Parties will be with us. Some won't like to be thought of as progressives, but others who are not currently part of the political system will. Some will talk of a realignment of political parties, but what we are seeking is a deeper realignment of minds to underpin the political change we advocate. No one has all the wisdom, but in a world as complex and rich as ours we need a political system that can offer an equally complex and rich response. To change our world we first have to change ourselves – and that is within our own grasp.

On one level all is gloom. The Conservatives are in office with a majority, Britain appears to be heading out of the EU. Austerity continues, climate change accelerates. The progressives are spread about the political battlefield, often more intent on fighting each other than on using their power and influence smartly. But things can change, and quickly. Old tribal loyalties that are blind to the good in others can easily die away, enabling people to find their voice and their power, as new technology enables new solidarities to emerge at speed and scale. And the more we find markets that are too free and states that are too remote and thus unable to deliver what society needs, the more there will be added motivation for the progressives to work together.

We might perhaps ask ourselves a couple of questions: is the country we want for our children really going to be created by the politics of their great-great-grandparents? And do we seriously believe we can address the threats we face as a society and a planet by using mechanisms that leave around three-quarters of the voting public feeling disenfranchised and lacking any meaningful say in who forms their government? If we don't, those who carry the hope for a better society, created by a better form of political governance, will have to be smart about the way they act over the next few years.

Ultimately we are looking to foster a belief in the best of people in other progressive parties (and none), not the worst. For many who have taken comfort over many years in tribal certainties, it will mean moderating their view of who the enemy is. And if we really want to enhance the practical prospects for compassionate social policies, respect for human dignity and ambitious action to tackle environmental threats, it *has* to be done. But for it to happen, the progressives will have to put aside at least some of their differences and work out a strategy that may not satisfy every aspiration, but that will be a lot more effective and more hopeful than the tired party politics of business-as-usual.

The process to find common cause and create the change this country needs is already beginning. With this book, we are setting out the prize to be won, identifying ways to address the practical challenges along the way, and – most urgently – calling on the progressives in British politics to get stuck in!

Lisa Nandy, Caroline Lucas & Chris Bowers

June 2016

SECTION ONE

PROGRESSIVE VALUES AND POLITICS

BUILDING A GOOD SOCIETY: AN ARGUMENT FOR RADICAL HOPE

Neal Lawson

There is a fine line between hope and wishful thinking. Wishful thinking is blind and blinkered. It believes that belief is enough, that history is on our side, and all that's required to bring about change is loyalty and endeavour. Hope is similar but ultimately altogether different. Hope is utopian, wistful even, but radiates, energises and directs us precisely because it is grounded in an instinct and an analysis that allows the desirable to become feasible. Hope is based on a realistic assessment of what is possible – the challenges, threats and opportunities we face. Why, despite so much of the evidence to the contrary, should progressives be hopeful today? Indeed, how does what's happening today help define what it is to be a progressive and what is to be done by progressives?

We live in two very different worlds at exactly the same time. We need to understand both and adjust our political strategy accordingly if we are to create a good society through a progressive alliance.

Let's start in world one, where we mostly are but don't want to be. In this world we have one foot in the past and it clamps us into a cycle of political failure. Whatever your stripe of progressivism – red, green, social, liberal, national and/or democratic – we are all locked into old ways of thinking and doing. It's the politics of 'one more heave', 'another throw of the dice', more doing the same thing and expecting a different outcome. Nearly always we position ourselves, our own little tribe, as better than the other progressive tribes, and grumble 'if only they would see the light and vote for us!' It is a world in which deciding who is not with, and therefore against us, is key. A world of purity, where betrayal, and the easy excuses that come with it, lies just around the corner. We forget who the real opponents are and never take on our real enemy: a system that is not just remorselessly burning parts of the planet while flooding others, but everywhere stretching social bonds to tearing point by guaranteeing not only that the rich get richer but also that with it they become more powerful, thus ensuring we can't even envisage an alternative, let alone create it. It's not that a good society doesn't feel feasible in this world; increasingly we can't even comprehend it as a commonly held desire. Mrs Thatcher spoke of 'TINA' (There Is No Alternative). Was she right, and has she won?

Sometimes it feels like it. The day-to-day, the immediate, the local and the purely reactive sap our energy and deflect us into comfort zones of action and activity that change very little. It's the politics of some small victories but ultimately of gradual retreat. As one activist has said, 'Goldman Sachs doesn't care if you raise chickens.' The idea that without politics a cacophony of little local actions will turn into a symphony of transformation, up against mighty global, corporate behemoths, is wishful thinking. As is the belief that any single party can, on its own, wield power and usher in a good society – in opposition to every other progressive not in their tribe. This world, based on very twentieth-century notions of hierarchy, predictability and controllability, and therefore the potential rule by one party, is being eroded fast by complexity and diversity, but also, of course, insecurity and anxiety.

Let's leave that world behind for a while and step into the other world in which we already co-exist. In this 'other' world, our lives reflect a much greater sense of joy and fulfilment. It is a world of connections and contact, of individual and collective action at a local and global level. Just stop and think about what you can achieve with a smartphone in your hand and a Wi-Fi connection. We can speak to anyone in the world about anything. We can find out which people in our community share our interests and concerns. In this world, injustice, through leaks and whistle-blowers, has no hiding place and the means to do something about it is at our fingertips. Obviously a political dimension is still needed, but that too can become more effective in a connected world.

In this world, we believe change is possible and we make it so. Accelerated by new technology, organising is now ridiculously easy. We can now express our solidarity with infinite ease at home and abroad. We sign, share, collaborate and co-create. And we begin to develop our potential as human beings as we become more aware of each other, of the planet and of other animals and species. We recognise in ourselves the need to create, to innovate, to express and to share. From solidarity with asylum seekers at home, to concern for the ice caps abroad, from Kickstarter to Avaaz, we are becoming local and global citizens. From the physical to the spiritual, people are pushing beyond old boundaries – both alone and together.

But there is a shadow side to this more joyous world. We are better informed than ever, but also more overwhelmed with data than ever. We can have video calls with our kids on their gap-year treks through Asia, but too frequently find ourselves in echo chambers. While we can connect with consummate ease, we can disconnect just as easily. And some struggle with the cost of being a digital actor.

Of course, all this hope and fear, the frustration and the realisation, co-exist at once in the same world. We experience them simultaneously with all the contradictions and paradoxes that must abound when an old world is dying and the new has not yet been born. And to continue the phraseology of the Italian politician and philosopher Antonio Gramsci, in this interregnum morbid symptoms abound. Nigel Farage or Donald Trump, anyone?

All of this is as complex as it is paradoxical. But if we stop to think about it, the second world has the potential to help us reshape and move beyond the first, and to help set an optimistic and predominantly progressive political trend in the future.

THE COLLAPSE OF THE LAST PROGRESSIVE WORLD

The world we defend today against the onslaught of market fundamentalism was created around the midpoint of the last century in the years after the Second World War. It was an optimistic new world, born out of a world divided – divided into tribes, classes and parties. Its intentions were good but it became a model of big, top-down, statist government; well-meaning, but ultimately elitist and paternalistic. It was progressive politics done *to* people and not *with* people. As such it was always going to struggle to create and sustain a good society.

But the progressive world of the mid-twentieth century was not just the invention of Clement Attlee and his colleagues in the 1945–51 Labour government. They helped create this progressive if paternalistic society but in effect were ultimately playing the role of site foreman, working to architects' plans drawn up over the previous decades. Its realisation was the culmination of what David Marquand calls 'a 100-year conversation' and what Paul Addison describes in his book *The Road to 1945* as 'the rich melting pot of ideas and activism well beyond a single party or ism'. It took the trade unions, the Methodist and guild socialists, the friendly societies, cooperatives, mutuals and building societies, the left-wing book clubs and the socialist clarion cycling clubs to make it happen. It was founded not just on the ideas of Labour thinkers but more importantly on social Liberals such as Keynes and Beveridge, and even Tories like Butler and Quintin Hogg (it was Hogg, later Lord Hailsham, who coined the term 'social security'). History is made not so much by the surfer but by the wave.

But it couldn't last. Once the post-war austerity gave way to growing prosperity, the sense of the collective began to be eroded by the desire of individuals for a greater sense of freedom. Choice, not conformity, became the cultural order of the day. The rich complexity that created that mid-century progressive alliance was gradually undermined and even painted in a bad light due to the predominance of its statism. The big and the bureaucratic, the centre and the technocratic – this all seemed a burden as the instinct for individualism and identity took hold in the 1960s. And the certainties of social class – reflected in Labour and Conservatives sharing all but a handful of votes and seats in the 1945, 1950, 1951 and 1955 elections – started to dissolve. Tribal affinities started to loosen and the days of two parties getting 98 per cent of the vote were gone for good.

The rest is history. The centre could not hold, at least not for long. It began to unravel, as much in the Soviet Union at first, and eventually in the social democracies of the West. The instinct for individualism and identity and the break-up of class forces stripped the progressive ethos of the crucial ingredient of agency. A new 'common sense' took hold, based on the view that the desire for individual betterment was seen to be a more legitimate aspiration than the pursuit of the common good. Progressives were on the back foot and have remained there ever since.

If a progressive economic strategy had been able to contain the recurrent crises of capitalism, it might have survived, but it couldn't. By the mid-1950s, progressives foolishly believed the political and economic job was effectively done, that the only task was to share the proceeds of capitalist growth in a mixed economy. Environmental limits and Thatcherism smashed that naive assumption, and out of it grew the aggressive creed of neoliberalism, a creed that sought to undermine the political and social basis for progressive politics and created the assumption that the only answer to an economic crisis was a new era of austerity to last until the books balanced.

We now live in the wreckage of that project. New Labour was an attempt to recreate a progressive society at the height of the Thatcher/neoliberal demolition work. For a while it did some good – around public investment and temporarily stemming the tide of inequality – but it failed as a political project because it looked only at the symptoms of excessive free markets and never built the political capital to deal with the causes. If the real test of progressive politics is not what it does for people but how it shifts the balances of forces away from the already powerful to the powerless, then it failed. Its big-tent approach tried to cram everyone into one space on terms dictated by a few at the top. It could last while the economy kept growing but had been long discredited before the spectacular success of Jeremy Corbyn in Labour's 2015 leadership election.

Today there is no going back to this past, either the paternalistic society developed under Attlee or the sticking of plasters over wounds caused by excessive free markets under Blair. Neither is feasible nor desirable. Instead, we must turn to the future.

RADICAL HOPE FROM AND FOR THE PEOPLE

Karl Marx may not have been everyone's idea of a progressive, but he had the magical insight that the economic base, and the way we make things and make things happen, shapes the rest of our social institutions. On this basis we could say that the factory defined the twentieth century. A word commonly used to describe the twentieth-century model of economic growth and its associated social order is 'Fordism' – after the big car factories set up by Henry Ford that divided up labour and put everyone in their place on the production line. Governments and other bodies ran in the same linear and organised fashion. It was a style of governance that meant well and for a while was effective.

But if there's a lesson from the collapse of the well-intentioned progressive model of the mid-twentieth century, it's that a good society can't be created by top-down and elitist means. We can never separate how we do things with the results they create. Means always shape ends. A good society requires the resources and legitimacy of the state but in service to people acting individually and collectively in the knowledge of the interdependence between what's good for society and what's good for them.

The good society is one that *we* create, it cannot be something that is done to us. Radical hope comes from the insight that the way we make things and make things happen in the twenty-first century allows the means and ends of a good society to be aligned.

Today, we are beyond even post-Fordism, which saw the break-up of single factories into smaller, just-in-time production sites and creative worker circles – with much of the work outsourced and scattered across the globe. Today, production is defined by even more diverse networks and clusters of companies and suppliers who compete and collaborate at the very same time. The building blocks of the last progressive era are gone for good.

However, the shift to an age of digital networks is doing two things, both of which are vital to progressives.

First, it is monopolising wealth around a few big multinational corporations like Google, Apple, Facebook and the finance sector. The upshot is the creation of a growing cohort who have no material interest in the survival of the system. The young have no hope of a secure job but have mountains of debt and little prospect of a home to rent or buy. This precariat, which arguably extends into an increasingly insecure middle class, creates the emerging social bloc for a progressive politics.

Second, the networked society is dispersing power to these people – allowing them to know, talk, learn, speak, join up and organise. And it is the nature, not just the scale, of this activity that is of interest to us as progressives.

For what is happening is that old hierarchies are disintegrating so that everyone has a more equal voice, where no one is inherently superior or inferior. Yes, we must ensure that everyone has access to the technology and is at ease with the new digital culture, but this 'flatter' structure makes possible, but does not guarantee, more egalitarian and democratic ways of operating, and therefore more egalitarian and democratic outcomes. If we all have a voice and a say – if we all have a sense of ourselves, can all organise and protest, build and dream together – then this potentially unites means and ends. We can only create the good society in a good way. And along the way, a new historic agent of change is created – no longer one defined solely by class but instead by being a networked citizen.

Thus progressives can hope to bend modernity to progressive values and not, as Labour did in the past, bend progressive values to either the remote state or, more recently, the free market.

Such a flatter or 'horizontal' culture doesn't mean that hierarchies or 'vertical' cultures are obsolete. We still need the state for many vital functions, like public finance, defence and environmental protection, and as a benign agent for society to function efficiently. That means we will still need political parties, both to represent different ways of doing things and to take responsibility for putting ideas into practice in governments (locally, nationally and globally).

We are only at the outer edges of this new digital age that will change our lives and society as much as every other technological revolution. The biggest factor at play here is the rate and extent at which new technology will displace jobs. This is an old fear with every new wave of technology, but even though the boy cries wolf, it doesn't mean he doesn't eventually get eaten alive. Every prediction says there will be a huge net loss of jobs due to algorithms, big data, robots, artificial intelligence, 3D printing and the rest. It's not a single technology that will eat up manual and white-collar jobs, but a unique combination of them. If Marx was right that our economic base and the way we make things shapes our social institutions, then it's fairly safe to say the twenty-first century will be defined by the internet and networked technology – and thus by the sentiment of Facebook and not the factory.

Progressives need to embrace this future, not fight it. Progressives always do well when they own the future: 1906, 1945, 1964 and, to some extent, even 1997. We must stop defending dreary, soul-destroying work and instead have a different conception of the good life – where we work, create, play and have time to care. Of course, we have to eat – but that will be determined by our skill in sharing and redistributing the productivity gains of the technological revolution so that everyone shares, not just a few Silicon Valley billionaires. Ideas like a universal basic income and a shorter working week must become the central planks of a new progressive politics.

One of the upsides to this revolution in how we produce and live is that it can cut our carbon footprint. Digitisation involves less energy than the first industrial revolution and we must conceive of a life that isn't based on buying things we didn't know we needed, with money we don't have, to impress people we don't know. No one dies wishing they owned more stuff. We die wishing we had more time with the people we love, to have lived a life that left the world in a better place than we found it. This is the kind of human insight that should guide our vision of a progressive future.

Great care has been taken here to describe what could happen, but there is no preordained future. History is never on our side, but at different moments it can be made more or less kind to us. While the trend might be towards a flatter and more connected world – with all that implies for progressive politics – there are dangerous factors that risk undermining progress. Social media allows both the creation of the Arab Spring and the vilification of anyone who doesn't agree with us. It empowers and liberates us while simultaneously creating these global digital behemoths. It sets us free – and puts us under constant surveillance.

But while these contradictions and tensions are real, we need to focus on the predominant trends towards greater awareness and connectivity. And, anyway, whatever we think of the technology, it is largely given. It cannot be undone. We shape it or it shapes us. So the question is, can we adapt it to our progressive values better than the right can? The answer to that question will depend on whether we can be smarter about our politics.

45-DEGREE POLITICS

Cooperation among the progressives – whether formally in the shape of an alliance for government or informally on an issue-by-issue basis – is not really a deal between progressive party leaders (although that might help). It is a state of mind, a sentiment, a culture, a way of seeing and being that holds within it the seeds and the hope of a good society. It comes primarily not from the top but from the bottom. Yes, it can and must be accelerated by the parties and, through them, the state, but it will grow from the new cooperatives, the sharing economy, the world of peer-to-peer activity, in civil society and purposeful companies, social enterprises and NGOs. The job of the politicians is to create the spaces and the platforms to help incubate, protect and grow these progressive new practices. Transformative moments never come only from the top down and cannot be sustained from there. Instead, they must emerge from everywhere.

The progressive politics of the future will have to recognise the need for both the vertical – party structures that allow for the effective and democratic management of the state and its resources – and the horizontal – the myriad civil society and social institutions that will eventually make this a progressive century. Indeed, they are already starting this process. The meeting point of the two is what we can call '45-Degree Politics' – the point between traditional governance and modern-day activism in all its forms. This fault line is the space progressives must understand, own and occupy if we are to shape the future of a politics that is of and for the people.

A realignment of votes and parties is essential, quite simply because – for all their valid differences – Labour, the Liberal Democrats and the Greens need each other. In the last century, change was possible through single-party domination. Our world is now too complex, there are too many contradictions, paradoxes and problems for any single party to solve them. And, anyway, fewer and fewer now sign up for life in a single political tribe. This is about more than votes and seats, although both matter. A deeper realignment of minds must underpin any political change. No one has a monopoly of wisdom. In a world as complex and rich as ours, we need equally complex and rich political responses.

But to change our world we first have to change ourselves. Indeed, that is the only thing we can really change. Because by changing ourselves we change how people react to us. It doesn't mean real differences should be glossed over; because we can and must learn from each other, adapt and, through the process of building an alliance for change, arrive at solutions that endure, because they have the wisdom and support of more than one narrow tribe.

If we understand our emerging world, and adapt not our values but our strategy, then we move beyond wishful thinking to hope. But there is no hope if progressive voices remain at war with each other – angry with anyone who stands in the way of them getting their hands on the levers of power (as if the machine hadn't rusted and corroded long ago). Neither the people nor the planet can survive if the Tories, as they are currently construed, remain the dominant force in British politics. Cancelling out each other's votes is bad enough, but fighting in essentially the same terrain for the same issues and the same set of fundamental beliefs is madness. Progressives share a belief in a much more equal, democratic and sustainable world. Increasingly we have the technical and cultural means to make it happen. It is beholden on all of us to find a way to make the desirable feasible. As ever for progressives, the only hope we have is each other.

Neal Lawson is a political writer, commentator and activist. He was an adviser to Gordon Brown, was co-editor of *The Progressive Century* (2001), is managing editor of the journal *Renewal* and is chair of the political pressure group Compass, which campaigns for a good society.

THE STRANGE REBIRTH OF FREE TRADE AND PRACTICAL ECONOMICS

David Boyle

When the first Liberal mayor of Birmingham, Joseph Chamberlain, addressed councillors in the 1870s, he told them to 'be more expensive'. This is hardly a phrase you hear much these days, partly because its meaning has changed: he probably meant 'more ambitious'.

But then, Chamberlain was nothing if not ambitious. He had just seized control of a city that was in a desperate state, with poisoned rivers, occasional water supplies and hideous poverty. He had also seized it from a group of independent councillors who met regularly in a pub called The Woodman, and who prided themselves on their ability to avoid spending any money at all. They called themselves 'The Economists'.

In this respect, Chamberlain is in some ways a very modern hero. He revived Britain's second city, paved it, lit its streets, infused it with enormous pride and built parks and galleries and concert halls. He did so, not by begging for central government subsidies or from Chinese investment, but by using the assets at his disposal – the foul water, the money flowing through, the local people. Chamberlain municipalised the water and gas supply and used the profits to reshape the city and fund the arts.

Now, fourteen decades later, we may be back to this kind of pattern. The investment is usually not forthcoming and the central government tap has run dry, rightly or wrongly. We could wait around until the political left controls the tap again, but there are more fundamental reasons why it has run dry that will make it more difficult to turn on again.

Local government is going to have to rediscover the entrepreneurial skills of using what assets lie before them. Unfortunately, they have been constrained over the past two generations by two generally accepted truths that have both proved to be completely wrong. One, that the economic levers are all in Whitehall, and economic decisions are supposed to be made there; two, that all they should do is to beg for government handouts or major corporate investment.

The absolute necessity for the progressives to be more practical in their approach to economics is most obvious here – the need to overthrow these twin assumptions. And at its heart is an old idea: that where people are gathered together, the basic necessities for growing an effective economy ought to be available. People have needs, skills and time; what they lack is partly the skills and confidence they require, and partly the business support to bring these elements together. So a progressive economic policy would look to provide the framework for economies at any level to thrive by exploiting the assets they have at their disposal.

The economic techniques for growing an effective economy have long since been forgotten and have not just atrophied – they have been undermined by the monopolies and semi-monopolies that have been allowed to dominate so many local economies, from groceries to energy and refuse collection. In that, there is the outline of a very practical agenda for a new economics of the progressives – economic devolution, local lending institutions and a major programme of monopoly-busting.

THE BACKDROP OF GLOBAL ECONOMIC TRENDS

It hardly needs emphasising that the real problem goes some way beyond this. An article by Michael Sauga in *Der Spiegel* in October 2014 ('The Zombie System: How Capitalism Has Gone Off the Rails') put the issue pretty succinctly: the global economy is no longer working as it should – the banks are not lending, and the huge sums to be distributed by them simply shore up their balance sheets. The middle classes struggle increasingly to make ends meet, and the poor just struggle. Meanwhile, the handful of those at the top – less than 1 per cent, actually – extract more and more.

The idea that the institutions of modern capitalism have become extractive – as institutions have occasionally done in history, with disastrous results – is becoming increasingly accepted. The problem is that there are few agreed solutions, even tentative ones. This is how Sauga puts it in the *Spiegel* article, describing the economist Daron Acemoğlu:

> He became famous two years ago when he and colleague James Robinson published a deeply researched study on the rise of Western industrial societies. Their central thesis was that the

> key to their success was not climate or religion, but the development of social institutions that included as many citizens as possible: a market economy that encourages progress and entrepreneurship, and a parliamentary democracy that serves to balance interests ... Extremely well read, Acemoğlu can cite dozens of such cases. One is fourteenth-century Venice, where a small patrician caste monopolised maritime trade. Another is Egypt under former President Hosni Mubarak, whose officer friends divided up key economic posts among themselves but were complete failures as businessmen. These are what Acemoğlu calls 'extractive processes', which lead to economic and social decline. The question today is: Are Western industrial societies currently undergoing a similar process of extraction?

In my book *Broke* (Fourth Estate, 2014), I drew a parallel with Spain at the height of its imperial power, where the gold poured in, the ability to manufacture withered away and inflation finally overtook the empire. It may be that deflation, not Spanish inflation, is the demon that will do for us – but, like sixteenth-century Spain, we have allowed our economy to become so dominated by the needs of finance that it tends to suck the life out of the rest. It does look increasingly as though our struggling big banks will go through another period of instability, as the big economies begin to unravel again. A new settlement is required, and one that can include people again. Fortunately, history has a habit of providing these things once the situation is really desperate.

What is more, those moments of reboot seem to happen pretty regularly every forty years or so. The last one was in 1979–80. The one before was the rapid political and economic shift in the UK and USA in 1940–41. Before that, it was the new settlement ushered in by the

People's Budget of 1909 and Teddy Roosevelt's busting of Standard Oil, which ended finally in 1911. The big political shift before that came with Gladstone's reforming government in 1868; before that it was the Great Reform Act of 1832. We are not quite overdue for a major reboot, but it is coming and – by my forty-year pattern – it should emerge around 2020. We don't know how it will happen, or what constipated failure to tackle the underlying forces at work will provoke it, but we can be pretty clear already about the kind of shape it will take.

This is why, when the next 'crisis' or 'moment of reboot' comes, we need an economic policy that is sustainable within its own terms. And here the *Spiegel* article reaches a parallel conclusion, quoting Acemoğlu again:

> What is needed, he [Acemoğlu] argues, is a new political alliance that takes a stand against the power of the financial industry and its lobby. He sees the anti-trust movement from the beginning of the last century in the United States as a model. It was a broad coalition from the centre of society and finally achieved its great victory after decades of struggle: the break-up of major corporations like Standard Oil.

That seems to me to be an important clue about our future direction, and the issue of monopoly – ignored for more than half a century by the left – emerges again here. The trouble with concentrating entirely on the control of monopolies is that it isn't enough. It implies once again that the function of the left is opposition, rather than proposition. Yes, the problems of the current system need to be opposed and criticised, but the time has come to put forward another model, and the sheer predictability of the left in its opposition seems to me to make it its own worst enemy.

There has been little thinking emerging recently from the progressive parties that would be new to most people in the voluntary sector or think-tank worlds. Most of the rhetoric in the Labour leadership campaign of mid-2015 revealed a longing for 1945. As for the Liberal Democrats, they appear to be divided between one faction (the Social Liberal Forum) that harks back to the 1970s and another (the Orange Book) that seems to nurture a fondness for the 1870s. Nor is either party challenging the right on their own territory: the ability to create prosperity. The left knows how to share it around but appears to now accept that only the right can create it. It is as if all the parties are splashing around in the same pool of exhausted ideas and mind-numbing rhetoric.

The emerging new left, from Syriza in Greece to Podemos in Spain, does seem to be asking tough questions about the privileging of finance over life, and opening spaces for debate. But Syriza's apparent capitulation to the European central bank reveals the same intellectual gap: there must be other ways to revive an economy than bleeding the patient – but what? It's the absence of an apparent alternative that causes the left to get increasingly frustrated and focus its attention on issues that it may be entitled to be indignant about – offensive jokes or statues of long-dead imperialists – but that don't lead it any closer to a coherent strategy to tackle the key issues that concern us most.

THE EMERGENCE OF A NEW ECONOMICS

So what can we do? We have to accept that the old Fabian compromise is over: the Fabians believed you could leave the economic system alone and then redistribute the proceeds. But we can no longer leave the economy to rumble on unmolested and then redistribute the wealth – partly because income tax is increasingly voluntary for the wealthy, and partly because the economy is now designed to funnel resources upwards to the elite. What we can do is develop an alternative approach to economics that is capable of creating prosperity on a wide and sustainable basis – not just because we can redistribute the wealth, but because we have shaped an economy that works, and works because it is designed to support the vast majority of people to lead meaningful lives and does what it is designed to do.

This is quite urgent. People are angrier – in the middle classes too, priced out of the places they were born – and if the progressives don't provide an answer, voters are liable to drift elsewhere, even further to the right. The sheer practicality of Chamberlain in Birmingham, however, seems to me to be a potential symbol of the new, more creative consensus developing among the progressives on economics. There is an emerging tribe that is overwhelmingly positive, highly practical, ideologically committed, but seeking new ways forward with energy and innovation, especially in the field of economics. You can see it primarily at local level, in local authorities like Preston or Enfield and among Transition Town entrepreneurs.

This is a powerfully local phenomenon, aware that centralism no longer works and using the language of renewable energy, social entrepreneurship, social enterprise, people-powered prosperity and the strange netherworld between small-business innovation and urban revival. What is fascinating, and rather unexpected, is that the sheer pragmatism of this emerging tribe is remarkably similar in one part of the political divide as it is in another. It is English in the sense that it goes for what works, and the most English political virtue is sheer practicality.

I recently found myself in Preston interviewing members of the council and found that I agreed with practically every word of the bold and innovative economic programme of the local Labour Party there: they are putting local enterprise at the heart of their economic efforts, and studying exactly where the money they spend on services flows to and whether they can make it continue flowing locally for longer. They have been examining where the public sector is spending their money, aware that it could have dramatic economic effects if pensions investment, waste contracts and other energy generation could use local resources and local people.

I'm aware of how difficult this may be to achieve in some places. I'm also aware that it hardly drives out the need for investment. But I agree with it, particularly as a Liberal, aware that its concern with enterprise could almost make it more right than left. It is certainly positive and pragmatic, but it is also radical. It was also put together by supporters of Jeremy Corbyn.

It is true that import replacement can only take us so far, and is only relevant to some classes of products and services. It also has to be about broadening choice, rather than restricting it. But if this is a symptom of a genuine realignment of the left, offering in effect a broad choice between the negative and backward-looking and the positive and pragmatic, then I'm on the side of the positive and pragmatic.

RECLAIMING FREE TRADE

Where this new economics will lead is far from clear, but there are clues. We know which intractable economic issues need a new frame: the way the global economy is geared to creating billionaires while leaving so many people struggling to feed and house themselves, the peculiar trend that makes modern middle-class life virtually unaffordable without state subsidy for the vast majority of the population, and the housing crisis.

New economic positions that just tinker with these will hardly survive because they will not be what the world needs. Nor is it just about investment, though people seem to understand the need for investment, and the new institutions capable of making it happen; nor is it about welfare either, because that harks back to the old Fabian compromise that left the economy untouched and relied on redistribution to make it work more progressively. We need to shape the ideas that answer these conundrums and test them out locally and regionally. One of the most interesting ideas recently in this category is the proposal for new public money creation or the ScotPound (see Duncan McCann and Josh Ryan-Collins, *ScotPound: Digital Currency For the Common Good*, London: New Economics Foundation, 2015).

What we can't afford to do is to make the thinking subservient to the business of political opposition – the idea that it is best to fail in Westminster in order to make a Labour government seem more urgent. Collaboration across the left is going to mean strategies to make things happen, not after an election fought under the pointless first-past-the-post, but here and now, in Westminster and outside.

But the return of the monopoly theme implies there is an opportunity worth discussing: a new approach to free trade. The term 'free trade' has become corrupted as an idea in the minds of many progressives. What began as a radical extension of the anti-slavery campaign in the nineteenth century, a way to siphon the rewards of economic activity down to the poorest, has come to mean the precise reverse:

the ability of the economically strongest to call the tune to the detriment of less affluent, but equally important actors in the economy.

For Chamberlain's generation, it was a recipe for cities and towns to claw back a measure of economic independence. It meant they could replace their imports, produce and grow things locally, create energy, excitement and diversity, and shape their own economic destinies. Not anymore. Some time over the last half-century, the idea became its own opposite. Instead of being a critique of monopoly, it became an apologia for it. Instead of being a recipe for economic diversity, it became a route to monoculture. Instead of being the antidote to economic slavery, it became the manacles. It became a means by which the urban poor stayed urban and poor.

Taking a practical lead on economic revival means clawing back the idea of free trade for the radical side again, to support individuals and communities in local economies all over the UK, including the poorest places, who are making things happen using existing resources. This is the new tribe I talked about before: overwhelmingly entrepreneurial, pragmatic and focused on creating the enterprises and institutions that can make change happen – like Bath & West Community Energy, Wessex Community Assets, the Digbeth Community Enterprise Quarter, Incredible Edible Todmorden, the Kindling Trust in Manchester, the Wadebridge Community Energy Network, and so many other places and projects. They are operating in the margins, often without support or official approval, pretty uncategorisable politically, but they are slowly edging towards a new economic diversity. The demise of free trade as a radical concept provides an opportunity for its strange rebirth as an underpinning for those local activists who are making things happen, promoting independence and sustainability. It is an idea that could, with recasting, be used to meet local needs.

There are limitations to this bundle of ideas, but there are also enormous possibilities when people take more charge of their economic destinies. It certainly isn't a panacea for everything. Nor does it imply that the new generation of business will be somehow altruistic in a way that the old one was not. But it suggests that, in fact, business itself is shifting – most business now is internationalist when the Conservative government wants to restrict foreign visitors. It is in favour of challenging the status quo and tackling monopolies, when the Conservative government is not. It is in favour of broader education in skills and apprenticeships when the Conservative government wants schools to be more academic. It recognises that business is, in some ways, a progressive force. The left has to embrace that.

Above all, the implication is that economic policy isn't just our responsibility to shape; it is our responsibility to put into practice locally. That means making sure local authorities are asking the right questions:

Are they concentrating on what they have got – wasted local people, local imagination – rather than what they haven't?

Do they know how much money is flowing through their areas and where it flows out?

What would it mean to concentrate their major effort, not on attracting rare outside investment, but on building networks of local enterprise to fulfil local needs?

Where does public money get spent?

Is the local authority trying to do everything, or are they aware of the imagination and energy locally that really ought to be taking decisions and bearing some of the strain?

What financial institutions do they have that are committed locally, and how can they launch more of them?

These questions might be asked by people in any political tribe, and the new pragmatic tribe that is asking them isn't really categorisable in the old way. But they lay down a challenge to radicals, which I think is this: if you want to shape a new kind of economics, then learn how to make things happen.

David Boyle is a former Liberal Democrat parliamentary candidate, a former independent reviewer for the Cabinet Office and co-director of the New Weather Institute. He is also the co-author of *Prosperity Parade.*

PUTTING THE SECURITY BACK INTO SOCIAL SECURITY

Ruth Lister

Social security (aka 'welfare') is regularly identified as a toxic issue for progressives. Public opinion is largely hostile, fed by an unrelentingly negative narrative from the media and politicians. Yet the economy is increasingly unable to guarantee a secure life that enables members of our society to flourish. Too many people are finding themselves part of the 'precariat', caught up in a 'low-pay/no-pay' cycle, working hard in jobs with little intrinsic reward and little or no security, often with insufficient income to cope with sudden crises or to save for the future. Many can no longer access secure and affordable housing where they can build a home. In the face of such chronic insecurity, and the poverty and inequality that scar our society, social security arguably has a more important role to play than ever. Yet making the case won't be easy politically, as John Curtice's essay (page 186) demonstrates.

His essay underlines the challenge that dominant public attitudes towards 'welfare' create for progressives. This essay doesn't claim to provide a simple answer – because there is none! Of course, progressive politicians must listen to, try to understand and respond to the messages that attitudes surveys convey, but we must also remember that these attitudes are not monolithic or set in concrete. Moreover, our role is not simply to follow or woo the electorate – it's also to lead it.

According to the veteran pollster Peter Kellner, polling evidence suggests that politicians are more likely to win backing not by appeasing the public mood but by demonstrating that they deserve respect. So how would we develop an authentic story on social security for people below pension age that might start to rebuild public support? To this end, it would help to go back to first principles in order to ask what we mean by social security and what it is for. I will emphasise the importance of security and the failure of the current system to provide it. In looking to the future, rather than offering a blueprint, I suggest some principles to guide reform, some short term remedial measures and two broad approaches to longer-term structural reform to help stimulate debate among progressives.

WHY SOCIAL SECURITY?

The first step is to go back to fundamentals and try to shift the framing of the debate. This means no longer talking about 'welfare' as a synonym for social security. Used in this way, 'welfare' does not conjure up the positive picture of its original meaning – the state of faring or doing well – or even the institutions of the wider welfare state with its promise of security for all from cradle to grave. Instead, it conveys a rather miserable, stigmatised, residual form of social assistance for people in poverty. This meaning has been imported from the US, where it's used to describe means-tested financial support for people below pension age. And with it came negative connotations of 'dependency' – a state that marks the human condition but that, in the demeaning language of the 'dependency culture', was turned into a label stuck only on benefit claimants, with associated implications of passivity, addiction and failure, as Fran Bennett, one of the UK's leading experts on social security, has pointed out.

We should never underestimate the power of language – particularly as used by prominent politicians and the media. British Social Attitudes reports have suggested that the stand taken by political parties can influence the views of their supporters. They point in particular to how the increasingly negative language and tough stance adopted by New Labour when in office appears to have been associated with the erosion of support for 'welfare' among its supporters. Research indicates that political rhetoric and policy stances are important drivers of negative media coverage, especially with regard to fraud and abuse, thereby contributing to the increased stigmatisation associated with benefit receipt. New Labour maintained that its 'tough' stance was necessary to rebuild trust in the system. But arguably, by constantly highlighting fraud and supposed 'welfare dependency', it reinforced the belief that these are endemic and that the system offers 'something for nothing' (that phrase so loved by many politicians). It's encouraging that Owen Smith, the current shadow Work and Pensions Secretary, has made clear his determination to eschew divisive language and 'set a more decent tone of debate'.

Let's unpack those two words 'social security'. Social security isn't simply a bureaucratic means; it also represents an *end* to which society aspires. It expresses the desire to achieve, insofar as is possible, genuine economic *security* for all through *social* means. And herein lies the clue as to how we might start reframing and leading the debate on progressive terms.

At a time of widespread economic insecurity seeping into more and more aspects of our lives, we need to remind people that social security is a shared mechanism for safeguarding the economic security of us all. Unlike 'welfare', social security is there not just to relieve poverty but also to help prevent it. It provides shared protection against a range of risks and contingencies that we each might face during the course of our lives. It does so more equitably and efficiently than private insurance because it can pool risk across the whole population rather than just a sector of it and includes those with the highest risks who would typically be excluded from private insurance by higher premiums. In the process it helps to act as an automatic economic stabiliser during times of high unemployment or under-employment. It also helps to share some of the costs associated with disability, caring or raising children, thereby achieving what is called 'horizontal redistribution' aimed at reducing inequalities arising from differential needs. It can contribute too to reducing inequalities such as those associated with social class, gender, ethnicity and age. Analysis by John Hills of the LSE and by the Institute for Fiscal Studies shows that its 'piggy bank' function – redistributing resources over our individual life cycles – is in many ways as important as its 'Robin Hood' function, redistributing from those who need the money less to those who need it more.

This is an important message to get across because it helps to counter the dominant idea that 'welfare' is for them and is of no concern to 'us'. As the Scottish government has recently underlined, 'social security is important to all of us'. This points to how we need to start talking about social security in the language of 'us' rather than 'them'. At the same time, though, we should not give up on the idea of social security as an instrument of social solidarity. It may not be a very fashionable notion these days, but it's sorely needed as the Tories vilify 'welfare' as an 'unfair' source of division between out-of-work 'skivers' and 'hard-working families' (a label first deployed by New Labour) or 'strivers' – the new Tory icon. Such divisive language and thinking constantly help stoke public antipathy and obscure the reality of many benefit claimants caught up in a low-pay, no-pay cycle that is all too typical of today's insecure labour market. The underlying causes of poverty, which the Tories constantly refer to, do not lie, as they claim, in individual behaviour, culture and attitudes, but in the failings of the market and of economic and social policies. Too little has been done to counter the Tories' individualistic diagnosis of poverty, which has become increasingly dominant.

WHAT'S WRONG WITH THE CURRENT SYSTEM?

Today's social security performs none of the above functions effectively. In particular, it does not provide genuine security or prevent poverty and only relieves it inadequately, with the growing reliance on food banks merely the most visible tip of an iceberg of unmet needs. As the social and housing charity Community Links observes, it acts too late and pays too little to ensure a socially acceptable standard of living and security against financial shocks such as the breakdown of basic household equipment. Their research found that, all too often, engaging with the system creates stress and insecurity, not least because of a culture of 'institutionalised suspicion' that is manifest in an increasingly punitive regime of conditionality and sanctions. This is designed to push people into paid work at whatever cost and has now been extended to those in work claiming universal credit if they are deemed not to be earning enough.

New Labour had a mantra: 'work for those who can, security for those who cannot', yet the second part has consistently been sacrificed to the first as paid work has been fetishised, regardless of whether it's decent work at a decent wage, and without adequate attention to the responsibilities associated with unpaid care work. Yet, paradoxically, the work of Community Links and others shows how inadequate social security benefits, and the recent raft of cuts to them, can make people less job-ready as their energy goes into everyday survival.

Underlying many of the problems has been a gradual shift in the balance between universal, contributory and means-tested benefits under successive governments. The result is that means-testing now represents the fulcrum of the system, thereby reinforcing the idea that social security is only for 'them', with associated stigmatising connotations. It also serves to trap people in poverty (in particular making it difficult for second earners – mainly women – to lift families out of poverty because the means test is applied to the couple), is inherently complex and can deter people from claiming their entitlement.

Contrary to popular belief, spending on social security is not 'out of control' or particularly high compared with other advanced economies; but it suffers from having to pick up the pieces of the failings of the labour and housing markets. The more secure jobs there are available at decent wages and the fewer the obstacles in the way of marginalised groups accessing those jobs (e.g. discrimination, lack of affordable and accessible child care, poor public transport), the less the need for social security. Similarly, housing subsidies have been deliberately channelled into housing benefit rather than 'bricks and mortar' so that spending on housing benefit is now vilified and cut when the answer lies in building more social housing and some form of private sector rent regulation.

When people claim benefits for the first time, the inadequacies of the system can come as a shock. This doesn't necessarily translate into pressure to improve it, but it could potentially widen the constituency of those who understand that benefit recipients are not typically, as ministers such as George Osborne proclaim, 'sleeping off a life on benefits' while others go off to work, with the insinuation that they're work-shy scroungers enjoying an enviable life.

LOOKING TO THE FUTURE

Principles

To some extent, the principles that need to guide social security reform flow from the functions outlined above. A good starting point is provided by a recommendation on social protection agreed in 2012 at an International Labour Organisation (ILO) conference. Among the principles it enunciates are 'universality of protection based on social solidarity' and 'respect for the rights and dignity of people covered by the social security guarantee' in recognition of social security's status as a human right. The aim should be the provision of genuine economic security through the pooling of risks, benefits sufficient to 'allow life in dignity', to quote the ILO, and what the literature increasingly refers to as an 'upstream' approach grounded in 'a culture of prevention'. As Community Links put it, rather than an ambulance picking people up at the bottom of the cliff, social security needs to provide a protective fence that stops people who trip up from falling over the cliff in the first place.

Social security needs to provide genuine economic security in the face of not just an insecure labour market but also of family instability. This is particularly important for mothers who can be trapped in unsatisfactory or abusive relationships if they lack any independent income of their own. Ideally, social security for adults should be paid as an *individual* right, enabling individual financial autonomy, but so long as the couple is the unit of assessment, as is typically the case in means-tested schemes, it's important to try to ensure that the woman has access to at least some of any benefit paid (which is not guaranteed under universal credit). A gender perspective also underlines the importance of what the New Economics Foundation calls a 'rounded approach', which values contributions other than through paid work – for example through care of children or older people, community building and creative work – which help to sustain what they describe as the 'core economy' that helps society to flourish outside the market economy.

Support for the core economy helps to nourish social relations. Likewise, the institutions of the welfare state help to shape social relations both between different groups in society (as argued above in relation to the divisive nature of current policies) and between individual citizens and the state. The current culture of institutionalised suspicion needs to be replaced by a culture of human rights in which claimants are treated with dignity and respect, are supported as individuals, and are listened to as experts through experience. In addition, a system that is less complex and easier to understand reduces to some extent the power imbalance between claimant and official, although simplification has always been something of a holy grail of social security reform within the constraints of heavy reliance on means-testing.

Less means-testing

These principles all point towards a long-term goal of reducing reliance on means-testing.

There is general acceptance that movement towards this goal will have to be gradual given the costs and disruption of a big-bang reform. It's important also that social security reform is set in the context of what Andrew Harrop of the Fabian Society has called the 'world of shadow welfare': the hundreds of billions of pounds spent in tax reliefs and allowances on policy goals more often associated with social security, largely to the benefit of the better-off. This helps to break down the 'us and them'-type attitudes discussed earlier, as well as to counter arguments that it's wasteful not to target help on those on low incomes through means-testing. This is especially the case in relation to child benefit, which replaced not just the family allowances introduced after the Second World War but also child tax allowances. It thus in effect performs the function of a tax allowance for children but, unlike with personal tax allowances, an increase helps families below the tax threshold.

Paradoxically perhaps, cross-national evidence indicates that more universalistic welfare states are more effective in combating poverty than those that target help on people in poverty. And Richard Titmuss's aphorism – that benefits and services for 'the poor' alone are more likely to be poor benefits and services – still holds.

From short-term to longer-term reforms

Before setting out two broad, longer-term approaches for reducing reliance on means-testing, there's a more immediate question as to what remedial measures are needed to undo or at least mitigate the grievous harm that the Tories are doing to the existing system.

The current benefits freeze is invisible but its cumulative effects are immense. If the living standards of benefit recipients are not to fall further behind those of the rest of society, a priority must be to restore the index-linking of all benefits. A whole range of nasty cuts, including the removal of means-tested support for third and subsequent children (predicted to increase child poverty significantly), the bedroom tax, disability benefit cuts and the benefits cap, will have to be reviewed. Reversing such cuts without doubt costs money. But there are also urgent areas needing reform that are more or less cost-free, such as the punitive sanctions regime, benefit delays and monthly payment of universal credit into a single account (to the potential detriment of women). And a commitment to a human rights culture that treats claimants with dignity and respect costs nothing.

Simply patching up the wreckage left by the Tories does not, of course, constitute a strategy for reform. If we want to reduce reliance on means-testing and create a social security system worthy of the name, there are two main options to consider: a revitalised, more inclusive contributory social insurance system or a universal basic income (with a third option, a participation income, as a variant).

Revitalised social insurance

The case made by the Commission on Social Justice (CSJ) for a revitalised social insurance system (in which entitlement is linked to contributions paid or credited), that is better attuned to labour market and family change, still stands today. It was based on a handful of arguments, namely that social insurance: can protect people against unemployment and sickness more cheaply, efficiently and fairly than private insurance; rewards personal effort and balances rights with responsibilities; and has a unique role in helping people distribute income across increasingly varied life cycles. In addition, as an individual entitlement, it helps to protect the financial autonomy of women and provides each member of a couple with what Fran Bennett and Holly Sutherland have called 'independence of action' in terms of earning.

However, the current social insurance scheme is premised on a traditional male model of employment that takes little account of contributions other than paid work, and provides poor protection for part-time workers. A key question will be what kind of work should 'earn' contributions. There's a strong case for including unpaid care work. This would be in tune with public attitudes, as a number of studies indicate that people feel that caring is undervalued by society. More difficult perhaps is the suggestion that formalised forms of voluntary work might count, but it should certainly not be ruled out for the longer term.

Other issues to resolve include the relationship between contributions paid or credited and benefits received. Among the suggestions made by the CSJ were the inclusion of more part-time workers and the option of paying higher contributions in order to earn higher benefits so as to bind more people into the scheme. Other ideas floated more recently have been the return to an earnings-related element (abolished in 1981) and Labour's suggestion of differential benefits according to length of time spent in the labour market (although it would be important that this didn't discriminate against people who have had time out of the labour market because of caring responsibilities, long-term sickness and similar reasons). Thought should also be given to whether the scheme could be extended to cover other contingencies such as parental leave and long-term care. A good discussion of all these issues can be found in a TUC pamphlet by Kate Bell and Declan Gaffney (see Further Reading). They also make clear that the value of reciprocity, embodied in social insurance, has to be balanced with that of solidarity – the recognition and meeting of need including those that arise from costs such as those associated with children or disability. As Beveridge made clear, social insurance will always have to be underpinned by a means-tested safety net.

Universal Basic Income

Commentators from across the political spectrum are heralding Universal Basic Income (UBI) as an idea with a long history whose time has come. A growing number of experiments are being undertaken around the world; in the UK, Compass and the Royal Society of Arts, as well as the Citizen's Income Trust, have modelled possible ways of implementing it; and the Green Party has been an advocate for some time. Part of its attraction lies in its simplicity (and therefore low administrative costs): every individual adult and child, subject possibly to some kind of residence test, receives an unconditional, flat-rate payment, without a contribution or means tests attached. In some schemes it would replace personal tax allowances as well as (in its pure form) most existing cash benefits.

Proponents see UBI as potentially transformative. They argue that it better meets social security's objectives and addresses the problems inherent in the current system. It supports people in how they choose to divide their time between paid work, caring, community and citizenship-focused activities, creativity, education, family and friends and leisure without being dictated to by an intrusive state. It's thereby better attuned to today's precarious labour market and forms of employment that do not conform to the old, male, full-time model. Moreover, many of those predicting that the new age of automation will mean the loss of many traditional jobs see UBI as the answer to the associated loss of wages as a reliable source of income, at the same time helping to sustain demand in the economy. As an individual income it promotes women's financial independence. Above all, it offers individuals a degree of genuine security in the face of whatever the labour market or family throws at them.

Criticisms of UBI have been both philosophical and practical. Most fundamental perhaps are those that emphasise the lack of reciprocity that underpins social insurance and fears that a totally unconditional scheme would act as a disincentive to paid work (disputed by advocates) and would not meet the test of public opinion if perceived as offering 'something for nothing'. While there's a feminist argument for UBI, there's also one against: that without other measures designed to shift radically the gendered division of labour between paid work and care and the continued gender pay gap, it could undermine women's position in the labour market by encouraging them to stay at home. And progressives need to be aware that one reason some on the right support UBI is that they would use it to replace welfare state services as well as existing benefits in the name of withdrawal of the state. Practical problems include how a simple flat-rate scheme can meet additional costs such as those associated with disability and housing without reimporting too many of the complexities of the existing system.

Another issue is how UBI can provide a politically and economically viable *adequate* income for those without other means given the cost, even allowing for some increase in taxation. This has led most proponents to accept that any such scheme would have to be phased in in some way, so that initially it would sit alongside most existing benefits rather than replace them. It could nevertheless provide a worthwhile secure income on which people can then build. An alternative halfway house, favoured by the CSJ and by Professor Tony Atkinson, would be a 'participation income', which would not be totally unconditional but would broaden the notion of contribution from that governing the existing social security system to include social contributions, such as caring and formalised voluntary work.

I have always been ambivalent about UBI, able to see its attractions but also very aware of its dangers. Moreover, I've feared that, by arguing for such a radical rupture with the present, more modest achievable yet nevertheless important reforms might be disdained as too timid. However in the face of growing economic insecurity and the possible effects of technological change, the case for a scheme that guarantees each individual a modicum of financial security becomes more compelling. And as proponents now acknowledge that any UBI would have to complement, rather than replace, most existing benefits initially, my fears that we could end up with a scheme that provided an even less adequate income than now for those without other means, if it were to be affordable, are allayed. Of course, the flip-side of that is that the complexities of the current system would continue. But a modest UBI could provide an important stepping stone to a system that provided genuine security.

WE'RE ALL IN THIS TOGETHER!

Progressives from different political traditions may differ on their priorities for both short- and long-term reform of social security for people below pension age. But I hope that we can agree on the broad principles outlined here and on the need to reframe the debate around social security in more positive terms. It's time that progressives stopped treating social security as a burden that 'we' bear on behalf of 'them', a 'cost of economic failure', a problem, and instead started seeing it as a *key element in a good and fair society*. If *we* don't believe in it, how can we expect the general public to do so? To this end, this essay has attempted to provide some pointers as to how progressives might think and talk about social security in a way that addresses the insecurity faced by a significant proportion of the population.

Looking at social security in this way makes a reality of the Tory slogan that 'we're all in this together'.

Ruth Lister (Baroness Lister of Burtersett) is a Labour peer and Emeritus Professor of Social Policy at Loughborough University. She currently chairs the Compass management committee and was a member of the Commission on Social Justice and the National Equality Panel. She is also a former director of the Child Poverty Action Group.

FURTHER READING

Atkinson, Anthony B., *Inequality: What can be done?* Harvard University Press: 2015, chapter 8.

Bell, Kate and Declan Gaffney, *Making a Contribution: Social Security For the Future*, TUC: 2012.

Commission on Social Justice, *Social Justice: Strategies for National Renewal*, Vintage: 1994, chapter 6.

Harrop, Andrew, *Beveridge 2020: Options For Social Security After Austerity* [working title], Fabian Society: 2016.

Hills, John, *Good Times, Bad Times: The Welfare Myth of Them and Us*, Policy Press: 2015.

Horton, Tim and James Gregory, *The Solidarity Society*, Fabian Society/Webb Memorial Trust: 2009.

Horwitz, Will (with Luke Price), *Secure and Ready: Towards an Early Action Social Security System*, Community Links Early Action Task Force: 2014.

Lyall, Sarah and Kate Wall, *Social security for a new social settlement*, New Economics Foundation: 2014.

Painter, Anthony and Chris Toung, *Creative citizen, creative state: the principled and pragmatic case for a Universal Basic Income*, Royal Society of the Arts: 2015.

Reed, Howard and Steward Lansley, *Citizen's Income – An Idea Whose Time Has Come* [working title] Compass: 2016.

REINVENTING PUBLIC SERVICES

Norman Lamb & Steve Reed

Labour and the Liberal Democrats trace their roots back to the same political tradition. Both see themselves as radicals; both cherish a heritage that includes the non-conformists, the cooperative movement and the friendly societies of an earlier age. After Labour displaced the Liberals electorally at the beginning of the twentieth century, both parties continued to fight over the progressive space in politics for the next century. The Liberals emphasised personal freedom while Labour emphasised collectivism – but both perspectives are stronger alongside each other. It was the great Liberal, William Beveridge, who shaped the NHS, and the great socialist, Nye Bevan, who brought it into being.

Today, progressives face a new challenge. On the retreat, electorally, in much of the developed world, progressives have failed to offer a compelling alternative to conservatives at a time of economic fracture. Opposing is not enough. In terms of public services, we must demonstrate both how we can improve them so that we achieve better results for people and how we can make them sustainable.

BETTER RESULTS

The Conservative instinct is to marketise public services, but this often leads to fragmented services and the same remote power: distant organisations unresponsive to individual need. They can get away with this because of an unfocused common perception that public services don't always represent good value for money, and that the monolithic state is too overbearing and unresponsive. The challenge to progressives is not simply to defend a declining status quo, but to listen to people's concerns and shape a new vision for public services that revitalises them for the future.

If we want public services to have a long term future, we have a duty to make them as effective and relevant as possible. In an age where more people exercise greater control than ever before over so many areas of their lives and lifestyle, public services must become more directly accountable, more personal and focused on outcomes that people define for themselves. They must fit the age we live in, not the very different world of the 1950s in which they were born.

Lack of accountability in public services and a sense that the citizen too often has no power to alter things should make us impatient for change. And it's always the most vulnerable who lose out the most. We have seen, too often, unacceptable treatment of people by organisations funded out of public money. The father of a patient with learning disabilities who was living at Winterbourne View, where the most shocking abuse took place, described how he tried to raise concerns with the commissioners. He said he felt completely ignored; no one would listen. He felt guilty that he could do nothing to help his son. What a dreadful way to treat people.

Then there is the shocking case of Connor Sparrowhawk, who was on the autism spectrum and who died as a result of drowning in his bath at an NHS unit in Oxfordshire. The inquest concluded that neglect contributed to his death. Connor's mother, Sara Ryan, fought to establish what had happened but felt that the NHS didn't engage with her. Eventually, a highly critical report into the Southern Health Trust was published, highlighting the fact that the trust had failed to investigate more than 1,000 unexpected deaths.

In our respective former roles as council leader and Minister of State in the Department of Health, we have witnessed how bureaucracies too often fail to respond and are too focused on self-preservation. Yet the paradox is that public services are full of people with amazing potential, committed to working for the communities they serve, although too often held back by systems and top-down structures. The key is to unleash the vitality of people working in public services and the insight of those who use them.

This represents a big challenge for politicians as well as those who run public services. Trust in politics is broken because too many politicians who claimed to have all the answers turned out not to. The days of deference will never come back, so trust can only be rebuilt if politicians first show that they trust people to take more decisions for themselves. In both politics and public services, people want more direct control and accountability for themselves; we are failing to meet people's growing demand for more power.

MAKING SURE WE CAN SUSTAIN VITAL PUBLIC SERVICES

The fight against 'austerity' has been a rallying cry for many on the left. The argument is that there must be an alternative to constraints on public spending and that there need be no threat to public services – it is simply a political choice for right-wing politicians to destroy the public sector. Whatever side of this argument you sit on, there is something more scary coming down the tracks that it will be impossible to avoid. It grows from the happy fact that we are all living longer. This results in a dramatic change to the ratio of people of working age – those who work and pay income taxes – to people in retirement. Traditionally, the ratio has been about four to one, but by 2050 it is projected to be three to one (according to 2014-based National Population Projections by the Office for National Statistics). This puts an enormous burden on people of working age to pay for the financial support and health and care services needed for people in retirement.

This is the way the Office for Budget Responsibility (OBR) puts it:

> The OBR expects the ageing population to force non-interest public spending upward once the current period of fiscal consolidation ends. At the same time it expects receipts to remain broadly flat as a percentage of GDP. Therefore the OBR projects the primary budget surplus, which it expects to be achieved during this parliament, to turn to deficit in the 2030s. The primary budget excludes interest payments. The OBR projects a primary budget deficit of around 1.9 per cent of GDP in 2064–65.

The main upward pressure on spending is set to come from health, state pensions and long-term care, all of which reflect the ageing population.

To see the impact on public sector net debt, the OBR adds financial transactions – notably student loans – alongside the primary balance figures. The OBR projects public sector net debt to fall to around 54 per cent of GDP in the early 2030s, before rising to around 87 per cent of GDP in 2064–65.

So, irrespective of the debate over 'austerity' policies in the aftermath of the 2008 crash, those of us who believe in the absolute importance of good quality public services have no option but to think afresh about how we sustain those services in circumstances where it becomes more and more difficult to spend our way out of a problem. This is a crucial challenge for all progressives. Unless we confront it – and start to come up with solutions – the right will win the argument and will shrink and marketise the state.

So our search begins for a better deal for people – both those who need public services and those who work in them. And, alongside that, we start the exploration of how we can make the money go further, how we can secure better financial and social value.

Many of the answers to these challenges are already visible. Great innovators across our country are getting on with the job of reinventing public services.

THE CHALLENGE TO REWIRE SERVICES TO THOSE WHO USE THEM

Power is shifting dramatically in the world around us. Technological change is opening up the economy to fast-moving start-ups that disrupt established markets or create new ones. Data and information are no longer restricted to a privileged few; they are shared openly and widely through the internet. People expect to exercise far greater control over the life they lead and the products they buy, and they don't see why public services, from education to healthcare to youth support, should be exempt from this growing sense of people power.

Decisions about public services are made in town halls and Whitehall and they frequently fail to take account of the experiences of the people who are affected by them. This leads to frustration when public services fail to do the things people really want, but it also means we sometimes fail to target resources on the things people really need, which, apart from anything else, wastes precious money.

It's time for a new model of public services that rewires them back to the people who use them, instead of to the politicians and senior officials who run them. That means decision-making where the people who use public services or live in communities have a bigger say over what happens. By making public services more directly accountable, we can make them more responsive and efficient, and make politics more relevant to people's everyday lives.

We wish to highlight five principles for better public services.

Power

The wealthy have always had the power they need to shape their own lives and the goods and services they use. Everyone else has less control, but the most vulnerable or socially excluded often feel they have no power at all. Their lives are determined by the decisions other people make about them, and that includes those who control the public services they rely on. Too often, services are still provided on a 'one-size-fits-all' basis. 'Take it or leave it' is the extent of the choice available. We have turned too many people into passive recipients when we could instead give them a bigger voice over the decisions that affect them.

This is about control, not just choice. Choice on its own is not enough since the choice between two bad alternatives is no choice at all. People need the power to make change happen on their own terms. That power leads to better decisions – and more effective use of resources – and it helps people who have become dependent rediscover the sense of well-being that comes from being in control of your own life.

Power, in this sense, can be exercised in many ways. Instead of forcing unemployed people to work for no pay in non-jobs or take pointless CV-writing courses that don't lead to anything, we can give them a bigger say in how they are helped back to work. There's a cost to whatever programmes unemployed people are sent on, so why not let them decide how the value of that budget will be spent? When Oldham Council piloted personalised budgets in this way, a group of unemployed people spent theirs on a van, tools and a training course that helped them find work as plumbers.

There are other examples, too. Rochdale mutualised their entire council housing stock, handing ownership as well as control to the residents who live in the homes. Managers, now directly accountable to tenants, quickly started focusing on fixing the issues that bothered residents the most rather than dealing with performance indicators seen as important by the hierarchy of senior managers at the town hall.

Personalisation of services is another way of giving service users more power. Instead of expecting older and disabled people to put up with whatever's allocated to them, they are helped to choose how to spend a budget designated to look after them. With good advice and support, this leads to better decisions, and it leaves people feeling they are still in control of their own lives, an important part of maintaining their well-being.

When the idea of personal health budgets was piloted in the NHS, one severely disabled participant spoke of how he had been stuck in the revolving door of A&E departments, in and out, as each new crisis struck him. Once he had control of the funds available for his care, he could decide what his priorities were. He got his life back and the frequent, disruptive visits to hospital became a thing of the past. Now, everyone on NHS continuing care has a legal right to a personal health budget. But the principle could be applied much more widely to all those with long-term, chronic conditions, to those with a learning disability, for people with severe and enduring mental ill health. These are the people most often shunted from pillar to post, without any real sense of control over their lives. We should give them the power to lead their lives as they wish, making crucial decisions about their care, challenging the tendency that still exists to put someone into an institution and leave them there.

This approach of transferring power to the citizen has developed over several years in social care. It is now a right, enshrined in law in the Care Act 2014. And others could benefit as well. Providing individual budgets to parents of children with special education needs would give them a bigger say over the kind of support they want their child to have. Pregnant mothers could choose how and where they want to give birth, and who supports them. This power grows stronger if budget holders can pool their budgets to give them greater influence over service providers. It's still public services, but power is placed in the hands of people on the receiving end. The challenge is to ensure that those without power and resources can get the same control over their lives as others take for granted – this cannot be just for the sharp-elbowed.

A bigger voice isn't just something that benefits service users; workers benefit too. A 2014 review of staff engagement and empowerment in the NHS, chaired by Chris Ham, found that employee-led mutuals deliver high levels of staff engagement. Far from being an end in itself, the review also found that staff engagement – where workers are strongly committed to their work and are involved in decision-making – delivers a higher quality of care. Organisations that allow staff a bigger say report higher patient satisfaction and lower staff turnover and absence.

The MacLeod review in 2009 found that employee ownership was a profound and distinctive enabler of high engagement. Also, importantly, the Nuttall review (2012) describes how employee ownership leads to enhanced employee well-being, reduced sickness absenteeism and greater innovation. The 2014 Ham review (see previous paragraph) reports that one of the public service mutuals that has spun out of the NHS reported an 18 per cent increase in the number of staff recommending the organisation as a place to work. The Mutuals Taskforce also points to better customer experience and satisfaction. They found that mutuals have lower production costs and higher productivity than conventional firms.

This all suggests that this model has great potential to combine both a strong public service ethos with a capability of being more fleet of foot than the traditional public sector.

There are now many examples in health and care of these mutual principles being applied. Sunderland Home Care Associates have reduced sick leave and staff turnover by giving their employees a stake in the ownership of the company. Decisions are made collectively, employees have an increased sense of control over their work, and as a result are happier and less stressed by what remains a very demanding job. Bromley Healthcare is one of many social enterprises now running community health services. They have very high patient satisfaction ratings. All profit is reinvested into improving services. All staff are invited to become shareholders. They elect staff governors, who then have influence over how services are delivered with the aim of providing excellent care and the best possible outcomes.

The evidence therefore suggests beneficial outcomes for users of the service, for staff and for the public purse – which offer the potential for significant productivity gains.

While the principle of giving power and voice to staff is highly attractive and should be pursued, we must always remember that, when it comes to public services, the most important person of all is the citizen, the user of the service. Services are there, after all, for people who use them, so choice and control for the user of a service to achieve the best possible results for them must override all else.

Prevention

If one challenge is to give service users a bigger say over the help available to them, another is to try to stop problems occurring in the first place. Too many public services try to manage problems rather than prevent them, and yet the benefits in financial and human terms of prevention are immense.

Violent youth gang crime plagues too many poor communities in inner-city Britain. Young lives are wasted and the whole community suffers as a result of drug-dealing, knives and gun crime. Young men involved in gang violence are often the victims of deep-rooted problems; experience of domestic violence is the single biggest predictor that a young person will grow up to be a criminal. So why does public policy not focus more squarely on identifying and intervening in situations of domestic violence, instead of waiting until some of the young people affected by it, having grown up in a household with no clear sense of right and wrong, fall into criminal behaviour?

Lambeth Council tried giving a bigger say to communities affected by youth violence over what help should be available for their young people. The Young Lambeth Cooperative is now the country's biggest youth services trust. Funded by the council but owned by the community, it works with people in their own neighbourhood to shape services the community believes will make a difference. Instead of putting up with whatever's on offer, whether it works or not, the community can play a more active role in tackling a serious problem that affects them so profoundly. It has helped cut violent crime on the estates where it operates by diverting young people away from gangs, and has given some of the most socially excluded people in the community a sense of control. This is prevention in action, cutting crime, cutting costs, steering young lives back on track – and it's people power that's driving it.

We also know that many young people who get involved in gang violence have a range of mental health problems – indeed, the evidence is that one in three young people who offend have an unmet mental health need at the time of the offence. Traditional services work off the basis of a referral to treatment in the clinic, but only after a mental health issue becomes really entrenched. Often, the young person fails to turn up and the book is closed. This is a hopeless failure to reach those who could most benefit from help. So MAC-UK, a brilliant third-sector organisation, does it differently. It takes what works in the clinic out onto the streets, working with young people where and when they need it. By intervening much sooner, it can prevent a deterioration of condition. It costs less and is much more effective – literally saving young lives and keeping communities safer.

Partnerships

Public services tend to operate as if they are the only service an individual is using, but for people with complex needs that is not the case. Attempts have been made to get health workers, social workers, benefits officers, the police and housing officers to coordinate better around individuals, families and even neighbourhoods with high levels of need, but never to the extent that is really needed.

It's difficult to effectively tackle crime and anti-social behaviour on a deprived estate without also tackling some of the underlying causes of social dysfunction – poor quality and overcrowded housing, mental ill health and stress, low attainment in education, high levels of unemployment and low pay, and discrimination. Partnerships at the neighbourhood level offer a way forward. By bringing all the key public service agencies together and pooling their budgets, it would be possible to reprioritise funding on tackling problems at source. The previous Labour government's Total Place initiative piloted pooled budgets for specific services, and subsequent governments have continued that work with community budgets, but both happened only on a fairly small scale.

One problem is that it's impossible to pool budgets if you don't know what's being spent in the first place, and most public services don't store data about how much is spent where. But why not? We already know that partnership working and pooled budgets can dramatically improve outcomes. We are too wedded to the idea of individual services doing the thing that makes sense to them, rather than looking at how it feels to a frustrated community on the receiving end that can't make sense of a jumble of disconnected initiatives. Communities with more complex needs often receive considerable amounts of public funding in total but it doesn't deliver the change that people want and need.

One of the largest pots of public money spent on deprived estates is the benefits budget. Here spending is heavily prescribed and has not been part of any community budgeting so far. So we have the ludicrous situation of large numbers of people who are out of work and who suffer from poor mental health but who do not get support to improve their health and to help get them back to work. It costs taxpayers a fortune and it leads to miserable lives. Yet it doesn't have to be like this.

A programme called Individual Placement and Support (IPS) provides intensive support to help those with severe and enduring mental ill health get into work. There is a very strong evidence base that demonstrates that it works. It can make a massive difference to people's lives, and it saves public money. Yet, every year, out of a total of about 250,000 people who could benefit, only about 4,000 people are actually helped in this way. Health commissioners, faced with ever-tighter budgets, shy away from the additional cost. And it is another department, Work and Pensions, that benefits. So nothing happens. Now exciting initiatives are emerging around the country whereby people who want to invest in a social purpose put up the money to provide the service. The deal is that the government pays a return on the investment if public money is saved as a result of getting people back into work.

Relationships

We overlook the power of relationships as a means of bringing about change. Human beings are social animals; we all value relationships in our own lives. Whether it's with family, friends, our peer group, work colleagues or our community, we are heavily influenced by the relationships around us, and we value those relationships highly.

If someone is unemployed, they are likely to go to their local job centre for advice or to be directed onto programmes intended to help them find work. But there are other approaches that can be even more effective. Backr is a project that successfully trialled a relationships-based approach to employability.

It's a fact that the majority of jobs are never formally advertised; they are filled by word of mouth. If you're unemployed, and if you come from a community where there are very high levels of unemployment, you are unlikely to ever hear about these jobs. But we can use people as bridges. We can link people who are part of social networks where people have jobs with unemployed people who are not part of those networks. You can take this a step further by training employed people to act as mentors who help those seeking work in the same sector. These human bridges transmit information about developing the right skills and networks as well as information about jobs that become available. Relationships have a role to play alongside more traditional skills development.

At another level, we've allowed communities to feel that we no longer value human relationships within them. If someone wants to stop smoking, they'll find it easier if they're not surrounded by smokers all the time. The same principle applies to persuading an offender to stop committing crime, or a drug abuser to stop taking drugs. Targeting services on an individual as if they weren't part of a community that influences them isn't enough. We need to find ways to harness the wider community to help change behaviours that damage everyone.

In every community there is enormous human capital. When it comes to care of elderly people or combating loneliness, neighbours can play a vital role. Nowadays, the extended family is often dispersed far and wide. Sometimes there is a mindset that the state can step in and take over, but companionship and friendship, giving people the chance of a good life, is more about people than the state.

New technology

New technology is changing the world around us. Nearly all of us are plugged into the internet at home or, via mobile devices, even when we're on the move. We can keep track of friends and family, read the news, download a book, watch a video, search for information and find others who share our interests, all pretty much as we please. One area in which new technology has not yet led a revolution is our democracy and our public services. That needs to change.

We have already argued that power and relationships matter; the internet gives us a means of deploying both. Casserole is a project set up by FutureGov. It works by linking people in a neighbourhood who are willing to cook an extra portion of food and give it to an individual living nearby who is unable to cook for themselves.

This initiative not only provides someone with a meal, it brings people together in a community who otherwise might never have met. This is about more than just food, it can also help tackle loneliness and isolation.

Good For Nothing is a movement that brings together people who use a particular public service with the people who run it, members of the community, and technology and data experts who help them think about how things could be run differently. They hold 'gigs' where everyone with an interest comes together to explore how they can solve a problem or run a service differently. They've tackled issues as diverse as waste management, energy generation, education and helping asylum seekers integrate into their host community. Using technology and open data to enable new forms of collaboration is a fantastic opportunity for public services.

MAKING THIS THE NORM, NOT THE EXCEPTION

The examples of innovation we have described offer a more human, more responsive and better-value approach to public services than the traditional model. First there is the challenge of how, and then you must make this the norm rather than the exception. Embedding citizens' rights in law is important in challenging the status quo. Here are some steps that could be taken.

A right to personalisation

We need to extend the legal right for citizens to control a

personalised budget across more public services. This becomes even more effective where budgets for different services can be combined, such as in health and social care. It should come with a right to have support in making the best, most effective use of the money available and the right to pool that money with other recipients so that they can, together, organise how that money is spent.

Citizen-led commissioning

Commissioning is the process by which needs are assessed, desired outcomes selected and services allocated to achieve them. Putting the citizen or service user at the heart of this decision-making process can transform how it works. Lambeth's 'cooperative commissioning' model aims to help individuals or communities choose the outcome they want for themselves, then helps them select the interventions or services to make it happen. With proper guidance and support, it is an approach that puts real power in the hands of the service user by making professionals more directly accountable to the people they serve.

A right to mutualise

Both front-line workers and service users should have the right to request mutualisation of the service they use. Proposals would need to demonstrate how service users would have more control over decisions that affect them, and could be required to demonstrate improvements in social value. Any right to a request of this kind would be subject to viability tests, including the knock-on effect on other related services so they would not be undermined.

CHALLENGING THE TRADITIONAL MODEL

Progressives must answer two crucial questions. First, how can we make sure that public services – those services on which we all rely at some stage in our lives – achieve better results for people? And, second, how can we sustain public services given the massive challenge of an ageing population?

The answers lie in challenging the traditional bureaucratic model of state-delivered services. We must shape an enabling state based on the principles of power, partnership and prevention, seeking to harness and strengthen human relationships and seize the opportunities presented by new technology. This will involve a fundamental shift of power to citizens, communities and front-line workers, and by developing a new citizen-led model of decision-making, it will break down the service silos that lock so much inefficiency into the system. Change on this scale doesn't just renew public services, it renews public accountability and democracy itself by shifting power to people so they can use it to improve their own lives, and we can all benefit from a fairer and more equal society.

Norman Lamb has been the Liberal Democrat MP for North Norfolk since 2001. After serving as a minister in the Department for Business, Innovation and Skills, he served as Minister of State for Care and Support at the Department of Health (2012–15). In this post, he worked to reform the care system and integrate health and social care, with a greater focus on preventing ill health. He also challenged the NHS to ensure mental health is treated with the same priority as physical health. He is now the Liberal Democrat health spokesperson.

Steve Reed is the Labour MP for Croydon North, a seat he won in a by-election in 2012. After graduating in English, he worked for sixteen years in business and education publishing. During this time he was elected as a councillor in the London Borough of Lambeth, and became the council's leader in 2006. In 2011, the *Local Government Chronicle* named him one of the most influential council leaders in the country. He served as a shadow Home Office Minister under Ed Miliband (2013–15), and is currently shadow Minister for Local Government.

REGENERATION WITH IMAGINATION

Jonathan Edwards

'Happy families are all alike,' writes Tolstoy at the start of *Anna Karenina*. 'Every unhappy family is unhappy in its own way.' One might easily transpose that observation to the different areas of the UK, or even the wider world – there is something consistent about areas that do well, but every area that does badly is in that position as a result of specific local circumstances. And therein lies the solution.

Growing inequality is not a specifically British problem, but the idea that the most deprived areas, those that widen the extremities of the inequality spectrum, can somehow be dragged into prosperity by a uniform strategy handed down from London needs revising. It has certainly failed thus far, despite the best intentions, pronouncements and sometimes efforts of those who recognise that something has to be done. The search for that 'something' to lift our most deprived areas out of their current state needs to focus on custom-built local solutions specific to the areas concerned, with London playing its part as a facilitator but not dictating what must uniformly be done.

Many of the most deprived areas of Britain are in Wales. The Gross Value Added contribution of each individual (GVA per head) is lower in Wales than in any other UK nation or region. Anglesey is now the poorest part of Britain, its average income barely above Malaysia's, and some of Europe's poorest smaller countries have now overtaken some Welsh communities. But it's not just about poverty. People are being economically marooned from the mainstream simply because of the places in which they live (or, rather, *don't* live), because everything is focused on Britain's biggest cities and metropolitan areas, most notably London and the south-east of England. There is no shortage of regeneration initiatives coming from Whitehall, but much of them are directed towards areas of greatest population, like the so-called Northern Powerhouse. And, anyway, regeneration is not a case of one-size-fits-all, which means Wales stands to hold on to many of the areas that contribute to the UK's inequality problem unless a more creative and imaginative approach to regeneration takes hold.

Plaid Cymru is a progressive party. Tackling inequality and enhancing opportunity are two of the core principles at the heart of every Plaid manifesto, along with other progressive themes such as a genuine commitment to the environment, support for the EU, and an intelligent approach to infrastructure (we must expand Wales's infrastructure, both physical and digital, but in ways that will help, which is why we rejected the environmentally harmful and economically dubious plans to expand the M4 motorway). To that extent there is no reason Plaid shouldn't be part of a broad UK progressive cooperative spirit. The 2015 election was the first 'multi-national' Westminster election, with Leanne Wood's appearance on the televised seven-way leader debate bringing home aspects of Welsh reality to English, Scottish and Northern Irish voters in a way that had never happened before. The 2020 election promises to be no different, but for Plaid to be part of UK-wide progressive cooperation, the progressive approach to the Westminster government has to include a deeply held commitment to area-specific regeneration.

THE NEED FOR IMAGINATION

It was Vince Cable who said in January 2014 that Britain was undergoing 'the wrong type of recovery'. Invoking the now-legendary British Rail excuse about the wrong kind of snow thwarting BR's best efforts to weatherproof Britain's rail infrastructure, he said the focus on reducing the deficit by massive cuts to public expenditure meant Britain's economic balance sheet looked better, but at terrible cost. Cuts to public expenditure meant less money was going to revitalise the areas where people were struggling most, so while GDP and other economic indicators looked good, it was a 'recovery' at the cost of deepening inequality, which is hardly good news in the long run, to say nothing of being morally wrong.

Money is vital to help deprived areas, but money alone will not solve the problem. We need to avoid the wrong type of regeneration, which means adopting a new approach to regeneration policy. The amount of big data and connectivity we have these days augurs well. The data help us understand local economies, in particular why certain industries do well and others don't. New research has established a correlation between the profile of specialised skills in a town or city and the likelihood of certain industries thriving or struggling there. This ought to allow us to better plan which sectors to encourage and support in which areas, so we aren't putting large sums of taxpayers' money on a wing and a prayer into locating companies in areas where they might thrive but might equally well go under.

There are plenty of examples of the kind of imaginative regeneration happening, many from overseas, but enough in the UK.

In Bristol, the city's historic tradition has been combined with a diverse cultural scene to create a local economic revival around one of the casualty areas of the austerity years: the arts. For example, the Watershed is a project that grew up in former warehouses in Bristol's harbour area. It is known for its three cinemas and spaces for other arts events, but it also hosts digital and media businesses. The Watershed's manager Dick Penny talks about 'real respect here for difference and invention; a culture where people want to help, even if they don't get what it is that you're trying to do; a sharing of ambition and engagement between artist and audience'. Another buzzword used at the Watershed is 'disruption', the term *du jour* denoting a changing of habits and doing things differently. Also in Bristol is the Engine Shed, a hub of activity for entrepreneurs, business leaders, academics, students and others to share good practice and ideas, and in some cases collaborate. It's called the Engine Shed because it's housed in Brunel's original station dating back to 1841, and activities in the Engine Shed cover not just the city of Bristol but also the Bristol and Bath 'city region'.

In the USA, the start-up guru Brad Feld has outlined his 'Boulder Thesis', a guide to creating long-term prosperity in places that have known better times, based on his experience of helping businesses to start up in the Colorado town of Boulder. Feld argues that creating a vibrant start-up community requires four things: good local leaders; a long-term vision (looking at least twenty years into the future); a real mix of people who all feel valued and included; and events to keep people inspired. Known as a strongly hippy city in the 1960s with a fiercely independent streak, Boulder appeared in *Forbes* magazine's 2013 list of best places for business and careers, and Feld says the city's business success is based on remaining attractive to those who identify with the 1960s hippy era. The Boulder model won't work everywhere, but it works for Boulder with its combination of a distinctive history and a willingness to embrace new realities (it was the first US city to levy a carbon tax in 2007).

And, closer to home, there is the example of Preston – highlighted by David Boyle on page 23 – where the council has made it a central pillar of their local economic strategy to study where the money it spends on services flows to and whether it can continue to keep it flowing locally for longer.

POLICY MEASURES TO MAKE IT HAPPEN

The key recognition here is that no two places are alike. Each place – whether town, city or mini-region – has its own character, geographical attributes and local skills, and any regeneration solution must take account of local features and not assume that what works in Manchester will work in Machynlleth.

Underpinning a strategy to find area-specific regeneration solutions, there has to be a commitment by central government to economic fairness. Wealth inequality in the UK has grown under successive Conservative and Labour governments to the point where Britain is now the most unequal country in Europe, where inner London is the richest area in the EU but parts of Wales are worse off than many parts of the former Soviet bloc. We need to look to models such as that adopted by Germany, where the state deliberately pursues a policy to reduce wealth inequalities. Service industries such as banking, which are mainly located in London and south-east England, have overtaken the pre-crash levels of 2008, whereas the traditional strengths of the Welsh economy are still weak – industrial production and manufacturing are 15 per cent and 10 per cent below their pre-crash levels respectively.

A progressive government should bring in an Economic Fairness Bill that introduces a legal duty for all future governments to gear macro-economic policy towards a levelling up of wealth per head – which would make for a much fairer economy in terms of prosperity and opportunity. Other measures that could flow from this legal duty include a UK convergence fund (like the European Union's cohesion and regional development funds) through which underperforming areas are supported; industrial policy to redress the balance in the economy towards manufacturing and advanced engineering and not so much in favour of financial services; and a system whereby areas with the lowest GVA are prioritised for infrastructure spending and investment.

While help from central government is needed, a sustainable recovery will require local finance to remain local. Local economic growth, if it is to be genuinely self-regenerating, needs to be funded by the proceeds of its own failure or success. It's all very well talking about localism for democracy and public services, but there needs to be a form of economic localism too. One obvious policy for a progressive UK government to embrace would be to allow the revenue from corporation tax to be spent locally if it is raised from companies with profits below an agreed threshold. Taking the contribution of small- and medium-sized enterprises to the British economy, if this threshold were set at £1 million, it would give mayors, councils and First Ministers around £20 billion a year, which in turn would encourage them to reinvest it in local businesses that are likely to succeed.

If the progressives were to adopt such an approach, it would not simply be a sop to get the Welsh on board to create a viable project at Westminster. It would benefit other areas of the UK (notably Northern Ireland) which fall between the stools of the formulaic regeneration initiatives driven by Whitehall. Tackling inequality is at the heart of the progressive agenda; a government that sets the framework for an imaginative and creative regeneration programme based on specific local attributes would be making a profound and tangible contribution to narrowing the gap between the poorest and the rest.

This is important, because the rest of the UK must not view Wales as some sort of poor relation who needs ongoing support. Wales is in some ways a shining example of what the Westminster government should be doing. Wales's response to the 2008 crash was held up as a beacon of best practice across the UK, and thousands of jobs were safeguarded because a Welsh economics minister (a Plaid Cymru minister, actually) showed leadership and brought together businesses, the unions and the public sector to weather the storm. Our environmental record should also stand as an example of what the rest of the UK should be doing – from our work holding threats at bay, such as keeping restrictions on GM crops and scrapping expansion of the M4, to positive measures, such as regenerating farming, planting more than 112,000 trees and launching a £34 million programme to drive forward cutting-edge research to secure a low-carbon future for Wales.

How long Wales remains a devolved nation as part of the UK,

as opposed to an independent sovereign state, remains to be seen. For the moment, we are part of the UK, but there will always be a limit to the ability of a devolved nation to fully realise its economic potential. If the next government at Westminster is serious about keeping the UK together, at least for the foreseeable future, it would do well to recognise the value of what Wales has to offer, and to nurture it with the funds and framework to allow Wales to thrive as it has done at various times in the past.

In 1969, the Welsh economist Professor Edward Nevin said, 'The Welsh economy is drifting not because the crew are fast asleep, but because the boat has no engine and the navigator no map. The Welsh economy is drifting because no one knows where it is, or should be going.' We are keen to give the Welsh economy a new engine and a different map – and the whole of the UK will benefit from helping us in this task.

Jonathan Edwards is the Plaid Cymru Member of Parliament for Carmarthen East and Dinefwr. Before entering Parliament in 2010, he was head of policy for Citizens Advice Cymru. He is Plaid Cymru's Treasury and economic spokesman at Westminster.

HOW WILL WE LIVE IN THE FUTURE?

Siân Berry & Stephen Joseph

We've become so used to poor housing and traffic-choked streets that it takes imagination to see that things could be different. Yet, in both rural and urban areas, the idea of a place with good, affordable housing, pleasant streets and green spaces that are good for walking and cycling to nearby, locally rooted shops and services, with good access to public transport for longer trips, is a vision people right across the political spectrum can subscribe to. And it's an area where progressives can develop policies that can offer an optimistic and exciting prospect for the future.

In theory, all the necessary principles are enshrined in planning policy, and so it ought to be possible for the places we live to be making steady progress towards being much better than they are today. More importantly, it ought to be possible to build alliances and majorities in favour of specific measures to make them better – plans for truly sustainable new housing estates and regenerations, with enthusiastic communities committed to making them friendly and attractive, the resources for good local services and green space, and, of course, good, affordable, sustainable transport.

But we are not there yet. Too often the provisions of the National Planning Policy Framework are being used to support the oldest of old-style suburbs and sprawl, backed up with bypasses instead of buses and trams. And although the county councils and government ministers responsible for the decisions that lead to these are usually Conservative, there is often a significant level of support from the left for these plans too.

Therefore, to make a real start on building the broad-based coalition in support of building the best, most sustainable places to live, there are some past shibboleths that need to be tackled. These include:

- thinking that any development is good development, even if it harms and excludes whole groups of people;
- an attachment to 'regeneration' without thinking about who this regeneration will serve;
- a blindness to car dependence and the problems this brings, for those with as well as those without access to cars;
- and criticism of anyone expressing concern about destruction of the countryside by new roads, housing or business parks, or about poor or substandard development, as Nimbys intent on 'pulling the ladder up behind them'.

Of course, poorer communities need jobs, housing and investment, as well as access to these, but too often they have been offered crumbs from the developers' tables. In addition, those promoting alternatives to, say, the Pathfinder initiative in Liverpool that involved the demolition of terraced housing, or the redevelopment of council housing in Newham, or for that matter new roads and upgraded airports surrounded by car-based development, have simply been dismissed as Luddites getting in the way of growth. More widely, there has been a failure to consider a good, high-quality built environment, or the need to have more equal shares of space and land rather than just wealth or income, as a key part of any progressive project.

The last Labour government did very little to tackle dysfunctional land and housing markets – if anything it fell prey to neoliberal ideas of 'freeing up' or deregulating and weakening the planning system, rather than valuing and strengthening it. On transport, the government – after the early years under John Prescott with a good Transport White Paper and the creation of Transport for London – did little to tackle poor public transport (indeed, in 2004 it actively stopped the building of trams in Liverpool, Leeds and Portsmouth), or promote cycling and walking. It did, however, having culled the Conservatives' road-building programme in its early years, revert to building and widening more roads. It's a sad fact that Labour governments have been responsible for the closure of far more rail lines than Conservatives have, seduced by an argument that railways are somehow for the rich and should therefore be replaced by buses.

TRANSPORT'S ALLIANCES NEEDED FOR HOUSING

However, in many towns and cities, the conditions are developing for a new alliance among progressives for more positive models of development. The ways in which housing, planning and transport policies and trends now work are disadvantaging large numbers of people and starting to create space and opportunities for broad coalitions of change.

These conditions are particularly severe in London, where we can see the beginnings of an acute hollowing out of the centre by high property prices driven by lax land ownership and deregulation, as well as the sale or redevelopment of the remaining low-cost housing on estates. But they also apply to many larger cities and towns as well, particularly in the south where home ownership is already following London in becoming out of reach for all but the richest.

Across the country we can see problems caused by land hoarding by developers, growing levels of homelessness, poorly regulated private landlords, new and old car-dependent developments, poor and expensive public transport, too much traffic, a growing awareness and concern about levels of air pollution, and concerns about obesity and ill health caused by too little exercise. With almost every citizen affected by one or more of these problems, we can hope for a renaissance in the broad-based coalitions for change that we have seen in transport in the past, and for these to expand to cover housing and other issues as well.

These problems, driven by a malfunctioning housing market, can also help to cast light on the wider failures of free markets and can help create the conditions in which these failures can be challenged.

Transport, of course, already has a track record of these kinds of coalitions achieving change. Campaign for Better Transport (for which both of us have worked) was founded in the early 1970s as Transport 2000 by the rail unions, who brought together a range of interests, including the Ramblers Association, the Women's Institutes, and the Railway Industry Association, to create a campaign that successfully stopped attempts by the Conservative and then Labour governments to close all or most of the rail network.

In that decade, local, broad-based coalitions were also successful in stopping destructive road building in some cities, including London where the Labour Party (having been in favour of the three large motorway-style Ringways) changed its view and won back the Greater London Council in 1973 on a 'Homes before Roads' platform.

Later, in the 1990s, opposition to the Conservatives' 'Roads for Prosperity' programme, which Margaret Thatcher described as the 'biggest road-building programme since the Romans', brought together unlikely alliances of radical environmental campaigners, aristocrats and Conservative councillors. Friends of the Earth successfully spearheaded a 'Road Traffic Reduction Act' with very broad support; this charged councils with a duty to come up with traffic-reduction plans.

ACCESS TO SERVICES, NOT JUST TO TRANSPORT

For the future, we believe we can hope for even broader and more coherent coalitions in support of better places and communities. The social and health implications of transport and planning policies are starting to result in campaigns within transport that are not focused only on the means or the mode, but on the outcomes expected.

For example, in recent years, our work has supported campaigns by bus users in rural communities concerned about reaching vital healthcare and other services, and a coalition of young people highlighting how public transport gives them access to training and education that would be impossible under their own steam. And, although the strongest outcry remains in London, growing awareness in many cities across the country of the health effects of air pollution offers similar opportunities for building broad-based coalitions to cut traffic, control lorries and vans, create space for cycling and give pedestrians more space and priority.

On public transport, there are opportunities for broad-based campaigns, but there is still a danger of confusing means and ends and a tendency to talk about public ownership and control as good things in themselves, instead of spelling out how they might improve people's daily lives. Better, more frequent and cheaper services, more accessible to people with disabilities, and with more staff who are better paid, better trained and better treated, with smart cards valid over whole networks, have social and economic effects that will attract lots of support if spelled out.

On housing, the opportunities are there to create similar coalitions for change. Our housing problems have many causes and need to be tackled from many different directions. Hundreds of thousands of new homes are needed, but supply alone won't solve the problem unless we also change the nature of what is being built, where it is located, how it is serviced and how it is governed.

There have been large-scale, broad-based campaigns against fuel poverty and in favour of good insulation. There have also been inspirational local campaigns against estate demolitions and communities being dispersed while the social housing they lived in is replaced by homes that are 'affordable' only to the few.

There is a growing ecosystem of housing campaigners: activists occupying empty buildings to highlight homelessness; communities defending their estates; private renters banding together to take on rogue landlords and lettings agents, and a growing discontent among younger generations who are realising they will never, under current conditions, be able to afford to buy their own homes. However, this is not yet a properly linked-up network. These are often locally based and under-resourced campaigns without the large, umbrella organisations to bring these concerns together and propose a clear alternative that the road campaigners of the 1970s and 1990s enjoyed. The large housing campaign groups themselves are often taken up with the day-to-day concerns of providing services for the homeless and those at the sharp end of the housing crisis, and not able to support these independent groups.

We can envisage the need for a 'Campaign for Better Housing' to emerge in the way that Transport 2000 and Friends of the Earth grew up and supported rail and road campaigners, playing a crucial part in the wider environment movement in the 1970s and 1990s, alongside grass roots networks such as Alarm and Road Block. By bringing together the groups fighting individual housing battles and building a coherent alternative vision to tackle the dysfunctional housing and land markets, such an organisation could have a real impact.

The conditions for change in housing might include restrictions on absentee ownership, more regulation of landlords and rents, open data on property ownership, and much stronger and more positive planning to restrict car-based urban sprawl and prevent the loss of social housing in inner cities.

But more fundamental change will also be needed – land value taxation or alternative forms of taxing 'betterment' of land to cut land speculation. This is going to be much more challenging, because it can be presented as a threat to existing home owners, and to a syndrome now deep in the national psyche about housing as an investment – another totem we need to tackle, which is much less entrenched in other Western European countries.

BETTER HOUSING MAKING BETTER COMMUNITIES

A housing campaign might also make the case for high-quality housing, rather than just more housing. Improving existing buildings – with proper insulation, streetside play areas, in-built traffic calming and better local services that people can walk or cycle to – needs to be treated by progressives as a priority, alongside building new housing. And when we do build new housing, we can and should build real communities, with all of these and more – high-density housing but with plenty of room and rooms rather than rabbit hutches, minimum space standards, built around good public transport, green space and safe cycling and walking routes to good local schools, health services and shops.

There are some examples of places striving for this, like the new housing development at Shawfair in Scotland next to the newly opened Borders Railway, and car-free developments such as 'BedZED' in Sutton and promoted in Islington by the Lib Dems when they controlled the council.

To get all this, we can find some unexpected allies, encompassing a lot of different people from very diverse backgrounds.

Although many people from the 'baby boomer' generation are

sitting on theoretical fortunes in their underused family homes, their own children and grandchildren in generations X and Y are struggling, and many are still living with their parents at ages not seen commonly for decades. The recognition that the value of their asset stands in the way of their 'own kind' getting on could be a turning point if we can make it more widely known. As 'buy to let' loses its attractions, the scope for getting widespread support for properly regulated private housing markets and landlords will grow. We might even start to question the idea that everyone must own their own home, and move towards a more European-style renting culture, recognising that land speculation is much less entrenched in other European countries.

More generally, there can be widespread support for affordable homes. London First has spearheaded a 50,000 homes campaign – this is not simply a call for less restrictive planning policies 'freeing up' developers, but a much more nuanced call for more affordable homes.

This has to be the right direction. A focus on genuinely affordable homes, of high quality and in the right places, can attract lots of support from across the political spectrum. It can unite those concerned about the loss of countryside to those wanting to see genuine urban regeneration. It can even bring in businesses increasingly concerned about their employees getting affordable housing. And it can unite people concerned about keeping car-based sprawl in check with people wanting genuine regeneration and support for communities in cities and towns. For example, countryside campaigners are concerned that the Green Belt might be opened up to development on sites around rail stations; they want to stop this because these sites are the most valuable in meeting the recreational purpose of the Green Belt. This kind of cause can unite transport and housing campaigners to oppose such opening up of the Green Belt and support town centres in existing urban areas being opened up to affordable housing around stations there.

With transport, there are even more potential alliances. The younger generation is much less enamoured by the car than their parents. The growing phenomenon of 'peak car', where car use, especially among younger people, has peaked, is now found in many developed countries. This means that when people under forty envisage an ideal community, the lack of traffic and the ability to get around on foot, bikes and public transport is a stand-out part of their vision.

We can see this being applied in the cycling campaigns in London, Manchester and increasingly other cities, where creative pressure for space for cycling is becoming a feature of campaigning and political consensus.

More progressive business interests are buying into this vision of 'smart' cities. Birmingham has seen Business Improvement Districts funding upgraded public transport. The debate in Cambridge is all about cutting traffic and finding new funding for public transport and cycling from developers, and maybe a levy on workplace parking spaces. And, with the help of grant funding secured by the Greens-run council, Brighton and Hove was named European 'City of the Year' for 2014 by Civitas for policies to promote clean transport, and shortlisted for the National Transport Awards 'Transport Authority of the Year' for its innovative design of cycle lanes. All of this has in common a recognition, whatever the siren voices on the right may say, that high-quality transport and liveable communities are social goods that need to be collectively paid for and provided.

This can be applied more globally. Resistance to airport expansion now brings together working-class communities in Newham with those around Heathrow and under flightpaths elsewhere. Rather than accepting spurious arguments about allowing poor people to fly, progressives should be looking at radical options, for example a 'frequent flyer levy' that would allow one tax-free flight a year, with taxation progressively increasing for subsequent flights. We should not be afraid to make the case for closing and developing some airports in more urban areas, as has been proposed for London City Airport, where this might offer better and more sustainable jobs and cut environmental pollution and noise.

If progressive forces seize this energy and work with it, and work together, the end result will be places that are safer, more pleasant and affordable to live and work in. If we make these a central part of progressive campaigning, we might be surprised how much support we get.

Siân Berry has twice been the Green Party candidate for Mayor of London and is a councillor in the London Borough of Camden and a former Principal Speaker for the party. A graduate in metallurgy, she worked as a writer for pharmaceutical companies but left to work for charities and academic institutions when she became politically active in the early 2000s. She was a founder of the campaign group Alliance Against Urban 4x4s in 2004, and was with the Campaign for Better Transport (formerly Transport 2000) from 2011 to 2015.

Stephen Joseph is the chief executive of Campaign for Better Transport, a post he has held since 1988. He was instrumental in opposing road building and rail privatisation in the 1990s and more recently has been involved in advising on various government initiatives on transport policy. He has shepherded numerous other initiatives on buses, slower speeds, rail and air transport. He was awarded an OBE in 1996 for services to transport and the environment.

REIMAGINING BRITAIN: A NEW APPROACH TO ENVIRONMENTAL ISSUES

Andrew Simms

'Towards what ultimate point is society tending by its industrial progress? When the progress ceases, in what condition are we to expect that it will leave mankind? ... [In an economy no longer growing,] there would be as much scope as ever for all kinds of mental culture, and moral and social progress; as much room for improving the Art of Living and much more likelihood of its being improved, when minds cease to be engrossed by the art of getting on.'

— John Stuart Mill, 1848

Behind the headlines even of partial environmental success stories – like the Paris climate accord in December 2015 – there is a culture of denial. Initiatives are designed and agreements signed with little recognition of whether they will actually solve environmental problems. From governments to anti-austerity opposition groups, the economic implications of the need to prevent irreversible climatic upheaval are not fully appreciated.

The Paris accord itself, though a great diplomatic achievement, rests on assumptions that could undermine its ambition. The UN Framework Convention on Climate Change recognises in the Paris text the need to keep global average surface temperature rises 'well below 2°C above pre-industrial levels and to pursue efforts to limit the temperature increase to 1.5°C above pre-industrial levels'. It gathers together pledges of action from nations to help achieve these targets. But if the point is to build a bridge of action to reach them, so far the promises don't cross the divide. Pledges by countries are non-binding, with no penalties for failure to deliver. A range of estimates indicate that current commitments would leave the world facing between 2.7–4°C of warming. Anywhere in this range is a step beyond the point that a domino effect begins, suggesting a course of potentially irreversible, catastrophic warming. Even worse, the models used to arrive at the lower, but still dangerous, levels of warming make unrealistic assumptions, for example that global emissions peaked in the past (when in fact they are still rising), and that purely speculative, future technologies will be able to remove vast quantities of greenhouse gases from the atmosphere. Hope depends on an obligation by the signatories of the accord to publish and regularly 'upward review' the targets, such that 'the efforts of all parties will represent a progression over time'.

No doubt the Paris accord represents as much as could be achieved at the time, and getting some form of global agreement was indeed an accomplishment. But quite apart from the need to recognise that the deal won't deliver what it promises, and even if it does it would still be insufficient to halt aggressive warming, it is typical of a world that talks the talk when it comes to environmental rhetoric yet turns its back on the environment when planning and shaping the economy of the future.

Part of the denial comes in the form of the politically tempting idea that somehow technology and efficiency alone offer the wealthy world a planetary 'get out of jail free' card. In other words, they suggest we can deal with climate change without having to change much. But this assumption is dashed by research showing that the long-promised (and longed-for) decoupling of growth from resource use has been mostly illusory and an artefact of incomplete accounting. Research published in May 2015 by the US Proceedings of the National Academy of Sciences found that 'achievements in decoupling in advanced economies are smaller than reported or even nonexistent... As wealth grows, countries tend to reduce their domestic portion of materials extraction through international trade, whereas the overall mass of material consumption generally increases.'

While subsequent, more sophisticated updates of the original 1972 work on limits to growth by scientists at the Massachusetts Institute of Technology (MIT) only confirmed those early findings, an exciting new debate on achieving prosperity without growth was opened by the UK Sustainable Development Commission in 2009 with an agenda-setting report. This pointed the way forward for dealing with the apparent non-appearance of an environmental Kuznets Curve in 'advanced' growth economies, one that might suggest that the more information- and service-driven an economy, the more 'weightless' and less demanding of resources it becomes. On aggregate, higher economic growth drives higher environmental impact, with the effects exported through the displacement of mining, manufacturing, offset schemes and waste being shipped to poorer countries.

Instead, a new economic model is needed, judged not by how quickly it grows, but by how well it allows us all to thrive within planetary environmental boundaries. The good news is that such a change in direction would bring both environmental and social benefits. Social justice, human well-being and a thriving environment are, in fact, the core and measure of success for a new economic model.

Our current situation portrays a tough landscape, but as Thomas Hardy once wrote, 'If a way to the Better there be, it exacts a full look at the Worst.' And the very good news is that the kinds of policies that can lay the foundations for a radical environmental transition in Britain, such as those laid out at the height of the financial crisis in the 2008 Green New Deal report, are policies that also address a number of social and economic challenges. They tackle fuel poverty; create countless 'green collar jobs' in places where they are most needed; make good, secure investments for our pensions; insulate Britain from fuel price volatility; and also pave the way to effective climate action. The first steps of such a policy package not only touch on much-needed reforms of the finance sector, but tackle one of the other great crises facing Britain: housing.

Many of the policies that are environmentally damaging are bad socially too. In 2015, the UN delivered a set of new, universal Sustainable Development Goals, one of which is poverty eradication, yet there remains an almost universal reliance on wealth trickling down within economies that are geared towards endless conventional economic growth. The problem is that the evidence of recent years has been the opposite: of wealth concentrating among small elites in rich and poor countries alike.

It has long been known that there is no automatic link between economic growth and human development. The UN Human Development Report shows, for example, how countries with similar income, like Chile and Equatorial Guinea, can have very different human outcomes, while countries with similar levels of development, like Gabon and Indonesia, can have different levels of income. Other policies to do with issues like education and distribution of income make the difference. Beyond certain levels of income, links between rising consumption and well-being break down. Just as growth does not guarantee human development (although for very poor countries it will typically accompany it), nor can we grow our way to reducing our environmental impact.

So not only is the very thing that is supposed to contribute to poverty eradication inefficient at best and generally failing the poorest, but it is also mortgaging the planet. The environmental footprint of the global economy has already outgrown the shoe size of the planet's biosphere. Climate change is one clear example. Governments speak of living within our financial means (which is, in reality, a very political and elastic concept) while globally we are casually consuming resources and producing waste faster than ecosystems can replace and safely absorb them, living far beyond our ultimately inescapable planetary means. In other words, we shouldn't take more than the environment can make in a given year. But, by the most recent, conservative estimate, globally we had used up a year's worth of nature's ability to provide resources and tackle waste by 13 August – only two-thirds of the way through the year! – and had thus run into 'ecological debt', continuing a trend in which the day when we begin overconsuming falls ever earlier in the calendar.

A POSITIVE VISION OF A GREEN ECONOMY

An old economic model of debt-fuelled over-consumption has steadily reasserted itself in Britain, with consumer debt rising again in a pattern that preceded the 2007–08 financial crisis, causing deep concern to the Bank of England. Our challenge is to learn how to flourish within planetary boundaries. People on the left of economics cannot provide a meaningful alternative to neoliberalism simply by criticising austerity for its failure to deliver growth. There needs to be a positive vision articulated for how everyone can live well, while respecting environmental thresholds. A new politics for Britain is nothing without a new economics, and the time has come to consider some of its core principles and ask what it might look and feel like.

The new economic model has to make sense from an economic, social and environmental perspective. We all have basic requirements, like food and shelter, so it needs to deal with housing and food production. We all require a certain amount of energy, so ensuring a security of energy supply that meets basic requirements while making the transition to meet climate targets is a core challenge. And we have to ensure that our use of resources is sustainable, not just to guarantee our current social and economic foundations, but to avoid exhausting resources on which future generations may rely. A circular economy with cradle-to-cradle production methods creates the base for this. It also helps prevent the accumulation of the waste from 'stuff' left behind by a consumer model built on disposability and the built-in obsolescence of 'upgrade' culture. It is another way of talking about the basic green economic principles, which employ both skilled and unskilled labour and are hence rich in job creation, of repair, reduce, reuse and recycle.

We have to challenge the notion that 'consumerism to fuel economic growth' is the only way to run an economy – not just for economic and environmental reasons, but because nobody is particularly happy with the consumerism we have. Data stretching over decades and from across the industrialised world reveals a common, consistent pattern: that while GDP has risen, reported levels of life satisfaction have generally flatlined or fallen. The idea that, once key needs are met, more 'stuff' makes us happier, is a myth. It prompts a rethink of our relationship with material goods.

A 'NEW MATERIALISM'

The great irony of neoliberal economics that struts beneath a flag of choice and consumer sovereignty is that it seems to offer no other choice than to live in an economy of debt-fuelled, growth-addicted, disposable consumerism. But is a different kind of economy, one that meets people's deeper needs while respecting and enjoying the real material world of diverse natural resources, so hard to imagine? Inescapably, we are part of the material world, so how then can we develop a better and healthier connection to it?

A green and more convivial economy can have at its heart a 'new materialism,' not only to significantly enhance our well-being, but as an essential step towards thriving within planetary boundaries. A new materialism would also offer a better solution to key, current economic challenges, such as the need to generate ample, good-quality jobs – and a way of making daily goods and services available without falling into the consumer debt-trap.

From environmental science to behavioural economics and neuroscience, data has piled up to reveal the personal, social and ecological harm done by materialism. At the heart of the new relationship we need with the material world are different attitudes toward making, owning, sharing and caring for things.

Until recently, if you tilted against the shopping mall and parade of endless consumer upgrades, you'd be defining yourself as an enemy of progress. By appearing to stand for a world drained of consumer novelty and pleasure, you're in danger of seeming to be part of a 'miserabilist tendency'. Such fears push claims about the benefits of living simply and of 'less being more' into the background. Perversely, the green movement, which works to save conditions for life on the planet, has been made synonymous with a rejection of the material world. As a result, it largely withdrew from a critique of growth and making the case for a fundamentally better economic model, instead hoping to 'green' the existing model from within. Two ironies stalk this version of events. Nothing has driven actual austerity like the collapse of the model of debt-fuelled overconsumption. And, in a green economy characterised by less passive consumerism and more active production – making, adapting, mending, sharing, repairing and repurposing – there is far more potential for novelty and pleasure. Yet, scared of criticism from the mainstream, many environmentalists took to preaching a green variant of consumerism, inadvertently reinforcing the very value system driving the lack of sustainability in existing economic models.

Ironically, when those models based on competitive, acquisitive individualism fail, it leaves many people in today's society having to make and mend out of financial necessity. But, more so, an economy based on local-level cooperation and mutual support, and reuse rather than waste, is precisely the model that has enabled people to survive when the conventional economy falls apart, as has been the case in Argentina and Greece. It is an economy of solidarity that underpins only the well-thought-through models of economic transition developed from the community level up, by movements from the Buen Vivir initiatives in Latin America to the expanding international Transition Town movement.

From some of the poorest communities in the world to rural and urban Britain, there are growing examples of different, better ways of meeting our needs that involve a great reskilling, local economic innovation, creating new job opportunities and access to goods that many would otherwise be deprived of, all based on more sustainable practices.

Workshops where people can share tools and ideas known as 'hack' or 'makerspaces' are spreading fast globally. From Albania to Argentina, Poland to the Philippines and Nigeria to Norway, people are meeting and making. The UK has dozens, and the movement is thriving in the home of old consumerism, the United States. In Britain, the Bicycle Hub website lists sixty projects that recycle and repair bikes, selling them at affordable prices and often incorporating training schemes; Swindon-based Recycles is a social enterprise run by people who were once homeless; Organic Lea, a workers' cooperative, has brought growing back to the Lea Valley, the original 'bread basket' of London.

Such enterprises are not just about economics and the environment – there's a dimension about our greater well-being but which is of great practical value too. By making and mending objects, we engage in a practice of care that connects us more directly to the world and one another, rebuilding local economies and, in the process, reweaving community. The attractiveness of a 'great reskilling' has been taken up by the enormously successful Transition Town movement, prominent in the UK and spreading quickly internationally.

The ecological economist Herman Daly describes the economy of the future as needing to be 'a subtle and complex economics of maintenance, qualitative improvements, sharing, and adaptation to natural limits. It is an economics of better, not bigger.'

Unambiguously, this presents a shift from a consumer society to a producer or 'great making society'. It suggests a world in which we roll back our gradual deskilling and the impoverishment of work. This is a world where we don't just consume collaboratively, we produce collaboratively too. In terms of economics, it is what Professor Victoria Chick, one of the world's leading Keynesian scholars, describes as meaning a collapse in the rigidly separate ways in which producers and consumers are understood. A programme of reskilling is called for.

It would be naive to expect such a different economy to emerge spontaneously in a contemporary world created by decades of deskilling, disposability and relentless conditioning on the consumer treadmill. Conditions for a better economy need creating. Available time and basic financial security provide important foundations for change. Key working policies, such as the shift to the norm of a shorter working week and schemes that guarantee people a basic income, have a track record of making life better for people from Europe to North America. Other economic pressures that stand in the way of change will need addressing too. Chief among these is tackling the UK's dysfunctional housing market – in turn distorted by a weakly regulated and bloated financial sector. Again, there are ample international precedents from Berlin to New York that we can learn from to prevent profiteering and guarantee affordable and social housing.

There are signs that some of this new materialism is happening by itself. The American magazine *Forbes* estimated that the revenue flowing through the sharing economy into people's pockets in the US surpassed $3.5 billion in 2013. Eighty per cent of British people say that sharing makes them happier. In thinking about whether to hire or buy, the majority of people work out the likely cost per use of an item and around one in six people already opt to hire over buying.

There is a body of evidence that suggests that more positive environmental behaviours follow from a broad shift away from the value system of 'old materialism'. Building on that, a world in which we all hold a wider range of practical skills has the potential to leave us less at the mercy of disposable goods and built-in obsolescence, and more in a position to shape and fashion the world around us in satisfying ways. Such a world would increase our own agency and give us real freedom to replace the illusion promised by financialised markets.

BOOSTING DEMAND WITHOUT INCREASING CONSUMPTION

A rare point of consensus about the current economic malaise centres on demand. Most economists agree that you have to boost demand to keep the economy ticking over, but how do you do so without increasing wasteful and unsatisfying consumption? How can we get away from an economic model that relies on persuading us to overconsume?

If environmental constraints hit an economy that demands ever-higher productivity being produced by fewer people, you have a problem. The only way it can keep going, increasing productivity, is by making more people unemployed. But with a new materialism

– a world in which we make things last longer and endlessly reuse them, and where there is a big shift to the services that keep things going – it takes a lot of hands, which creates a lot of employment. A study on job creation by the waste agency WRAP and think tank the Green Alliance showed that a confident expansion of the circular economy – which is just another articulation of Daly's economics of 'better not bigger' – could create half a million new jobs in Britain. The International Labour Organization sees the global potential for tens of millions of new jobs in the so-called 'green-collar economy'. In this different economy, there is also greater emphasis towards spending on the great joys of life, experiences rather than disposable goods – a shift in consumer spending, which is already proving popular – that are both appealing and also labour-intensive. It points towards the necessary shift from an economy based on material extraction, throughput and waste, to a circular economy of care and conservation.

This new economy will need investment. But there is no shortage of money in the system and there is a slow cultural shift beginning in the world of investors opening up new opportunities. A movement to divest holdings in dubious investment funds is burgeoning; early adopters have, for example, begun a substantial movement to divest from fossil fuels, a movement already representing $2.6 trillion in assets under management. Orthodox economists say that, while such moves may be worthy and are legitimate in reflecting the beliefs of investors, they fail to promote conventional economic growth. Similarly, some financial advisers tell private investors that ethical funds are likely to underperform compared to those unrestricted funds with no ethical criteria.

Not only is this often untrue – some ethical funds have impressively outperformed non-ethical – but it misunderstands that the quality of economic activity is vital to our quality of life. Economics has a purpose beyond and transcending mere scale. It fails to see that persisting with an economic model that does not serve anyone, and is undermining the very life support systems we depend on for our survival, is fundamentally self-defeating.

AWAY AHEAD

Mainstream politics and economics tend to wave away calls for a new economy by telling people to live in the 'real world'. The great irony is that the same voices tend to dismiss the actual real world upon which our livelihoods directly depend – home to forests, fields, climate and ocean – leaving them as afterthoughts and externalities in their economic models.

Against that, a new politics must take back exactly what it means to live in the real world, and offer a better way for everyone to care for and thrive in it.

The way ahead lies in action being taken both at individual and structural level. Governments can't do everything on their own; they need the support of people. But the two working together can create a self-reinforcing dynamic. Manchester's free city centre bus service, which helped reduce car-dependence, and government funding for local council kerbside recycling, which successfully reduced the amount of waste going to landfill (a requirement that originated at EU level), are among the many examples. The kind of low environmental impact, high well-being economic model imagined here requires a comprehensive revitalisation of local economies. That can only come from mutually supportive action by local communities and local and national government. A wide range of measures to achieve such a transition was spelled out in 'Re-imagining the High Street' (NEF, 2010), a report summarising the insights of years of work on the economic forces creating ghost towns and clone towns.

The government formed after the 2020 general election will have to take distinct policy decisions to allow the new economy to evolve. At the very least these will need to include:

- A new, triple-line policy test to apply to all measures taken at national and local government level. Just as every government decision currently has to go through the Treasury, under this new policy test, every decision will need to be assessed on the basis of the best evidence available for whether it is, on balance, likely to raise or lower our well-being, more or less equally share the benefits of economic activity, and increase or reduce our ecological footprint.
- A comprehensive package for high street revitalisation to promote dynamic, local green economies. This should include measures like those laid out in 'Re-imagining the High Street', such as powers to make empty properties available to local small and micro-enterprises and for high street 'transition' hubs; designing well-being, distinctiveness and sustainability indicators into Master Planning processes and making residents equal partners in them; establishing a Local Competition Ombudsman as recommended by the former Competition Commission to rein in the power of the big chain stores; levelling the playing field for new, local sustainable businesses; promoting local procurement; and giving local authorities powers to offer discretionary business rate relief for new low-carbon businesses moving onto the high street and to existing small- and medium-sized independent

businesses who commit to reducing their carbon use and adopting best environmental practices.

- A basic citizen's income – a social support system that replaces means-testing with a single payment to which every citizen is entitled. It has economic potential through encouraging enterprise and creativity, and offers some basic security at a time of the so-called 'gig' economy where people are moving in and out of short-term work. (It is currently being trialled in parts of the Netherlands and Canada.) (See Ruth Lister's discussion of Universal Basic Income, pages 39–41.)
- A new boost to Britain's apprenticeship culture, partly funded through a Green New Deal training programme, itself supported by more effective, directed Bank of England operations to support the productive economy. (It would mean, for example, using public money creation such as quantitative easing to support the emerging low-carbon economy rather than commercial banks.)
- A new approach to the housing supply. There is a huge lack of supply – which greatly restricts people's ability to change economic behaviour – but it cannot be solved simply by building our way out. We need policy innovations such as controls to prevent private profiteering, bringing empty properties back into use, increasing the supply of social and genuinely affordable mutual housing, supporting low-carbon community self-build schemes, and measures to separate land prices from housing costs. And any new build schemes must be to the highest environmental efficiency standards.
- A shift to a new norm of a shorter working week, bringing a range of economic, family, community, citizenship and environmental benefits.
- A review of taxes and charges on materials and services so the

full economic and environmental costs and benefits of repairing or adapting an object are taken into account, designed to create an incentive against waste that may be justified on 'full price' grounds.

- Plans, pathways and resources to achieve the rapid, short-term decarbonisation of the energy supply with a shift away from a 'predict and provide' approach towards active demand management. A Green New Deal to transform domestic and commercial properties and industrial energy use, with aggressive demands for reduction and promotion of renewables, could see the UK's energy supply become 90 per cent renewable by 2030, offering the win/win/win of eradicating fuel poverty, promoting massive job creation and being an adequate action to avert irreversible climate destabilisation.

Leading up to and since the Paris climate agreement, far from resisting change, many major businesses, like the Renewable Energy 100 group of companies, have been ahead of governments, committing to 100 per cent renewable power and calling for clear direction, purpose and support from policy makers and regulators. Time and again, even when some complain initially, businesses innovate and adapt in response to progressive regulation. As the OECD chief economist pointed out recently, 'Governments should stop working on the assumption that tighter regulations will hurt their export share and focus on the edge they can get from innovation.'

The challenge is for the progressives to agree on their core principles and, because there is no single right answer, unite in their willingness to innovate, explore, experiment openly and be prepared to adapt policies that will most effectively steer us towards a new economy. A successful strategy will be one that takes us out of ecological debt, reduces poverty – both in the UK and abroad – and improves life satisfaction in British villages, towns and cities. If we can succeed, people may finally see environmental action as an inextricable part of a new political contract to reimagine Britain and a set of measures ready to be enacted by the post-2020 government.

Andrew Simms is an author, analyst and co-founder of the New Weather Institute. He is a research associate at the Centre for Global Political Economy, University of Sussex, and a fellow of the New Economics Foundation, where he was policy director for over a decade. He wrote the book *Tescopoly* on the impact of supermarkets, coining the term 'clone towns' to describe high-street homogenisation, and co-authored the *Green New Deal*. His latest book, *Cancel the Apocalypse: the New Path to Prosperity*, is a manifesto of new economic possibilities.

NO SUCH PLACE AS 'ABROAD' – A FOREIGN POLICY FOR PROGRESSIVES

Peter Hain

Not always, but at its best, Britain's left has been synonymous with internationalism. From the courage of Jack Jones and George Orwell travelling out to fight fascism in the Spanish Civil War, to the unyielding support of anti-colonial struggles by Fenner Brockway and Michael Foot. From the anti-apartheid zeal of Neil Kinnock, Barbara Castle and David Steel, to the passionate Europeanism of Tony Crosland, Roy Hattersley, Shirley Williams, John Smith and Robin Cook.

In a world riddled with growing inequality and conflict, it is today the progressives' belief in internationalism not isolationism, in multilateralism not unilateralism, in transparency and accountability of power, and in protecting the interests of the many not the few, which offers a much better way of meeting the new threats faced by humankind. The contemporary British right's tendency to unilateralism and isolationism means continuing global insecurity and instability.

So does its dogmatic advocacy of neoliberalism. New mixed-economy models based on government intervention, state ownership stakes and policy-driven regulation offer a much better alternative than the neoliberalist orthodoxy that has been gripping global economic governance since around 1980.

Furthermore, many of Britain's chief economic competitors practise different systems of 'state capitalism'; their governments support significant industrial restructuring and sponsorship of new technology developments in order to stay competitive. Sovereign wealth funds in Asia and the Gulf, increasingly important to both UK domestic and foreign inward investment, are of course state-controlled or -influenced.

The US is often viewed as a model of free-market capitalism. But its iconic car manufacturer General Motors, its insurance giant AIG and its large banks were all bailed out by state funds after the financial crisis. Even Britain's free-market, small-state Conservative government, facing uncertainty over energy supplies, has sought investment in nuclear reactors from the largely state-owned French EDF and Chinese nuclear operators owned and controlled by their Communist government.

Today, international intervention and collaboration by governments is necessary to regulate the global financial system to prevent it from self-destructing again. Although of course governments have always cooperated in the past over natural disasters, or to prevent war, or to combat the proliferation of weapons of mass destruction, there are new, growing and universal threats to the whole planet from climate change, food and water insecurity. These are intertwined in a way that means no country can act on its own; and it is risible to suggest that market forces left to their own devices are any sort of a solution. Together with more familiar threats – international terrorism, cyberattacks, unprecedented levels of migration, population growth, global poverty, cross-border crime and pandemics – these constitute all the ingredients for a 'perfect storm' to hit humankind. And surely nobody can seriously suggest the old nation-state solutions will successfully tackle it? These global threats require global solutions.

SHIFT IN GLOBAL POWER

That in turn requires a recognition that there is a new global politics. In past centuries, Britain may have been able to go it alone. More recently, as a medium-sized nation state, we have sheltered under America's superpower umbrella. But now we are in a multipolar world.

The European Union is the largest, richest single market in the world and plays a significant role in international affairs. But the BRICS countries (Brazil, Russia, India, China and South Africa) symbolise the shifting economic and global power away from the old countries of the west and the north towards the new ones of the east and the south. These emerging economies are forecast by the United Nations to constitute 85 per cent of the world's population – twelve times Europe's at 7 per cent – by 2050.

By 2013, China had become the second biggest economy in the world, the number one trading partner for 128 countries, the biggest holder of foreign reserves, the world's biggest polluter, the biggest consumer of Middle Eastern oil and gas, the country with the fastest growing defence budget and the biggest contributor to

United Nations peace-keeping missions among the five permanent members of the Security Council.

And – notwithstanding China's 2015–16 economic instability – over the next decade and a half, it is likely to be transformed both in relative power to the West, and in the structure of its economy, politics and foreign policy. Its economy could grow to twice the size of America's. Rather than being an exporter of cheap products, it could have the world's biggest consumer market and the largest spending on research and development. And its passive foreign policy of recent years could well mutate into an active strategy in defence of China's global interests.

This means that for European countries like Britain, Pacific alliances and not just our traditional Atlantic alliances will assume increasing importance. And nor should Africa continue to be sidelined. Having been written off as 'The Hopeless Continent' on the cover of *The Economist* in May 2000, in recent years it has seen the fastest growth rates anywhere.

By contrast, the Middle East/Gulf region is a continuing source of huge threat and instability to the world. Jihadis, refugees, war, sectarian conflict, unspeakable human rights abuse: there seems no end in sight to what could even become the equivalent of Europe's Thirty Years' War. Unless four key countries – Saudi Arabia, Iran, Turkey and Israel – put aside their deep differences and begin to work together for peace and reconciliation rather than conflict, the prospects are dire. An end to the apocalyptic Sunni–Shia battle, together with justice for the Palestinians and the Kurds, is a prerequisite to neutralising the global barbarity and mayhem spreading from this region.

Again, this underlines the importance of internationalism not isolationism, with Britain a leading player in international institutions like the United Nations, NATO, the Commonwealth, the

International Monetary Fund, the World Bank and (until the Brexit referendum of 2016) the European Union. Increasingly, we will have limited impact if we try to act alone. This was demonstrated when Britain under Gordon Brown's leadership – and backed by key EU leaders – galvanised the April 2009 G20 meeting to increase public spending in order to prevent the credit crunch from triggering a global depression rather than a recession.

The sheer scale and depth of the global threats of our era make 'little Englander' isolationism – whether from Eurosceptic Tories, UKIP or the BNP – futile. For they offer unilateral responses to multilateral problems.

FOOD AND WATER INSECURITY

Although starvation and shortage of clean water have always been with us, there is now a new and serious problem from a ballooning world population of 7 billion, increasing by 200,000 people daily. It is expected to reach 9 billion by 2050 and over 10 billion by 2100. It has been estimated that fully 50 per cent more food and water will be needed by 2030.

Already, nearly a billion people are undernourished or starving. Food reserves are at a fifty-year low. Although Africa is host to 60 per cent of the world's undeveloped arable land, in eleven countries, stretching from West Africa to Mozambique, only half of usable land is currently being farmed.

But there is a new twist to the problem of food security, born from urbanisation and a rapidly growing middle class. In China, a fundamental change in diet means traditional staple foods such as rice and corn have been eclipsed by meat, fruit and vegetables, consumption of which has quadrupled over the last fifty years. But, compared with cereal crops, these each need considerably more land and water to grow and produce. Beef, for instance, requires about twelve times the amount of water to feed the same number of people as can be fed on rice and wheat. And China is by no means alone in experiencing this phenomenon – as almost all developing economies urbanise and industrialise at great pace, those modern lifestyles require huge additional amounts of water. Yet, over a third of the world's population lives in a water-scarce region. Nearly a billion people have no accessible clean water: in sub-Saharan Africa, that's 40 per cent of the population.

Indeed, conflicts over water are becoming more widespread. In 2001 and 2013, Egypt's presidents threatened military action against Ethiopia to uphold Egypt's access to its main source of water, the Nile. In 2014, Iraqi rivers, canals, dams, sewage and desalination plants all became military targets in the country's civil war. Regular and extreme water shortages in the country give a strategic advantage in cities and the countryside to those who control water supplies. The embittered Israel–Palestine conflict also concerns access to scarce water supplies, with Israelis often controlling or corralling water in Palestinian territories.

The UN Panel report of March 2014 also found evidence that 'climate change can indirectly increase risks of violent conflict in the form of civil war and inter-group violence', for example riots triggered by food shortages and spiralling prices.

More demand for food and water means more demand for energy. Yet there are global energy shortages and volatile fuel prices, which are adding pressures for migration into countries like Britain, its political toxicity uncomfortably demonstrated in the 2016 EU referendum.

MIGRATION

International migration is also a product of globalisation opening up unparalleled opportunities and incentives for people to move to seek better lives. This means it is not easy to make the distinction between 'refugees' and 'economic migrants'. Some 200 million people (the size of Brazil's population) are now on the move globally every year. In 1970, the figure was 70 million.

Contemporary Europe has faced an even bigger crisis as millions have fled from tyranny and economic misery in the Middle East and North Africa, after terrible wars partly promoted by disastrous failures of US/European foreign policy, especially in Syria where a Western-led bombing campaign was pursued instead of serious diplomacy involving also Iran and Russia.

The result: huge strains on every European member state's jobs, housing and race relations, triggering ugly authoritarianism, right-wing extremism and go-it-alone isolationism. But, Europe-wide in nature, the refugee problem could only ever be solved by a Europe-wide solution: it required 'more' Europe not 'less' Europe – an uncomfortable truth for Eurosceptics, notwithstanding the 2016 EU referendum.

Memories proved to be short. Modern Europe was born after a terrible war and the Nazi Holocaust, a time of deep austerity with millions of European refugees fleeing: stateless, homeless, starving and freezing. The people of Europe, Britain included, were saved because governments accepted the moral responsibility for all peoples: allies and ex-enemies alike. We acted together, empowered by the generosity of the US via the Marshall Plan, and we promoted economic policies for growth, not austerity, that were successful both in rebuilding shattered societies and bringing down sky-high levels of wartime national debt. And many of those refugees made distinguished contributions to our societies, from medicine and science to business.

Ominously, as David Miliband, Chief Executive of the International Rescue Committee, observed in 2014: 'There are three forces that are driving this rise in the number of people fleeing conflict: an implosion in the Islamic world, weak states that can't hold back different ethnic and political differences, and a weakened international system. Those are secular trends, not short-term trends, so I think ... that this is likely to be a trend, not a blip.'

GLOBAL SOLUTIONS FOR GLOBAL PROBLEMS

What may appear domestic threats in any one country – like migration, food and water insecurity or drug and people trafficking – are invariably internationally rooted. Rainforests are destroyed to satisfy the global demand for raw materials, and individual decisions by millions of consumers and thousands of corporations also encourage global warming.

The inability of poor Americans to repay mortgages that they probably ought never to have been granted activated a banking crisis in 2007–08, which ricocheted through the entire global financial system, gridlocking private sector credit and investment across the world in countries like Britain. Millions, completely unaware they were at the end of a complex financial chain to those poor American householders, lost their jobs and were forced to hand back the keys to their own mortgaged homes. In turn, the ensuing global recession led to deep cuts in public spending by Western governments, including on their overseas aid and development budgets. The victims: previous beneficiaries of anti-poverty programmes, again oblivious as to the cause of their sudden plight.

British tourists infected with malaria or HIV/Aids while travelling abroad might have been better protected had British-funded programmes been in place to combat these diseases at source. International flu pandemics, cyberattacks on home computers from thousands of miles away, lone American jihadis motivated by internet appeals from Syria-based terrorists, floods of refugees into Europe from Middle East conflicts, British pensioners dependent upon investment returns in China – all this means that 'foreign' and 'domestic' policy are now inextricably intertwined. Multilateral, intergovernmental responses are therefore the only answer, internationalism not nationalism the necessary focus.

Globalisation is now ubiquitous and unstoppable. But while some on the left embark upon a futile mission to defy it, the neoliberal right turns a blind eye to gross exploitation of foreign workers who produce the cheap goods on which richer countries and their citizens have become dependent, and also to the environmental degradation caused by certain production processes.

However, the neoliberal stranglehold on globalisation has also generated a serious backlash in the richer countries. Since the early 1980s, the relative decline in the incomes and job security of the bulk of the population – and especially white, male, working-class citizens – has encouraged support for populism. The surge of popular anger behind both Donald Trump in the 2016 US presidential election and the Brexit campaign in the 2016 British referendum is a part of this backlash.

But the nationalistic, protectionist, unilateralist right in the end has no answers to problems or threats that are global and universal.

Nor is its worship of unrestrained free markets and shrinking government capable of delivering greater prosperity and social justice for all.

It falls to the left to make the case for progressive internationalism. Because interests and problems are so globally interconnected, not only do they require collective action by governments, but we cannot sustain global stability without global justice. Abuse reported in social media on one side of the world becomes almost instantly transparent on the other. The progressives' values of human rights, democracy and equality therefore become not only moral imperatives, but also necessities for stable and sustainable development.

STRONGER, MORE INCLUSIVE GLOBAL INSTITUTIONS

That in turn requires strengthening, not undermining, international institutions and international rules.

Progressives should reclaim and reform key international bodies: the United Nations Security Council, the European Union, the G7/G20, NATO, the Commonwealth, the International Monetary Fund, the World Bank and the World Trade Organization. For example, the composition of the law-making UN Security Council still reflects its origins in the post-Second World War colonial age of 1945. How can Germany, Japan and India be denied the permanent membership enjoyed by the USA, Russia, China, Britain and France? Why is no African or Latin American country a permanent member?

However, like nation state governments, the influence of international bodies has waned, with power ebbing away from the West to the Rest, and also from nation states to non-governmental organisations, both creative (such as Greenpeace) and destructive (such as Daesh). Moreover, the legitimacy of established institutions is threatened: in the US from the reactionary fundamentalism of the Tea Party, to the spirited progressivism of Occupy Wall Street; in the Middle East from the Arab Spring to anti-government people protests in Turkey.

A new progressive internationalism must take account of these complex trends.

EUROPE

Although the European Union can be a frustrating caricature of its progressive origins as a vehicle to deliver peace and stability across a continent where more wars were fought in recent centuries than on any other, and although the architecture and therefore performance of the euro is deeply flawed, Europe's achievements have been enormous. It would be unthinkable for its member states to go to war with each other as they did so often in the past, for they are linked together in a trading bloc underpinned by democracy and human rights. It is inconceivable that Spain, Portugal and Greece would lurch back into fascism, and that former communist dictators in central and Eastern Europe could be reincarnated. A competitive single market that enforces high social and environmental standards has raised both prosperity and the quality of life.

Progressives must challenge the Eurosceptic charge that the EU undermines 'national sovereignty'. Member states do not surrender their sovereignty in the EU, but pool it and thereby become stronger than they would be on their own in a world of huge global challenges. Each country retains its own national identity and very significant domestic parliamentary control but shares sovereignty, enabling common challenges to be confronted together and mutual interests to be promoted. Member states are thereby stronger together where they would be weaker apart, experiencing an illusory 'sovereignty' in an interconnected world. Although that argument may have been lost in the 2016 referendum, it nevertheless remains valid.

But progressives must drive forward an agenda of cooperation across the European Union for public investment and Keynesian growth, not the neoliberal austerity that both dominates and imperils Europe. Imperils because it cannot and does not deliver economic opportunity for all, and therefore breeds disillusion and dangerous populism, evidenced by the strength of the Front National in France, UKIP in Britain and right-wing parties across the continent. Perhaps the starkest evidence was the popular support among working-class voters for Leave in the 2016 EU referendum, which was as much an expression of anger and left-behind alienation at the political elite for pursuing neoliberal policies.

Moreover, although the European Union already contributes over half of the world's overseas aid and negotiates as equals with the US, China, India and other important nations over international trade, Europe needs also to be a serious global force: not so much a rival *for* the US, as a force to be reckoned with *by* the US and the emerging powers in the emerging multipolar world.

SOCIAL JUSTICE AND GLOBAL STABILITY

Since 1950, global economic output is up fivefold and per capita incomes have increased by 350 per cent; and since the early 1980s,

660 million Chinese have been lifted out of poverty; indeed, extreme poverty in Asia has been massively diminished. Nevertheless, in January 2016, an Oxfam report highlighted obscene global inequality: the sixty-two richest billionaires have the same amount of wealth – $1.7 trillion – as the entire bottom half of the earth's population, 3.5 billion people. Sixty per cent of the poorest people in the world are women and, while gender inequality continues, climate change and food and water insecurity will have a disproportionate impact on women.

Another example: although high levels of growth in Asia have created new levels of prosperity, according to *The Lancet*, over 2 million people a year are dying prematurely from air pollution in the cities of Asia.

Progressives should insist that the benefits of globalisation are not at the expense of social responsibility and social justice; and that there is an agenda for sustainable development around the world, based upon equal opportunities regardless of race, gender, religion, nationality, sexual orientation or disability. But, in doing so, we should explain that progressive internationalism is not only about fairness to all, it is also in the self-interest of everyone, including the rich and powerful, because, especially in a transparent world where aggrieved citizens can view alternative and better lifestyles, injustice and oppression are recipes for instability and conflict.

PROGRESSIVE VALUES

Some on both the right and left suggest that progressive values of liberty, pluralist democracy, the rule of law, freedom and human rights are primarily 'Western' and should not be pressed upon countries, such as those in the Middle East, that have not enshrined such values in their structures. Of course they should not be 'imposed' upon such countries, but these values are surely universal. After all, they are enshrined in the UN Charter and the Universal Declaration of Human Rights; indeed, they were expressed by Egyptian protesters occupying Cairo's Tahrir Square in the revolution of 25 January 2011, which gave birth to the 'Arab Spring'. Some – though by no means all – of the resistance to Daesh barbarianism in Syria and Iraq also expressed democratic values.

Nevertheless, there are good grounds for being suspicious of neoconservatives – who had their comeuppance over the war in Iraq – and who also preached 'democracy and human rights'. But that is no reason for progressives to abandon or deny our values to others across the world – more to align ourselves with, and give support to, those elements in other societies who share them. Aung San Suu Kyi was always very clear on this: 'Use your liberty to promote ours,' she said during the freedom struggle in Burma. Nelson Mandela was similarly insistent that boycotts and solidarity campaigns in the West played a vital role in overthrowing apartheid. It was in fact racists defending apartheid who objected vehemently to progressives across the world fighting for democratic rights in their country. The British left, who joined in the fight against apartheid, flatly rejected consistent attacks from apartheid supporters and their British apologists of 'interfering' in their country's affairs and trying to 'impose' democratic values on an African majority 'who weren't ready for democracy'.

That is one argument. Another one entirely is the fraught – and after Iraq often understandably toxic – question of military intervention in the name of democracy, freedom and human rights. That came to a head when the Tory Prime Minister David Cameron tried to bounce Parliament into voting for military strikes against the barbarous Assad regime in 2013. MPs rightly blocked this because it would have sucked Britain catastrophically into the quagmire of the Syrian civil war – a civil war of Sunni versus Shia Muslims, Saudi Arabia versus Iran, and Russia versus Europe and the USA. Also hanging over this decision was MPs' anxiety not to have a rerun of Western military interventions in Afghanistan, Iraq and Libya, especially their poisonous after-effects. However, in Sierra Leone in 2000 and Kosovo in 1999, British military intervention was fully justified and very effective in stopping horrific ethnic cleansing, gross abuses of human rights, mass murder and aggressive threats to peaceful neighbouring nations. Each case should be assessed on its merits against progressive values, with on the one hand a wary reluctance to act without United Nations support, and on the other a refusal to do nothing, as the world so shamefully did over genocide in Rwanda in 1994.

GLOBAL WARMING

Climate change provides perhaps the clearest case for concerted and urgent action by every nation coordinating together. Indeed, it cannot be tackled in any other way, for there is no escape for any part of the world from its destructive consequences.

The costs are already hitting hardest and earliest in the developing world, despite the fact that much of the climate damage has been done by industrialised nations. Lord Stern's 2006 report commissioned by the last Labour government predicted a decline in crop yields in parts of Africa already scarred by famine and desertification, affecting hundreds of millions of people, and some of the world's poorest countries, which are likely to lose 10 per cent of their economic output. Key agricultural areas – including the Mekong Delta, the source of much of the world's rice – face ruin from storm surges of salty sea water, in turn triggering starvation and mass flights of refugees.

The Stern report also made a compelling case that the undoubtedly high costs of preventative action to stop global temperatures rising by 5°C above pre-industrial levels, and a 5–20 per cent cut in global living standards, are nevertheless very much lower than the costs flowing from the disastrous consequences for humankind of not taking such action. If anyone were in any doubt, Stern stated seven years later in 2013 that he had, if anything, been wrong; actually things were already very much worse than his report had projected.

Five thousand years of cooling across the northern hemisphere has been reversed, with the past three decades warmer and stormier than any previous decade on record. Food stocks – including staple crops, wheat and fish – are shrinking fast. Wetter regions are getting wetter and drier areas drier. Already monsoons are more extreme and frequent, and so are typhoons, hurricanes, flooding, droughts, wildfires and famine. One analyst, Jeffrey Mazo, showed that there were already 300,000 deaths and $125 billion of losses, which were 'seriously affecting 325 million people every year' by 2009, as a direct result of such climate change.

Only agreement among the major powers – north and south, east and west – will resolve the gridlock over effective global action to combat climate change, which is why the agreement at the 2015 Paris Climate Change Conference was so welcome. But that does not absolve each citizen from changing their behaviour. For example, by those who can afford to do so installing renewable energy systems in our houses or voters insisting that politicians design them into all new-build. Each citizen has a responsibility to act.

• PETER HAIN •

OUR FATE BOUND TOGETHER

Global climate change is binding our fates together, blurring the distinction between the 'national' and the 'international'. No country can tackle climate change alone but no country can afford to postpone doing so until every other country does either. We have to act now and we have to act together as soon as we possibly can. Concerted progressive internationalism is essential to deliver an answer to the fast-gathering 'perfect storm'.

Which is why, where in the past progressive internationalists were perhaps viewed as mere well-meaning idealists, we are now the new realists – indeed, the hard-headed diplomats – of our era. Labour, Liberal and Green politics can therefore command the future foreign policy agenda – provided that we build new alliances together. We will continue to fight each other *domestically*, but the stakes are so high we have a duty to work together *internationally*.

Peter Hain, since November 2015 Lord Hain of Neath, was a Labour MP from 1991–2015 and from 1997 served as a British government minister for twelve years, seven of which were in the Cabinet. A former leader of the anti-apartheid movement, his critique of, and alternative to, neoliberalism *Back to the Future of Socialism* was published by Policy Press in 2015. His memoir *Outside In* was published by Biteback in 2012.

CELEBRATING THE MOVEMENT OF PEOPLE

Tim Farron

For hundreds of years, migration has enriched our language, culture and society, and has helped to drive innovation, productivity and economic growth. Over the decades, we've seen ebbs and flows in how many people come into the UK, but over the last decade, due in large part to the adoption of free movement of people in the European Union, we have seen sustained higher levels of immigration. Sadly, misreporting and exaggeration by some politicians, pressure groups and sections of the press have turned this debate toxic, with immigrants blamed for all the ills of the country. This culminated in immigration playing a central though bogus and misrepresented role in the EU referendum debate, and following the narrow Leave vote, there is a bigger responsibility than ever for sensible, progressive politicians to frame the arguments in favour of immigration in a way that first acknowledges genuine concerns and then seeks to address them. There are challenges posed by high levels of immigration, and we should address them positively, not ignore them.

A quick glance at national polls in the early part of this year – before the referendum debate got into full swing – shows that most people consider immigration to be the biggest challenge facing the country at the moment. However, it is striking that when people are asked what challenges face them and their family, immigration concerns drop out almost completely. Most people are scared of the abstract principle, rather than because they feel the impact of any problems themselves.

Some of this has been to do with the pressures behind the EU referendum, but it is very unlikely that it will change. People will still come to the UK from overseas, whether under freedom of movement within the EU (in the short term) or migration from anywhere in the world. We will still face many challenges, and the fact that the refugee crisis in the Mediterranean is expected to be three times bigger in 2016 than it was in 2015 will ensure that the issue will not go quietly away. Too often progressives have resorted to burying their heads in the sand and hoping nobody asks about immigration on the doorstep or in media interviews, or, worse, defaulting to the easy attack of implying that everyone with worries about immigration is stupid or bigoted. It is high time for progressive politicians to take a fresh approach that address the concerns head-on. We need to have positive solutions and a clear vision.

Progressives need to be making the positive case for immigration. There are many reasons and arguments for this. Firstly, a very simple view – immigrants are people too. They deserve opportunity and freedoms. This applies especially strongly to those seeking asylum. We know that people driven from their homes as a result of war and persecution deserve our help and support. The British public are at heart fair-minded people, and just as there was mass support for the Kindertransport, to save thousands of innocent children from the horrors of Nazi Germany, so we must muster support for the millions displaced from Syria and elsewhere. Of course we cannot house all of them, but then not all want to be housed – most just want to be able to go and live in their homes in peace. But we can make a difference to many thousands of people who need our help.

So there is a clear moral case for immigration – and for many of us that is compelling. But we should also not be afraid to make other, more pragmatic cases – especially to persuade those unmoved by the moral arguments. We should be comfortable highlighting the benefits immigration brings to those of us already here. We should demonstrate that self-interest and generosity are in this case aligned. We need only to look to the National Health Service to see how important immigration is – statistics produced by the Health and Social Care Information Centre (HSCIC) showed that, in 2014, 26 per cent of NHS doctors were non-British, and the British Medical Association have been clear that, without immigrants, 'many NHS services would struggle to provide effective care to their patients'. With an ageing population placing more pressure on the NHS, immigrants will be instrumental going forward.

The challenge for progressive politicians is to formulate and articulate an immigration policy that makes the most of the many benefits of immigration while reassuring British nationals that the overall balance is right. Changes to the current rules will happen as a result of the EU referendum – progressives need to use what influence they have to ensure that the new system is fair to everyone. Sadly, there are those who exploit the rules – we must be robust in tackling labour exploitation and those who abuse the spirit of Britain's willingness to welcome people from abroad.

MIGRATION DOES NOT BENEFIT EVERYONE EQUALLY

A good place to start is to accept that, without certain policies in place, immigration does not benefit everyone equally, all the time. Much like trade, the overall economic benefit of immigration is indisputable, but that does not automatically equate to better circumstances for all. Current policies in the UK combine with immigration to make life harder for some people.

The cry 'immigrants take our jobs' is crude and reductionist, but, as is the case with the trade of British versus Chinese steel, ultimately capitalism is driven by competition, and immigration introduces more competition into the labour market at the same time as it fills its holes. As the Migration Advisory Committee (MAC) highlights, where immigrants do compete with the native work force, it tends to be a very localised problem and very much dependent on the specific industry of the area (MAC, 2015). This is supported by research by Christian Dustmann from the Centre for Research and Analysis of Migration (CReAM) at University College London, which shows that while the majority of workers are either unaffected by migrant labour or positively affected, there is a negative impact on those with the lowest incomes. Often this is not because most migrants are low-skilled themselves, but because educational attainment and work experience do not translate well across borders, meaning many migrants find themselves 'downskilling' on arrival in the UK. Thus, when an employer has the choice of a British employee with low-level skills or an immigrant with greater skills who is willing to take lower-paid work, the British worker is likely to lose out.

So how can we make sure that migrants in the labour market do not undercut local wages or lead to the exploitation of workers by paying under minimum wage?

Proper enforcement of the minimum wage is vital. The Gangmasters' Licencing Authority has done excellent work in this area – clamping down on unscrupulous businesses and helping exploited workers. Increased penalties for those who break the law, which came in as part of the Immigration Act that passed through Parliament in early 2016, are welcome. This is especially important given that the government is set to increase the minimum wage in this parliament. Without sufficient safeguarding, there is a serious risk that more companies will seek ways to prevent having to pay the increased rate. This method also creates a more predictable tax revenue from both native and foreign-born workers, and diminishes the risk of exploitation of other regulations, such as those around health and safety.

Further research by CReAM shows that most migrants only stay downskilled for a short period of time – often it's just two or three years before they move on to higher-skilled placements. This means the low-skilled, low-paid part of the job market remains constantly busy. This trend could be mitigated by stronger policies around transference of qualifications between countries and sufficient investment in English language education. This first suggestion is especially critical when you consider the currently increasing holes in our labour market. In 2013, the so-called skills gap was particularly problematic in science, technology, engineering and maths ('Stem') industries, with an estimated shortfall of 30,000 graduates per year (CEBR, 2013). Where businesses can be confident that foreign *educated* workers have the transferable qualifications, they can hire them into those roles immediately and avoid any unnecessary pile-up in other parts of the job market.

It is also worth emphasising at this point that we cannot continue to allow high-skilled immigration to make up for the continual failure to equip British people with the education needed to fill this shortfall themselves. More needs to be done to ensure that our school system gives children the best start in life, and that it is accessible to those at all stages of life who wish to train for higher-skilled, higher-paid jobs. The coalition made enormous leaps forward in increasing apprenticeships in the 2010–15 period, and this should be built on further. Immigration should complement the skilled workforce we already have in Britain, not replace it.

One huge tragedy in UK immigration policy is the way that some of those on the right have attacked non-EU migrants excessively. New rules that came into force in April 2016 will see the majority of Tier 2 visa immigrants from outside the European Economic Area (EEA) having to earn £35,000 or more to qualify for indefinite leave to remain (ILR) – a move that will significantly impact immigrant teachers, nurses, scientists and IT professionals. It is possible that such rules will apply to immigrants from the EEA once Britain leaves the EU. Meanwhile, British citizens are separated from their wives or husbands, if they hold foreign passports, if the British partner earns below £18,600. Or, to put that another way, almost half of the British population do not earn enough to fall in love with a foreigner. This is cruel and unBritish.

The right are obsessed with having a debate about numbers of migrants, which is a fight they cannot win without severely damaging our economy in the process. Until now, these measures could be applied to workers who come to the UK from within the European Union, so they have chosen to hit non-EU workers much harder and more brutally. With Britain's exit from the EU imminent, everyone from overseas stands to be treated with equal brutality. Such proposals do very little to ease pressure on the low-income labour market, while simultaneously having a negative impact on our universities and high-tech industries – and our humanity.

THE MYTH OF DILUTED WELFARE

Another topic that has dominated the debate on immigration is the notion that British citizens are benefiting less from the welfare state as a result of migrants coming here to receive state handouts. In many ways, this narrative is the fault of politicians, who have realised that tweaking welfare access for migrants is something that has very little impact but which is populist and within their ability to effect. Various parties have set their standards at different levels and use this as an easy policy to point to when attempting to prove they are strong when dealing with immigration. The most recent example of this was the current government's EU renegotiation plan, which included measures that would be used to deny EU migrants access to in-work benefits for four years. Despite what this race for longer waiting periods suggests, there is little evidence to prove that benefits are a 'pull-factor' for migrants to choose Britain, and consequently that making people wait longer for in-work benefits is in any way a deterrent.

People do rightly raise concerns about limits on housing, on school places, and on the NHS. And they are right to do so – these are problems in many areas. But the solution to a shortage of school places is to expand schools or build new ones, not to blame the migrants that are coming here to contribute to society. They should not be blamed for government incompetence.

Decades of failure to build sufficient housing, to provide adequate school places and to properly fund our NHS were exposed by the economic crisis in 2008, allowing migrants to become a convenient scapegoat for what had been a system left to crumble. Migration tends to be predictable, with areas of rapid population growth easily identifiable. However, it is surprisingly difficult to find localised information on migration and therefore difficult to analyse how immigration actually impacts on local services. The census is the only standardised model of collecting this data at the moment, but once a decade is not frequent enough to make use of the information for proper community planning. High priority should be given to developing mechanisms that take better account of pressures on public services in local areas facing rapid inward migration. And where pressures are identified, sufficient resources should be allocated to relieve them. In fact, the European Union has specific funding available for this, the European Social Fund, but the option of such funds being tapped and spent in areas where public services are strained has now gone with the Brexit vote. Calculations made by the Liberal Democrats in 2013 estimated the UK would be eligible for £1 billion from the ESF. This would not simply have assisted new provision for new residents, but would have been a genuine investment of help for the whole neighbourhood and community.

If we accept the overwhelming evidence that immigration – from the EU and elsewhere – is good for our economy and, indeed, sustains our welfare system by reducing the ratio of workers to non-workers, we must ensure that we invest in using that strong economy to benefit all people. This is why progressives were in favour of Britain remaining in the EU – because freedom of movement helps our economy. Research by CReAM showed that over the period from 2001 to 2011, European immigrants contributed more than £20 billion to UK public finances. We can use that money to support public services like schools and hospitals in the areas where immigration is happening – and still leave more left over. Part of any progressive ethos should be to ensure that as much freedom of movement is protected as possible, and we have the example of Norway as a country that is outside the EU but has signed up to freedom of movement.

Another look at the polling reveals that the other big issue that concerns people is the economy, and evidence in a couple of our close European neighbours, Denmark and the Netherlands, shows that populist anti-immigrant policies can soon become less popular when clampdowns on immigration do start to have an economic impact.

A PROGRAMME FOR POSITIVE MIGRATION

It is the job of progressive politicians – both during and after the period when Britain's exit from the EU is negotiated – to set out a programme for positive migration, one that voters can see is credible and works for them. This vision should be based on four things I have identified above:

- Positive and clear language about the overall benefits we get from immigration.
- Understanding and reacting to the genuine concerns of those parts of the population who feel threatened by mass migration.
- Clear and strong control of borders that allows better management and more precise information about migratory trends.
- Separating out asylum from the immigration debate as far as possible.

We should not shy away from the fact that we want to maintain control of immigration – this is not an issue just for the right. We need to show that progressives are just as concerned about, and willing to invest in, secure and well-managed borders. This means handing powers currently with the government back to Parliament. It should be Parliament that decides and votes on what measures are needed each year to ensure that we are open for business to the best and brightest, and those who want to contribute, while maintaining control to keep us safe, secure and prosperous. It would be naive to insinuate that by handing this over to Parliament rather than the government we can deflate the political football that migration has become; however, by embracing independent advice and allowing for lengthy and intelligent parliamentary debate, we can at least help to mitigate the spin and force Members of Parliament to come face to face with the facts.

In addition, we should proudly say that we are open for business and growth without being blind to public concern. This concern stems from fear, and that can only be fought by raising the UK workforce's confidence, and showing that we are investing in 'UK plc' not at the expense of losing foreign talent but in conjunction with it. Apprenticeship schemes in the UK have proved to be hugely successful and there is no reason that these could not be extended so that an element of the 'training up' of the native workforce is included as an element of the visa requirements for highly skilled migrants coming to the UK. By highlighting the tangible benefits migration brings and creating people-to-people links, we can strengthen our hand as well as strengthening our economy. Progressives are well placed to make this argument that unites opportunity and economic interests.

Finally, it is the job of progressives to ensure that we do not allow immigration and asylum to get confused. We have seen that the general public sympathise with the plight of genuine asylum seekers; however, all too often politicians and the media confuse – whether on purpose or not – asylum seekers and economic migrants. We need to continually and robustly fight against this conflation and this will mean fighting for further separation of the systems. For example, the indefinite detention of asylum seekers paints these innocent people as criminals. It is our duty to not only help dispel these myths when we speak out but also to seek change in legislation to ensure that our asylum system is humane and treats these people in accordance with the demands of international law.

Anti-immigration rhetoric has been an easy win for the political right, and if progressives in politics hope to prevail, it is time to meet the challenge head-on and reclaim the debate. Though our exit from the EU is deeply regrettable, it means the immigration debate can become clearer, in that the right can no longer shamelessly blame the EU. This is therefore an opportunity, but one that will require us to address the real fears behind the rhetoric, like jobs, communities and welfare.

Tim Farron is leader of the Liberal Democrats and has been the MP for Westmorland and Lonsdale since 2005.

TRADE UNIONS: AT THE HEART OF A PROGRESSIVE FUTURE

Frances O'Grady

Try this for a paradox, or perhaps we should call it hypocrisy: the developed world views a developing country's attitude towards trade unions as one of the measurements of how civilised it is and how safe it is to do business with, yet we currently have the government of a developed nation undermining trade union rights in its own country in a way that would cause it to bristle elsewhere.

The right of people in work to organise themselves for the purpose of negotiating collectively is rightly considered a fundamental human right. Indeed, Article 23(4) of the 1948 Universal Declaration of Human Rights enshrines this by stating: 'Everyone has the right to form and to join trade unions for the protection of his [*sic*] interests.' Despite this, the British government's Trade Union Act amounts to the biggest attack on organised labour in a generation. As well as making it much more difficult for workers to take strike action, the Act imposes many other restrictions on unions that are designed to weaken working people's bargaining power.

Any new government – especially one of a progressive hue – must pursue an industrial relations strategy that strikes a fairer balance between employers' interests and the rights of workers to get a decent deal. In today's globalised digital economy, the balance of power has shifted significantly against working people. Stronger unions provide an essential economic service in working to counterbalance unbridled corporate might, to humanise work and to introduce a degree of economic democracy. According to a TUC study, eighteen EU countries plus Norway already practise some form of workplace democracy. And there are very sound reasons for this. Research across a range of indicators – from employment rates to expenditure on research and development – shows that countries with the strongest workers' participation rights reap the rewards.

And it's not difficult to see why. Trade unions hold management to account, leading to more effective decision-making. They ensure the ingenuity, expertise and experience of working people feed into the way organisations work. And there is a positive correlation between unionisation and higher skills and more workforce training. With economic power increasingly concentrated in the hands of a small number of overseas shareholders, on average for a matter of just months, the notion that shareholders are the sole and best stewards of the long-term interests of a company is well and truly bust.

Workers have a unique interest in the success of the enterprise employing them; they invest their time, labour and skills in the firm, and their livelihoods ultimately hinge on its long-term performance.

A strong voice for working people can also help address growing inequality in the workplace. Managers have always earned more than workers, but most of us expect the ratio between what workers and management earn to remain in reasonable proportion – after all, there can be no management without workers (even in a strongly computerised world). And yet, it takes Britain's highest paid director just *forty-nine minutes* to earn the same amount that a worker on the national minimum wage earns in *a year*. That is a sign of an industrial culture gone wrong, and an indicator that the relationship between capital and labour in this country is seriously awry.

OLD REPUTATIONS DIE HARD

Trade unionism still suffers from outdated stereotypes. Even as midwives took their first ever strike action last year in protest against the government's refusal to honour their independent pay review body's recommendation of a 1 per cent pay increase, the news was accompanied by old TV footage from the Winter of Discontent and the miners' strike.

Today's trade union world is a million miles from that. For a start, women full-time workers are more likely to be union members than men, and the spread of professions represented is much greater too. The people whose labour creates the wealth on which Britain's future depends include scientists and engineers devising the solutions to our technological and environmental challenges; manufacturing workers building planes, trains and automobiles; entertainers and educators who inspire the next generation; hi-tech, energy and transport workers; postal workers who strive, come rain or shine, to network the nation; and dedicated medical staff who tend our sick. You will find all these professions, trades and vocations – and many more – in unionised workplaces.

The portrayal of strike-happy workers willing to down tools at a moment's notice conveniently neglects the fact that the 1970s was Britain's most equal decade and that the election of Margaret Thatcher's government heralded an era of neoliberalism that would see workers' share of wealth decline significantly, both in the UK and globally. A series of Trade Union Acts in the 1980s ensured it became progressively difficult for workers to withhold their labour and hold back the juggernaut of deindustrialisation and mass unemployment.

In my experience, the decision to strike is never taken lightly, particularly as it means losing pay that most workers can ill afford. So when there is an item about a strike, or even a potential strike, in a newspaper or news bulletin, it should automatically tell the reader or listener one thing: that these workers feel they have no alternative. Despite regular headlines in the right-wing press about union militancy, the number of days lost to strike action in Britain is at a historic low.

Margaret Thatcher sought to neuter institutions she called 'the enemy within', not least trade unions. Her government reshaped the industrial relations landscape with the two Trade Union Acts shepherded by Norman Tebbitt, not to mention using the full power of the state to crush the NUM during the year-long miners' strike. Working people have been living with the consequences ever since.

Scarred by four election defeats, the New Labour governments of Tony Blair and Gordon Brown were very tentative about trade unionism. Although they introduced a new right to union recognition and brought in a minimum wage, they left the Thatcherite industrial relations architecture largely intact. Barely were the Conservatives freed from the need for coalition compromises following the 2015 election than they published their Trade Union

Act, which seeks to take Britain back to the dark ages of industrial relations.

THE TRADE UNION ACT

The Trade Union Act seeks to attack the very principle of the right to strike. It gives employers the right to bring in untrained casual staff on a temporary basis when the regular workforce is out on strike – effectively granting an official right of strikebusting (if you can just replace strikers overnight, you undermine the power that workers have to bring their employers to the table). And the proposals to restrict lawful protests and pickets during a strike are draconian and will lead to a surveillance culture in industries, some of which already carry the scars of industrial-scale blacklisting.

The Act has attracted plenty of criticism from far beyond the labour movement: from the Conservative MP David Davis, who has suggested some of its provisions are reminiscent of Franco's Spain; from the Chartered Institute of Personnel and Development, which says it addresses yesterday's problems; from the UN's International Labour Organization, which is concerned that permitting employers to use agency workers during strikes contravenes international labour standards; from the government's former adviser Bruce Carr QC, who believes it will undermine good industrial relations; and from Amnesty, Liberty and other human rights campaigners, who see it as an attack on civil liberties. Even the government's own independent regulatory watchdog has said this Act is not fit for purpose.

The TUC campaigned hard against the Act and it won some important concessions as the draft legislation passed through

Parliament. As well as engaging the Labour Party, we have worked closely with representatives from the Liberal Democrats, SNP, Plaid Cymru and Greens to build a wide, diverse progressive alliance against the reforms. In seeking to repeal the Act, trade unions are not attempting to turn the clock back to the 'bad old days' of the 1970s, but merely to bring labour law into the 21st-century European mainstream. Our neighbours on the Continent do not expect trade unions to operate within a legal and regulatory framework so crassly rigged in favour of bad business, and nor should we.

The Act is not just the biggest attack on trade unions since the 1980s, but on our best chance of raising productivity, pay and demand. There is a simple truth: you can't create wealth without the workforce. And if that workforce does not have the right to strike, the employer has the whip hand – and, as we have seen with the likes of Sports Direct, some employers can be unreasonable, unfair or just plain greedy. If an employer believes workers can't strike, they won't bother to bargain. And it's not just about money – without strong trade unions, we wouldn't have safe workplaces, we wouldn't have paid holidays or family leave, and we wouldn't have decent pensions. Under such conditions, workers become demoralised and productivity goes down.

AN INDUSTRIAL RELATIONS POLICY FIT FOR THE TWENTY-FIRST CENTURY

For all these reasons, we would hope that the government elected in 2020 would, as its first step, repeal the current Trade Union Act. But it's about more than that.

Any government concerned about optimising industrial

efficiency and productivity must adopt a modern industrial relations framework based on a strong voice for workers and workforce participation in organisational decision-making. A stronger worker voice is essential to tackling inequality and building a more inclusive economy, and the TUC is actively lobbying and campaigning for policies to promote it. We believe democracy matters just as much economically and industrially as it does politically. An attack on our democracy would rightly be greeted with screams of a creeping dictatorship, yet few such screams are heard when workplace democracy is attacked.

There is a very strong case for worker representation on company remuneration committees and boards. Although countless overseas companies have been adopting this approach for years, the transport company First Group is one of the very few in the UK to have a worker director on its board. But there are many other examples of unions and employers working successfully together here in the UK. BMW Mini in Oxford has worked with its unions to develop a world-class apprenticeships scheme; Nissan, Honda and Toyota worked with their unions to avoid redundancies during the downturn; BAE Systems has a very good model of workforce engagement; and there are more. The challenge is to make success stories such as these the norm.

Trade unions are particularly interested in raising Britain's dire productivity performance, as it is the only sustainable way to improve our members' job security, living standards and pay. Research from the likes of the OECD and Work Foundation shows that, where there is a positive engagement between unions and employers, the productivity gains can be significant. Our interest in productivity is part of a wider aspiration to build a new economy that delivers prosperity for all. Recent research from the University of Greenwich and the New Economics Foundation shows that higher levels of unionisation would add over £27 billion to the UK's GDP.

The TUC is working with the New Economics Foundation and other progressive think tanks to develop economic and industrial policies fit for the 2020s. Among the ideas it is exploring are the jobs, growth and productivity potential of low-carbon technologies; reforms to build better companies with a strong focus on long-term investment; and the role of Modern Wages Councils in setting decent standards for whole industries in a way that avoids the decent employer being undercut by the bad.

Tackling inequality must be the lifeblood of a progressive government's programme. Britain is crying out for change. If you rank the thirty-four OECD countries in terms of inequality of earnings, Britain would come fourth from top, and we were the only G7 country to see inequality rise in the period 2000–14. In the recent economic recession, it was not only the gap between the top earners and the bottom that got bigger, but the gap between men's and women's earnings also widened. If you think equality of earnings is a nice aspiration but a luxury in tough times, think again: the economic costs of inequality are profound. The OECD has calculated that the British economy would be more than 20 per cent bigger had the gap between rich and poor not widened since the 1980s.

Another huge challenge for trade unions and a future progressive government is rapid technological change, which is unleashing a wave of creative destruction across the economy and automating many of the jobs workers do. We are now in the midst of an information revolution arguably many times more transformative than its industrial namesake. So far the headlines have been dominated by driverless cars, pilotless aircraft, delivery drones, 3D printing and robots performing surgery. Just as important, though, are the more run-of-the-mill changes. Self-service kiosks and checkouts, online shopping and banking, internet flight and hotel booking have all had profound implications for retail workers, bank cashiers, travel agents and others.

But automation and apps are not just transforming the jobs people do and the way they work; they're also accelerating the so-called 'gig economy'. Instead of permanent contracts with guaranteed pay, hours, holidays and pensions, workers are self-employed and take whatever assignment they can get. For the lucky few this means genuine freedom to create. But for the majority, it means freedom to be exploited. And so we have the Uber driver competing for the next fare; the CitySprint courier paid for each drop off, rather than by the hour; the Sports Direct or care industry zero-hours worker waiting for the next text to confirm a shift – it may come; it may not. And it's not just low-paid, blue-collar workers who are feeling the force of disruptive technology and insecurity. Airline pilots, medical professionals, university lecturers, teachers and journalists are all discovering that this 'casualisation' of labour does not discriminate between class or collar.

All of this has profound implications for trade unions and the way we organise workers and build bargaining power. As Gavin Kelly, chief executive of the Resolution Trust, has written, 'In time, new forms of protection and worker organisation will be needed. Just as business faces an imperative to innovate, so too do those who believe in social protection.' Trade unions certainly need to think creatively about new forms of membership; new ways of supporting workers who have few rights and no formal employer; and new ways of exploiting the huge organising and bargaining potential of digital technology.

THE TUC'S PROGRESSIVE AGENDA FOR 2020

The TUC's job is to work across the spectrum to further the interests of working people. Of course we share values with Labour, and some of the TUC's unions are affiliated to the party. But we know that the political landscape is constantly evolving, with some of the smaller parties gaining ground, underlining the importance of our cross-party lobbying work. We recognise, too, that trade union members vote for a range of political parties.

What we most hope for from a progressive government – however it is constituted – is a fundamental change of direction on the big economic questions. Trade unions believe it's time to ditch the free-market fundamentalism that landed us with the biggest crash since 1929, the deepest recession since the Great Depression and the longest crisis in our living standards since the Victorian era. In its place we need a fairer, stronger, more equal economy; good public services in public hands; and a strong focus on better work. We would like to see change in five key areas:

1. Investment for the future

The Conservative government's clamour to shrink the state is undermining public services, choking off growth and hitting the most vulnerable communities hardest. In place of austerity, we need policies to promote fair growth, long-term investment and good public services; this is the best way to reduce the deficit over the long run. We would also like to see the 2020 government have a little more faith in the virtues of public provision. Whether it is the NHS, criminal justice, the welfare system or the railways, we have to get away from the simplistic and wrong-headed philosophy of 'private good, public bad' and rediscover our mission of protecting the common good.

2. Decent jobs and wages at the heart of a new economy

This means an intelligent industrial strategy, nurturing the success stories of the future such as aerospace, biotechnology and green manufacturing; investment in vocational education; financial reform that ensures the banks work for us and provide the funds we need to reconfigure our economy; radical reforms of corporate governance; and measures to promote fair pay, including a proper living wage.

3. A fairer labour market

Britain already has the most flexible, most deregulated labour market in the OECD, so we need to get tough on casualisation and insecurity. We need stronger employment rights, enforcement of rights and equal application of those rights irrespective of employment status. We need to address both the causes and the consequences of gender inequality – from the motherhood penalty to poor-quality part-time work – which means delivering decent, affordable childcare and offering genuine flexibility at work. The race pay gap needs closing too, with TUC research showing that black workers with university degrees earn around a quarter less than their white friends.

4. Stronger trade unions and more collective bargaining

More trade union membership and collective bargaining mean less income inequality. Research by Ewan McGaughey from

King's College reveals an astonishingly close historical correlation between unionisation and greater income equality. After the Wages Councils Act of 1945, union membership was on a rising trajectory for the next thirty-five years – as was income equality. After 1980, income inequality increased sharply as trade unions declined. Today unionised workers still earn more than their non-unionised counterparts; the latest official data shows the trade union pay premium is worth over 16 per cent overall, and for women it rises to a colossal 30 per cent.

5. *Co-creation*

Nobody is arguing that the German model of social partnership and co-determination should be imported wholesale into the UK, but it would be arrogant to ignore lessons from that approach in developing a British model of co-creation. From more competitive companies to better vocational skills and a more even distribution of reward, the German system of industrial relations has much to commend it.

In Britain, we have the best-educated generation of workers ever, yet many feel they have no voice and little control over their working lives. A government genuinely committed to empowering people would recognise that the days of workers – like Victorian children – being seen but not heard must end. As the only independent and democratic organisations of working people, unions have a crucial role to play. Of course that means, in a digital age, unions must up their game too. But from the carbon challenge and technological change to workforce planning and investment decisions, co-creation takes as its starting point that all wisdom will only reside in the boardroom if workers have seats there too.

TIME FOR CHANGE

Whether it's tackling inequality, nurturing a new economy or building a different kind of industrial relations architecture, trade unions have a pivotal role to play in changing Britain for the better. And the TUC stands ready to work with political parties that share our commitment to fairness, equality and social justice.

With the UK having narrowly voted to leave the EU, the TUC will be working with parliamentarians from across the progressive spectrum to defend the diverse range of workers' rights we have won from Europe. The referendum exposed deep fractures within society, a profound disconnect between working people and politics, and real anger at years of stagnant living standards. With the Leave campaign scapegoating migrants for social and economic problems made in Westminster and the City, this is a critical moment for everyone who believes in a more inclusive society. Trade unions and progressives must work together to tackle divisions within our communities.

A more progressive future for Britain can be within our grasp if we have the courage to seize it. And any progressive politician worth his or her salt should campaign actively for strong, effective trade unions to be at the heart of our national life. As Martin Luther King once said:

> The labour movement does not diminish the strength of a nation but enlarges it. By raising the standards of millions, labour miraculously created a market for industry and lifted the whole nation to undreamed of levels of production. Those who attack labour forget these simple truths, but history remembers them.

Frances O'Grady is the General Secretary of the Trades Union Congress (TUC). The daughter of a car plant worker who was also a shop steward, she worked for the Transport and General Workers' Union before joining the TUC in 1994. In 2013, she was judged the eleventh most powerful woman in Britain in a poll for BBC Radio 4's *Woman's Hour* programme.

RADICAL DEVOLUTION: WHAT THE SCOTTISH REFERENDUM CAMPAIGN TAUGHT US

Mhairi Black & Chris Law[1]

In 2012, when the campaign began that would culminate in the referendum of September 2014 on Scottish independence, the Yes side were on 22–27 per cent in the opinion polls. By the time the vote happened, the Yes side polled 45 per cent. And one opinion poll in the lead-up to 18 September 2014 put that figure at over 50 per cent.

The result of the referendum (55 to 45 in percentage terms) is still the source of considerable grieving to Scottish nationalists – made worse by having a Conservative government at Westminster, of which more shortly – but that does not negate the fact that their

1 Where the first person ('I', 'me', 'my' etc.) appears in this essay, it refers to Mhairi Black, but this essay was written jointly with her fellow SNP Member of Parliament Chris Law.

performance in the referendum campaign is still remarkable. Taking mid-range figures, the Yes campaign doubled its vote. And the reasons why should be of interest to progressives across the UK.

This was not a campaign for independence for independence's sake. It was independence to grasp genuine democratic power to enable many changes to bring about a fairer society. Many of the people who were part of the broad Yes church became involved as a result of specific issues, for example fracking. What the independence movement did was create the sense that influencing things was suddenly possible, or could be if we built a better nation. People were engaged; they felt they owned their destiny rather than feeling as if it was ordered from on high. There was a genuine opportunity and prospect of a blank canvas to design something new and better.

This is why so many people who were down as unlikely Yes voters at the start ended up supporting the idea of Scottish independence. It wasn't that Alex Salmond edged Alistair Darling in the TV debates. It was the creation of a 'can do' culture that energised and enthused so many people, not just those who felt they'd been left behind by politics but by many who never thought they were interested in politics in the first place.

EDUCATION AND CONFIDENCE

The key to this enthusing of people lies in two related points, both of which apply to politics anywhere in the world. The first is knowledge; the second is confidence.

When you receive knowledge, confidence comes naturally. What happened in the referendum campaign is what happens when politics becomes understandable: people connect with it. What I loved seeing on the campaign trail was the look on someone's face when they made the connection between a reason their life was a struggle and the policy that had caused it. The minute they understood why their wages had not gone up but prices had was the moment we connected. That did not always mean they were automatically going to vote Yes or vote SNP in party elections, but it meant we could engage and have genuine and frank discussions. The minute people understand that politics is very simple, that you can break things down and explain policies in simple terms and apply them to everyday life, they feel confident and can understand what people – whether it's politicians, commentators in the media or their opinionated next-door neighbour – are talking about. In turn, they can then read a newspaper or watch *Question Time*, and if they hear a smug, arrogant, 'educated' person talking about a particular issue, they will feel confident in being able to recognise when they are talking rubbish, rather than feel they are somehow not on that person's level. We made politics less arrogant, and that helped people realise not only how politics affects their life, but helped them feel confident enough to argue. That's when politics becomes natural.

The more knowledge voters have, the less vulnerable they are to spin. We found ourselves up against very hostile traditional media during the referendum, and to an extent we still do, but one of the ways you reduce the power of the media is to have enough people with sufficient knowledge that they can see through the attempts at manipulation.

In order to give people the knowledge that leads to confidence, you need to educate them. Or if that sounds too high-handed, put information their way so they build up their own picture. One of the best ways of doing this is simply to talk about politics, so that we change the mindset that people have that politics is a specialist subject and a specialist area. Ever since I was young, I always wondered why it was frowned upon socially to talk about politics or religion given that they are two of the most influential elements in society. So I did talk about them. I come from a very large family, and I first brought up the need to engage in politics at my cousin's birthday party. I remember getting so into it that my dad mentioned that people can become uncomfortable if you bang on about politics for a long period of time, but I remember feeling so enthused and excited by the fact that I genuinely was talking more sense than people older than me on topics that I had not engaged with before. I had aunties with whom conversations went a bit like this:

'I'm not interested in politics,' my aunties would say.

'But don't you care what your wages are?' I'd answer.

'Aye.'

'Do you care that you can still go to hospital for nothing?'

'Aye.'

'Well, you care about politics then.'

They were all No voters and die-hard Labour supporters four years ago; by the time of the referendum and the 2015 general election, they all voted Yes and all voted SNP. I have seen how they progressed over those two years. They are thirty years older than me, but I won the argument simply by helping them realise why this was important. And this was reflected right across Scotland.

So I would talk to him, to her, to you, to my aunties, and they all talked to other people. Suddenly we were spreading pyramid-like, and our voted ended up at 45 per cent. People pin the referendum on Alex Salmond and Alistair Darling, but it wasn't about them – well, it might have been for older voters, but for the vast majority of people who swung from No to Yes, it was conversations in pubs and staff rooms and on streets. My colleague Chris Law took a simple approach: 'If I persuade one person, that's twice me. If I persuade five, that's 500 per cent of me. And if they can persuade others, then we're making real progress.'

Word of mouth is very powerful, but it's not enough on its own. You have to get information out there, and this is where another of Chris's initiatives was very effective. He bought a 1950s Green Goddess fire engine and converted it into a mobile information stand with leaflets, which he took around Scotland on a 'Spirit of Independence' tour. He let all sorts of campaigns display their literature, even ones that weren't specifically about Scottish independence. Then there was the 'Margo Mobile', started by veteran SNP politician Jim Sillars. This was a mobile theatre, with music, and Jim coming out to speak. I remember a day when a union official came and started screaming at Jim, so Jim argued back, just making his case. This went on for a few minutes, and before long there was an audience. And I thought, 'This is politics in my street – I've never seen anything like it.' This was people getting engaged. It was politics that was not stale. It was politics with a blank canvas, and a sense that anyone could contribute to the painting.

We in the SNP had one balancing act to pull off that actually had a positive side effect. Our party campaigns for an independent Scotland, but we also have political views of our own, which are generally cast as left-of-centre. So we had to make the case for Scottish independence without assuming that the government of an independent Scotland would be an SNP government. We wanted people who supported Scottish independence but who might want a Conservative government in Scotland to still vote Yes.

Out of this arose a phenomenon, or an ethos, in which we answered a lot of questions by throwing them back at those who had asked them. For example, if I had an undecided voter asking me,

'What would an independent Scotland's policy on the currency be?', I'd often reply, 'What do you want it to be?' Of course, there's a time when a political party has to say what it would do so that people know what they're voting for, but we were making the point that independence would put power in voters' hands, that people could shape the newly independent Scotland, and people have got so unused to that idea in today's politics that it had real sway and helped create the momentum for the Yes campaign. In throwing the question back, people were forced to think for themselves and, before we knew it, most people soon became well-informed and were debating with each other as to what they thought was best, and why, on what has traditionally been seen as an incredibly complex policy area.

There has always been a sense that Scotland as a nation was always heading in a different political direction than what England votes for. The eighteen years of Conservative rule from 1979 to 1997 broke the social contract that had dated from the immediate post-war years. That's important in Scotland, where we have a sense of the common weal. Many Scots remember Thatcher's poll tax, particularly how Scotland played the guinea pig for this failed policy, which was rolled out here in 1989, a year before the rest of the UK. Meanwhile, the creation of the Scottish Parliament in 1999 gave us a sense of who we are, and allowed us to say that the neoliberal rejection of the caring society that emerged after the Second World War was anathema to us. Then, in 2010, the Conservatives returned to government at Westminster with more policies that to us seem rather callous. Frankly, we don't understand them. Why would you want to create policies that are harmful to society? Why are we creating bigger exclusions? Why don't we create a more human system?

THE ROLE OF SOCIAL MEDIA

Many people in politics discuss how important social media is. You can find many successful modern-day campaigns that have used it (the Obama campaign in 2008, for example), and equally you can find many people who say it's a distraction and there's no substitute for good old-fashioned face-to-face campaigning. Making it into an either/or issue rather misses the point.

What we found in 2014 was that getting people politically educated required the message to get out, and in getting it out there's no question that social media played a massive role in creating the knowledge base that was such a big part of the Scottish referendum campaign. But it was about more than just spreading information – it was about spreading the debate. A lot of us shared articles, often without comment so that people didn't feel we were ramming our views down their throats. If somebody shares something, it forces you to think, it exposes you to different ideas. This is what politics should be – and it should be done in a way that's not aggressive or antagonising.

Face-to-face contact is important, but sometimes that comes at a meeting that's only well attended if you publicise it. If you've got 5,000 people in a Facebook group, your influence can spread to the point where you get to talk face-to-face with more people, and of course listen to them.

Leaflets are also important, and here we're going back to the Chartists who handed out leaflets in their campaign for fairer votes. But what happens if you have several boxes of leaflets to be delivered and no delivery network? Social media can help you put out an appeal for deliverers, and suddenly the literature is on its way to doormats.

We knew we wouldn't achieve much through traditional media. If the progressives in England think the press is against them, consider this: thirty-six out of thirty-seven national newspapers were against Scottish independence. We could not make a dent in terms of how the press or television viewed us. Just after the referendum, the BBC in Scotland was found to have a 48 per cent satisfaction rating, which means 52 per cent did not think it was fair. So people turn off, but where do they go instead for their information? We had to work through hall meetings and conversations in corners of pubs, and it was social media that oiled the wheels for these interactions with voters.

So it's not about social media doing the work for you, it's about using social media to spread whatever word you want to disseminate. There was almost something subversive about it, because the traditional media were saying one thing by pushing the No line, while social media platforms were saying something else by building the enthusiasm for the Yes line. (These days, a lot of the news I get comes first on social media, and I then check it out in the mainstream media.)

BROADER LESSONS FOR PROGRESSIVES

Some of the features of the referendum campaign were based largely on specifically Scottish factors, but many apply more broadly – in the rest of the UK and overseas.

The biggest lesson learned is that you simply have to have a system of proportional representation for elections. First-past-the-post fails everybody, even those who win under it, because they have little or no legitimacy. If you live in a shire outside London and you want to vote Labour, Lib Dem or Green, you have very little to no chance of your party winning. A lot of people still do not fully grasp how a proportional system works, but they do understand that they can use it to make changes, and through it they can hold the balance of power. Once people believe that their vote has the potential to really change the status quo, it opens up debate and discussion and disagreement, which is healthy.

Proportional representation in Scotland meant thousands of people found their own voices. When the SNP came to power in 2007, it was as a minority government, which meant it had to seek compromise and agreement with other parties who wouldn't traditionally align themselves to the SNP. So the SNP became associated with listening to what people wanted, which encouraged a sense that things could be done through the Scottish Parliament. It's one thing having a raft of policies about the country we want to live in, but you have to be confident in the structures of government. All the progressive parties need to be committed to changing first-past-the-post.

Those structures include the two Houses of Parliament, and there has to be reform of the House of Lords. The second chamber has to be elected in some form, ideally attracting people who are of society but not necessarily of the political classes. People will only believe they can change things on the ground if they have a sense that they can do things through the structures of government. The House of Lords is an embarrassment, and it's holding back a modern Britain.

There also needs to be a written constitution. It's not that *everything* has to be set in stone, but that every society should have a set of beliefs or tenets that it is committed to and that are entrenched in law. Whoever is in government, we should be committed to putting an end to homelessness and poverty, to fighting threats to the environment, and such like. As a society we need to set a standard, and a written constitution would do that. Governments can then take politics in different directions, but this way there's always the golden charter that each must respect.

Equally importantly, the constitution needs to be written by a broad stream of people from across society, not just by politicians and lawyers. The progressive parties also need to reframe their relationship with non-party-political organisations fighting for social and economic change. What happened in Scotland in 2012–14 was that thousands of groups campaigning for various things – independence and specific issues – set themselves up and a grass roots movement was born across the progressive spectrum. The sense of having a new clean slate, of getting back the social values we had after the Second World War, and of showing the world what can be done, didn't come from a political party, it came from a broad movement in which political parties played an important role. If a party thinks it has all the answers in-house, it will continue to put people off.

There needs to be a commitment towards political education. There is a link between people's knowledge and their willingness to vote for progressive ideas. Many of the values we hark back to date from the middle of the twentieth century, when there was an explosion in secondary education. It means that, if the progressives are to succeed, they need to frame their arguments in a way that's open to dialogue, not simply telling people what's right and what isn't. The minute you open up the discussion in this way, politics will flourish. It's like a flower – if you hold it too tight you'll strangle it, but if you give it a bit of support, water it and let it grow, it'll flourish all by itself. Pushing political education won't be easy.

I have sensed a fear among the establishment that having too many people asking too many questions is a threat. To me, it's an exciting threat – once you start getting people engaged and asking questions, there is no turning back, and the scope for an inclusive society is magnified.

Connected with this, the established parties need to look at who they're allowing to be politicians. Politics affects people's lives, so politicians have to look and feel like normal folk who discuss things in the same way as voters. Jim Sillars's advice to me was, 'Be confident, but never arrogant.' One of the great characteristics of the SNP group of MPs is that many of us have not been politicians before. It's understandable that parties try to choose candidates who look as if they have the gravitas to stand up for their communities in council chambers or national Parliaments, but if that gravitas comes from an arrogance that includes trying to exclude people, then choosing them will make the problem worse.

When I made my maiden speech at Westminster, I reached out to Labour. I said we had to work together – with other parties – to form an effective opposition to the Conservative government. But I was not appealing to the Labour Party that lost the 2015 election. It lost that election because it bought into the Conservatives' narrative. The Tories spun the line that it would be horrendous if the UK was run by a Labour–SNP coalition, and Labour bought into that, so Ed Miliband started falling over himself to deny that Labour would work with the SNP. But why would a Labour–SNP government be horrendous? No one seemed to ask the question. The right-wing press pushed the idea that a Labour–SNP government would break up the UK, but the break-up of the UK is much more likely with the kind of government we have in Westminster now because its callous attitude to society reminds people in Scotland why we have continually rejected the Conservative rhetoric and yet have to endure it anyway as part of the Union.

This was why I and so many of my SNP colleagues were so demoralised by the general election result. We went through a grieving process after the referendum was lost, but our compromise was to work for many of the things that had inspired the independence campaign by using our influence at Westminster. Not only did we lose the chance because of the Conservatives' overall majority, but Labour has refused to work with us in opposition. It is strange, because Jeremy Corbyn's leadership campaign was like a mini Yes campaign – he engaged people with politics who had felt excluded before. So the hand I was reaching out to Labour was to a constructive Labour Party, one that didn't let its agenda be dictated to by the Conservatives, but that trusted in the decency and good sense of the people. I hope it will eventually be accepted.

People ask me whether, if the Scottish National Party can be part of a progressive government at Westminster, that will reduce my eagerness for Scottish independence. The answer is no. I believe that Scotland can only reach its full potential if it has complete democratic control and influence to allow the flourishing ideas and imagination of its citizens to become a reality. But what I would say is that if the Conservatives continue to run the British government in the same way they currently are, then it will certainly hasten the break-up of the UK.

Mhairi Black MP is the youngest member of the House of Commons (a role traditionally known as 'Baby of the House'). She was elected to represent Paisley and Renfrewshire South at the 2015 general election despite not having completed her degree in politics and public policy from the University of Glasgow. She completed her degree two months after getting elected to Westminster, and was still twenty when she made her maiden Commons speech.

Chris Law MP was elected to represent Dundee West at the 2015 general election. He trained as a chef, then studied cultural and social anthropology at the University of St Andrews. Before becoming an MP, he worked as a financial adviser, and operated tours of the Himalayas on 1950s motorcycles.

SECTION TWO

MAKING IT HAPPEN

REDISCOVERING THE SOUL OF PROGRESSIVE POLITICS

Jonathan Rowson

If there is going to be a progressive alliance, it has to be about more than political marketing. Being a progressive is not just about being a socialist with a makeover, a social democrat looking to downsize to one word, a green seeking a larger palette, a civic nationalist looking to appear civil, or a liberal who cares about more than freedom.

Instead, we're looking for deeper conceptions of progress that are inclusive, viable and inspiring enough for diverse interests to coalesce around and campaign for. We won't create that idea of progress by committee, but we may get there if we look beyond partisan affiliation and get personal in the right way. Your *personal* idea of progress matters, not just because you can find yourself by fighting for it, but because, as the early feminists foresaw, the personal is usually more political than it looks.

While many take progress for granted, the philosopher John Gray is probably the most persuasive contemporary voice for a long history of (mostly conservative) political thought that argues progress may not extend beyond the scientific and the technological: 'The myth is that the progress achieved in science and technology can occur in ethics, politics or, more simply, civilisation. The myth is that the advances made in civilisation can be the basis for a continuing, cumulative improvement.'

Gray's point is not that we never make progress. Wars end in peace. Billions escape poverty. Literacy spreads. Beautiful works of art are created. Emancipation seems inexorable. But such gains are extremely fragile, and often offset by losses elsewhere. The global economy appears to be stable and growing, then the financial crash and recession happens. Nations meet their climate change targets, but global emissions continue to rise. We think we've stopped torturing people, but then pictures from Abu Ghraib emerge. We have long since abolished state sanctioned slavery, but de facto economic slavery remains ubiquitous. We hope world wars are a thing of the past, but nuclear bombs are built, terrorism spreads and ISIS cut people's heads off, using *technological progress* to amplify their barbarism. The progress of civilisation is not a given. Indeed, there is a case for not believing in it.

A LARGER LIFE

What then, are we striving for? Which way is north on our compass? The political theorist Roberto Unger offered a helpful touchstone for progress in an interview for the BBC Radio 4 programme *Analysis*: 'A progressive is someone who wants to see society reorganised, part-by-part and step-by-step, so that ordinary men and women have a better chance to live a larger life.'

A *larger* life. I believe this idea is a good lodestar for progressives to unite around because it is capacious, deep and generative. Unger's conception of larger life is 'a life of greater scope, greater capability and greater intensity', and that's not so difficult to comprehend. We can all do and be more, with growing aptitude and wisdom, and experience life more fully and deeply as a result. Of course, that means we need ecological viability, a place to live, work to do, and the education and time to do it, but those things are the technocratic means to the experiential ends that ultimately matter.

Unger says 'to die only once' is the heart of his vision, not to suffer many small deaths in daily frustrations, but to continually overcome and thereby live fully, dying only at the end. As the poet Rainer Maria Rilke puts it, 'The purpose of life is to be defeated by greater and greater things.'

Talk of larger lives and dying only once will not directly win general elections, but we should be equally wary of ignoring the political power of such philosophical ideas. Impatience to act is often a form of ethical cowardice and epistemological panic. Throughout Europe, social democratic parties are struggling to rediscover their sense of purpose, and that's partly, I think, because we are a little scared of ourselves – scared of what we'll see if we look closer at what really matters to us, and why.

WHAT IS MOST PERSONAL IS MOST UNIVERSAL

The psychotherapist and humanist Carl Rogers said that what is most personal is most universal, so let me start there; not because I have a particularly edifying biography, but because one thing progressives can be sure to have in common is a case history that formed our idea of progress. For me, the main ingredient in personal freedom will always be interdependence.

I was born in Aberdeen in 1977, during the Cold War. My father is an artist who became schizophrenic and latterly a 'Care in the Community' success story. I was raised partly by my extended family but mostly by a working single mother who climbed from nursery teacher to Head of Educational Services in North Ayrshire. My parents separated, we moved house a lot, and I took refuge in chess, later becoming a Grandmaster and professional player. I'm a type-one diabetic deeply dependent on the NHS and I gained entry to Oxford University via comprehensive schools. I watched my father's two commercially astute brothers thrive in Thatcher's Britain, but I was closer to my maternal grandfather, who worked in a granite quarry, bet on horses, and fed me stovies.

I grew up amidst ambient invective against 'the Tories'. Now, as an educated adult, I am impressed by some aspects of classical Conservative thought, have many Tory friends, and I even admire some Conservative politicians, but personally I could never vote for them. They will always be, with all due consideration and affection, 'the bastards'.

So I welcome the premise of this book, not merely to unite *against* a shared opponent, but to share what we might also unite *for* by clarifying what it means to share the progressive cause. In this collection, some are focused on the proximate target of winning the next general election, perhaps through some kind of progressive coalition. The ultimate target, however, is the prevailing ideology of our time in which inequality is a not a problem but a design feature, climate change is noted but disavowed, the shrinking public sphere is celebrated not mourned, and democracy is thinly understood as a last resort against tyranny, not as a form of life.

It is in that broader ideological context, and not just the immediate political one, that we need to keep on asking: what does it mean to be progressive?

POLITICAL HOPE

If being a progressive means anything, it means having political hope. Progress may not be constant, linear or easy, but a progressive believes things can get better, and that such progress can be 'continuing and cumulative' in Gray's terms. The world is better on balance now than it was 100 years ago, says the progressive, and though challenges are legion, bit by bit we can make it still better 100 years from now.

But such progress sounds obtuse in the context of ambient debt and the urgency of climate change, and it won't happen if we don't try. In this sense, progressives are defined by being proactive. They would take issue with Michael Oakeshott's idea that thinking our way to societal solutions is somehow hubristic. Established institutions should be given some benefit of the doubt, but they still have to prove their worth. There is great wisdom in the House of Lords, and perhaps even in the idea of an unelected second chamber, but that doesn't mean we can't replace it with something much better. Being progressive means you are not content to let things unfold, trusting in providence. You feel you have some *responsibility* for changing the world.

And it goes beyond that, because while all politicians want 'change' of some kind, progressivism is about more than incremental tinkering. Political hope is grounded in visions of wholesale transformation and renewal – not merely change, but changing the *way* things change. Progressives seek new social, political and economic structures, rather than just trying to optimise outcomes on the basis of existing ones. That's why constitutional and electoral reform is a defining aspect of most progressive policy platforms – if all the axioms and algorithms remain the same, you'll keep making the same mistakes.

Progressive imagination is premised on worlds with safe and sound ecologies, which all but the greener elements tend to take for granted too often – there is a constructive tension here that the UK's recent carbon net zero target should bring to the surface. But most progressive visions feature societies that are above all more equal: in opportunity, outcome, and ideally both. To be progressive is to place a high value on sharing the bounties of life on principle, but also for morale and collective dignity. '*Progressive* taxation' is appropriately named in this sense, but several decades of political and economic learning mean we know we cannot rely on this instrument alone.

Anthony Painter, the political writer and director of policy at the Royal Society of Arts, says the minimal conditions for being a progressive are being a liberal and a social democrat. That translates as a commitment to individual rights and a belief in the value of a mixed economy. This framing explains why being progressive has been defined largely through being 'anti-austerity' in recent years. Fighting major cuts to public expenditure is grounded in recognition that such services are necessary to militate against the inequalities of opportunity built into the market, and that losing them often undermines individual rights and freedoms.

Being a progressive therefore means *not* being a neoliberal, who valorises the market and deeply distrusts government, caring principally for aggregate wealth in abstraction and not the imbalances of power and inequalities in welfare that result. Progressives believe governments have an important role to play in redressing the unfairness and negative externalities of markets, but the state is only part of the story. More generally they tend to be animated by all the other freedoms of association and expression that democracy affords.

Less obviously, and perhaps contentiously, being a progressive means *not* being a communitarian. While many progressives value solidarity and often campaign in solidaristic ways, enhancing individual autonomy remains a central objective. Yes, they may be fighting for class interests or the common good of particular communities, but usually because of the life chances of individuals that depend upon them. When people on the right say 'progressive' is just a socially acceptable term for 'socialist', they overlook that a qualified respect for individual freedom and markets are legitimate points of divergence.

Progressives can freely acknowledge that capitalism is by far the best way to generate wealth, but should be just as resolute in arguing that it's a terrible way to distribute and channel it. In all cases, being progressive looks like a middle way; the desired economy is neither unfettered capitalism nor old fashioned socialism, and the desired society is neither painfully atomised nor stiflingly communal.

It's no surprise, then, that in terms of the conventional political spectrum, 'progressive' can meaningfully apply to everything from the relatively innovative and compassionate end of 'one nation conservatism', through all the Liberal Democrat tribes, past most forms of civic nationalism, beyond the Greens, all the way to the soft centres of the hard left. Put like that, it looks like a centrist political project. Who would have thought that being a progressive could mean being a conformist?

IDEAS OF PROGRESS

But we have forgotten something. Beyond sharing an egalitarian disposition and an emphasis on social justice, progressives can and do differ in how they give content to the idea of progress. It is here that there is great scope to be radical. Although it is sometimes pictured as an arrow pointing left, being progressive is arguably a way of *not* being left-wing or right-wing. Progressivism questions the validity of a political spectrum that views our relationship to the state as the pivotal issue and thereby relegates other major aspects of political life, for instance movement building, networks, values, agency, media, finance, technology, ecology.

There are many forks in the road at this point. Perhaps we need a deeper engagement with the way technology determines political and economic outcomes, intrigued by blockchain technology and inspired by the American philosopher Jaron Lanier's increasingly pivotal question: who owns information? You might want to believe in green growth, but unless you can tell a credible story of absolute decoupling of growth from emissions with sufficient speed to safeguard our habitat, the key question might be making post-growth economics work. If you think nothing happens without relationships, and that the requisite changes will come from forging new forms of networks, Compass are developing work in this space. If you feel we need to democratise the experience, expression and rewards of creativity, the Royal Society of Arts now build their work around 'the power to create'. All these progressive stories are relevant and there are many other stories to be told. There are also those witty 'unknown unknowns', who will no doubt change the agenda.

A progressive, then, is somebody who believes in progress, fuelled by political hope and informed by a vision of ecological sanity, democratic renewal, inclusive economies and human development. The kind of progressive you are is mostly about what gives you that experience of political hope.

SPIRITUAL ROOTS OF PROGRESSIVE REVIVAL

Speaking personally, my political hope comes from the Gandhian ideal of trying to be the change we want to see in the world. This particular aspiration does not seem to me to be optional, which means the progressive challenge is to spread the kinds of human *experience* that we most value, including the experiences of meaning, development and direction, forged and expressed through our social and political engagement.

I therefore think it's time for progressives to speak about experience as such, in the explicit and evocative terms we need to cut through ambient distraction – the language, for instance, of the deepest currents of life: love, death, self and soul. When Russell Brand said the problem is 'primarily spiritual and secondarily political' it was a minor tragedy for progressive thought that this timeless message was subsumed by its messenger.

Whenever there is uneasiness with language, progressives should remind themselves of the contention by another American philosopher, Richard Rorty, that 'a talent for speaking differently, rather than arguing well, is the chief instrument of cultural change'. If progressivism is to be more than political conformity masquerading as radicalism, and if we are to convincingly argue against the likes of John Gray, we need to find the courage to speak differently, not least about the spiritual content in the idea of progress. (For more on this, see Carys Afoko, page 318.)

As author of a recent report on reimagining spirituality, I know this emphasis is vague and awkward for many, but that awkwardness can be viewed as grit in the oyster. To reconnect personal transformation and political transformation, we may need to move closer to the edge of our comfort zones to reclaim ownership of the language of the spiritual. After all, the most celebrated political progressives of all time – Gandhi, Martin Luther King, Nelson Mandela – are defined precisely by the spiritual content of their political commitment. Their struggles and victories show that this confluence of spiritual and political is not about quietism but about activism. You come to know who you are, and what matters most in life, through your efforts to bring about the world you want to live in.

As Unger puts it in *The Self Awakened*, 'If spirit is a name for the resistant and transcending faculties of the agent, we can spiritualise society. We can diminish the distance between who we are and what we find outside of ourselves.'

Diminish the distance between who we are and what we find outside of ourselves? Who would have thought we'd end up with *this* challenge when we asked what it means to be a progressive? But now that we're here, what's stopping us?

AESTHETIC UNITY

That question is not merely rhetorical. Two of the biggest things that need to be unlearned are how to approach issues often unhelpfully deemed 'environmental' and the awkwardness felt over sentiments that are broadly spiritual. To put that more positively, how will those who are ambivalent about seemingly 'green' issues come to realise that they lie at the heart of economic and social renewal? And how can we make democratic politics feel less transactional and more soulful; less like an episodic ritual, and more like a meaningful form of life?

I believe the answer to both questions lies in understanding and creating 'aesthetic unity'. We need visions of progress that are beautiful enough to make us feel whole as we work towards them. Aesthetic unity sounds abstract but is deeply visceral; it's what we feel and sense in a good book, a good film, a good song. In a moment I'll use the Yes campaign of the Scottish referendum as a political example, but the renowned ecologist Gregory Bateson frames the broader challenge like this:

> Mere purposive rationality unaided by such phenomena as art, religion, dream, and the like, is necessarily pathogenic and destructive of life … Our loss of the sense of aesthetic unity was, quite simply, an epistemological mistake … more serious than all those minor insanities that characterise those older epistemologies which agreed upon the fundamental unity.

Bateson's concern here is the relationship between knowledge and purpose in a post-religious landscape. Some aspects of religious belief may be 'minor insanities', but the major insanity – one many of us suffer from – is to live without a consciously chosen myth or meta-narrative to serve as a touchstone for the myriad details of our lives. In so doing we either lose our way, or latch on to one unconsciously like 'growth' or 'the market'.

'Mere purposive rationality unaided' was arguably part of what lost Labour the 2015 general election. The so-called retail offers were not enough because they lacked any overarching vision.

In contrast, 'Long-term economic plan' may not float your boat, but it has a form of aesthetic unity that millions bought into.

Creating a progressive sense of aesthetic unity is not easy, but is perhaps the defining challenge of our time. The erosion of institutions – churches, unions, political parties – matters because the fragmentation and diffusion of authoritative knowledge leaves the notion of purpose orphaned. When something we sense should be collective, intuitive and visceral becomes atomised, partial and contentious, we feel fundamentally lost. This sense of being lost, unmoored, simultaneously saturated with meaning and mythically deprived, is arguably also the root cause of growing mental health problems – another reason for spiritual life to be a more central progressive cause.

Whatever the value of religion in channelling civic energy, there can be no naive turning back to it as a source of political power. To be meaningful, and therefore 'work', the frame we need has to connect with every aspect of us, which is why it needs an aesthetic dimension.

Rediscovering aesthetic unity matters because the external world is undermining the stability and coherence of the forms of personal identity that shape political activism beyond single-issue protests. We are no longer in a traditional world where roles were clear, norms were given and political tribes knew themselves ideologically.

At the time of writing, in May 2016, our relational, institutional and cultural references are increasingly porous and malleable. We are asked to play multiple roles and feel obliged to have opinions on multiple issues that we barely understand or, on reflection, really care about. As the political scientist Peter Grosvenor put it, 'Disoriented denizens of neoliberal societies may look for satisfying and durable identities in, for example, nostalgic, reactionary, nationalist, or fundamentalist ideas and movements. More commonly, they seek solace in consumerism.'

To make sense of how to regain our own sense of wholeness, we need to realise that we are in some ways victims of a wholeness that was not of our own choosing. However pernicious and harmful it may be, neoliberalism has its own kind of aesthetic unity: markets deliver utility in the form of growth and profits, private interests trump and ultimately subsume the common good, market norms are efficient and productive and therefore helpful in every sphere of life. Such ideas may be utterly wrong or immoral, but they have their own internal consistency, which makes them appear like common sense to the unreflective citizen, and allows attacks on particular policy parts (e.g. 'abolish the bedroom tax') to be absorbed by the ideological whole (e.g. 'live within your means').

In Rowan Williams's review of Michael Sandel's book *What Money Can't Buy*, he pinpoints the core critique of excessive marketisation and points towards forms of resistance as follows:

> The fundamental model being assumed here is one in which a set of unconditioned wills negotiate control of a passive storehouse of commodities, each of them capable of being reduced to a dematerialised calculus of exchange value. If anything could be called a 'world-denying' philosophy, this is it ... a possible world of absolute commodification. If we want to resist this intelligently, we need doctrine, ritual and narrative: sketches of the normative, practices that are not just functions, and stories of lives that communicate a sense of what being at home in the environment looks like – and the costs of failure as well.

YES!

Williams refers to the need for 'stories of lives that communicate a sense of what being at home in the environment looks like'. Here again I think we have to plunge into personal experience. As a Scot, I am not alone in finding the campaign for an independent Scotland politically transformative. Whatever your view of the objective we sought, that *experience* offers a clue about what progressive renewal might look like. For a few months leading up to the vote in September 2014, I was fortunate to find myself advising some senior members of the Yes campaign, and reached an alacritous audience through one of the main online platforms in Scotland, Bella Caledonia. That summer, politics felt meaningful in a way that it rarely does, and life as such was revitalised by a constitutional question in which I had a stake and a voice.

What happened to me happened to many others too. Amidst the clamour of the debate about the future, the daily experience of the campaign offered glimpses of meaningful integration – of the myriad aspects of life somehow coalescing. Fundamentally we were parts in search of a whole. Scotland – the nation as such – was abstract and porous and loveable enough to help us transcend policy contention, acting as a lodestar for our memories, identifications and projections.

But that's only part of it. The deeper point, I think, is that many loved the prospect of an independent country not in spite of fears but *because* of them. I certainly had huge doubts, as I wrote in *The Guardian* at the time:

> There is something horrifying about the wilful destruction of a relationship that has evolved over centuries to a unique state

> of geopolitical complexity. There are troubling questions about technocratic imponderables, a palpable sense of guilt and betrayal about the prospective loss of kinship with fellow Brits, and a sense of anti-heroic embarrassment about the pragmatism of a British currency union. And while I do see a path towards a revitalised social democracy, at ease with ourselves and our place in the world, I don't see us getting there for a decade at least. I see lots of risk along the way, huge scope for regret and inevitable heartache. It all feels so unnecessary.

And yet, I was drawn by a sense of courage in the body that told me such matters were not fundamental. I sensed aesthetic unity in the idea of an independent Scotland in a way I regrettably didn't in the UK. I wanted my country to have creative agency, to be free to make its own mistakes and form relationships on its own terms, and I felt that this risk – and it was a risk – was worth taking. I felt sure that my beliefs did not have to be conclusive to be valid; I *felt* that nations are not negligible things; that statehood is their necessary maturity; that facing and overcoming fears is what it means to grow, and that growing is what we should all be trying to do.

The centrality of this point was brought home to me on the BBC's *Question Time* in the referendum's aftermath. One of the foremost Yes campaigners, the journalist Lesley Riddoch, was asked whether it was time to accept the final result and draw a line under the constitutional question. She acknowledged the result but qualified that with a remark that went much deeper:

> The level of activism, the commitment, the imagination, the friendship, the camaraderie … It was the best year of my life; from the point of view of the humanity and optimism that was

> generated. If you were a part of that … it's so precious, it's so unusual, that you really feel you do not want to see that go. Particularly younger people, older people, people in estates, people who are not usually involved.

POLITICAL COURAGE

This notion that the experience of courage is politically pivotal reminds me of the story (which can be appreciated figuratively) that, when we die and reach the gates of heaven, God will ask us, 'Where are your wounds?' And if we say, 'I have no wounds,' we will be asked, 'Was there nothing worth fighting for?'

What then are the things we deeply believe in but lack the courage to advocate? What are the things that we know to be risky, but that we value *because* the risk makes us feel like we are doing something worthwhile?

Opposition to Trident renewal is a bit like that. Advocating shorter working weeks is like that. Proposing a universal minimum income is like that. Campaigning for a post-growth economy is like that. There are many more such policies, but I think their flavour is clear. We need a range of big systemic ideas where we see ourselves as part of a big and beautiful whole; where we feel the fear and do it anyway. If a progressive alliance is going to succeed and endure in the UK, it will need to have soul, which means building aesthetic unity and finding political courage.

Jonathan Rowson is co-founder of Perspectiva, a new institute that examines complex policy challenges by integrating perspectives from systems, souls and society. He is a chess Grandmaster and three-time British chess champion, and was formerly director of the Social Brain Centre at the Royal Society of Arts, where he led a range of influential projects on social innovation, spirituality and climate change. His book, entitled *The Seven Dimensions of Climate Change: Rethinking the World's Toughest Problem*, will be published by Palgrave Macmillan in early 2017.

FURTHER READING

Rowson, Jonathan, *Spiritualise: Revitalising Spirituality to address 21st Century Challenges*. RSA: 2014. Available online: https://www.thersa.org/globalassets/pdfs/reports/spiritualise-report.pdf.

The final output of a two-year thought leadership project involving over 300 people featuring a range of public and private events. Most of the report tries to clarify the meaning and function of the spiritual and the final section unpacks the connection between the spiritual and the political.

Unger, Roberto, BBC Radio 4 *Analysis*, 18 November 2013. Programme available online: http://www.bbc.co.uk/programmes/b03hvn6n

Transcript available: http://downloads.bbc.co.uk/radio4/transcripts/20131118_analysis_robertounger.pdf

The political philosopher is interviewed about what it means to be 'a progressive' at LSE and unpacks his notion of reorganising society so that more people can live what he calls 'a larger life' in which they 'die only once'.

Rowson, Jonathan, 'As an exile I can't vote in Scotland's referendum, but I know I'd vote yes', *The Guardian*, 2014. Available online: http://www.theguardian.com/commentisfree/2014/jun/09/scotland-refendum-yes-economy-confidence

My rationale for deciding to support the Yes campaign in the Scottish independence referendum, and how it related to political courage and 'the sanctity of personal power'.

Bateson, Gregory and Mary Catherine Bateson, *Angels Fear: An Investigation Into the Nature and Meaning of the Sacred*, Rider Books: 1987.

The idea of 'aesthetic unity is introduced here in a dialogue between father and daughter, two extraordinary transdisciplinary thinkers known for their work on cybernetics, ecology and metaphor.

'John Gray says human progress is a myth', interview with Johannes Niederhauser, *Vice Magazine*, 2013. Available online: https://www.vice.com/en_uk/read/john-gray-interview-atheism

The original source for John Gray's quotation on the myth of progress.

Rowson, Jonathan, 'Why our Politics needs to be more spiritual', *Prospect* magazine, 2015. Available online: http://www.prospectmagazine.co.uk/life/why-our-politics-needs-to-be-more-spiritual

UNDERSTANDING MODERN BRITAIN

Yasmin Alibhai-Brown

Britain has been a multi-ethnic and multi-racial society for centuries. The minority communities ought to be drawn to progressive politics and the principles of equality and justice. However, there is a real risk that the progressives will languish and rot on the wrong side of history because they do not understand the current political landscape and, therefore, cannot negotiate the complexities of social engagement.

The mistake they are making is a well-intentioned one, arising as it does out of post-colonial reparative sentiments. Good people are keen not to make the same mistakes that were made in the past. The history of European colonialism, when Britain and other colonial powers rode roughshod over the cultures of the countries they ruled, has created on the left a desire to do the right thing today. The imperative is respect, given readily and expected by culturally distinct groups, nations and individuals. These responses are laudable but are leading to blind spots, the tolerance of the intolerable, lazy moral exceptionalism. And it's also worsening tensions between different social groups, not just between white and ethnic minorities, but between men and women, even between the working and middle classes.

The political right has owned the debate about race for decades. They have used slogans exhorting immigrants to 'be British', 'be like us', 'behave like us', and when they don't behave 'like us', the response is punitive rejection, racism or unfair scapegoating. The political left has tried to counter this by arguing against such ethno-centric attitudes. In doing so it has put a protective shield around ethnic communities that has also shielded them from fair scrutiny. This is unethical and patronising. All people in this country should have the same rights and responsibilities, whether indigenous, immigrant or anything in between.

For the progressives to simply oppose the hostile rhetoric of the right is no longer feasible. Progressives need to understand that there are barbarians and decent people across all nations and societies. The cultural war today is between barbarianism and enlightenment, authoritarian values and liberty, rather than the old-world schisms between Judeo-Christian and Islamic thinking, between the West and the Rest, between white and black, or anything else. The ideological struggles of the twenty-first century are playing out in India, Turkey, Arabia, the US, Europe, Russia, the UK – all over the world.

THE CURSE OF LOYALTY

At the root of this challenge is the concept of loyalty. The word can have positive connotations – we admire people who are loyal, we praise them for their loyalty, and we demand loyalty in a team player.

However, I think loyalty causes some of the most intractable problems in the world today. I'm not loyal to my family, nor to my race, nor to my country. And I don't expect anyone to be loyal to me. Loyalty imposes on you the duty *not* to be scrupulously fair and frank about what's going on but to stand by someone because they're somehow linked to you. So I'm not loyal to Muslims, or women, or Britain. I will defend Muslims, women, my country, my friends and relations where I think they are right or being treated unfairly, but to do so simply because of their association with me would make me a tribalist, my activism would be meaningless, and it would quite rightly create a backlash from good people who are trying to solve a problem and see the inconsistencies in my stance.

Many people accuse me of being flaky, because sometimes I stand up for women or for Muslims, and sometimes I don't. The charge has some merit. But my only loyalty is to what I believe is right – in the sense of basic right and wrong – and if something is wrong, then it doesn't matter who is perpetrating it: I will come out against it.

Take the controversial issue of Muslim women wearing the full veil. It is not a strict requirement in Islam (except perhaps Saudi Islam, and we have to challenge that view). Men and women are asked to dress modestly. Today veiling is ubiquitous and girls as young as two are seen with their hair and bodies covered up. The liberal left does not question this anti-feminist symbol. I would ask progressives this question: 'If your daughter came home and said, "Daddy/Mummy, I want to put on the full veil," what would you say? Would you say "OK, it's your choice"? Or would you say, "Can we discuss what message you are giving out about yourself by wearing this veil, and how this message will work in your life"?' If a responsible progressive doesn't want to send their child to a Muslim school because of concerns that the nature of the teaching and the general school environment is not promoting good all-round citizenship, then there have to be serious questions about whether that school is good for society, and the fact that it's run according to the teachings of Islam should play no part in addressing those questions. I have the same objections to all other religious schools. Faith has no place in state education or institutions.

Equality and human rights are universal, borderless principles, not Western impositions. If you have a young woman who is married in a village in India, and then ends up in a refuge having been horribly burnt as part of some religious punishment, she doesn't say, 'Oh, it's my religion that made them do it' – she says, 'I'm a human being and they didn't treat me like a human being.' Why should we treat her any differently because she's in a different culture? And why should an Indian tolerate such treatment simply out of the loyalty that comes from it being meted out by other Indians?

A NEW MORAL TEMPLATE

The way forward for all of us who are progressives is to develop a template for judging behaviour that – if applied fairly and across the board – should provide ample defence against unfair accusations of racism, homophobia, sexism, etc. This template should encompass equality, dignity, human rights, gender parity, autonomy for young people, and for women, all classes, indeed, for all citizens. The UN promotes and defends universal human rights standards, and some of the most committed human rights defenders are non-Westerners in places such as Afghanistan, Syria, Pakistan – indeed, some have been killed for fighting for human rights. No one should have difficulty with us adopting these as our measuring sticks of basic decency.

If you take that template and apply it to all people in all situations, you develop clarity of purpose and a new morality. So if, for example, you know that groups of Pakistani men are grooming women and children for sexual exploitation, you shouldn't be afraid to say so out of a fear that people will think you're being racist. By condemning it, it doesn't mean you're denying that there are white grooming gangs too. All men (and women) who exploit children should face justice and social ostracisation. Class, race, poverty, loyalty and other factors are too often used as excuses. Furthermore the underpinning culture too should be scrutinised. Jimmy Savile got away with it because he was protected by fame; Asian men get away with it because their own families and communities protect them and share their repulsive prejudices about 'promiscuous' white females.

I sometimes find my heart sinking when good liberal white writers push the apologist line, as if we Muslims are only ever put upon and always blameless. It doesn't help us modernist Muslims when good people don't see what's happening, or know what's happening but worry that criticisms of Muslims would unleash anti-Muslim racism. Racists don't need any encouragement, they are who they are. They look out for and snatch negative stories, and turn them into propaganda. Progressives should not waste time on haters. We must be clear-headed, and have a responsibility to make fair and brave judgements about all individuals and communities, otherwise we are guilty of a perverse moral order that accepts a lower standard of rights and protection for those who are not white and middle-class.

THE NEED TO BE BRAVE

If the progressives are to reclaim credibility in today's multi-ethnic Britain, we will have to be brave. It will mean standing up against certain traditions that we know are wrong but that we have felt unable to question for fear of encroaching on the sacred ground of other cultures and religions. It will mean an implicit recognition that some unacceptable and antisocial practices exist in communities that have grown up out of the abuse of colonial times, but that post-colonial guilt is no reason to tolerate such practices. We have found determination and courage when it comes to female genital mutilation. It's time now to turn to other cultural misdemeanours and to stop pussyfooting.

One of the policy areas the progressives will have to tackle is state support for all faith schools. These are policies that knowingly encourage separation. In essence, we have to be able to say we don't want separate faith schools in the state education sector, and the fact that they have existed for many years is not an excuse to keep them today. The practical fact of their existence means that abolishing them overnight is not an option, but the progressive parties need to signal in some way that state support for faith schools will end, even if it is phased out over the school career of your average school student (five or twelve years).

By the same token, we don't want imams propagating illiberal values in prisons. We shouldn't ban them, just as we shouldn't ban clerics from Judeo-Christian strands – religious figures can often be a force for good in helping people who have gone off the rails find their way back on track. But any religious support must fall within the framework of encouraging our rehabilitated criminals to respect the template of equality, dignity, human rights, gender parity etc., and not be part of a code of ethics that tolerates certain behaviours that are unacceptable.

We must also question 'choice', which has become the mantra of our times. It sounds so reasonable, and it appears to enforce the freedom that we all seek, but it has become a way of disengaging from the issues. We say women choose the veil, or men choose to stay within their ethnic communities, but how many actually do choose this? If the choice is out of a sense of fear that their security will not be guaranteed, that they will be cast out or somehow abused if they don't make certain choices, then they are not choices at all. Standing up against false choices will take a lot of political bravery.

A progressive manifesto would call on white liberals to integrate much better than has happened to date. Integration is a dance, so both sides need to know the steps, and to do them. David Cameron talked about racial integration, but how many Asians get invited to his house? How many black people get invited to his parties and functions? Ed Miliband was no better, and the Liberal Democrats are the whitest of the lot.

And the progressives must make a really strong case for migration. We need to make the case that it's not just about money or economic survival – but unstoppable global connectedness. We need to grow up and get over it, teach our children that this is the world they will be adults in. Next to a white child there could be a Bangladeshi child who may be working twice as hard. The Bangladeshi child might be very good at maths but not English, while the white child would be a fluent English speaker but might be rubbish at maths. Think of what they could do for each other. Interculturalism is the key.

We have to oppose neo-colonialism and contemporary colonial attitudes, whether they are multinational corporations profiteering in the developing world, or governments fighting neo-imperialist wars, such as those in Iraq and Libya. Progressives must not repeat the mistakes of empire (there are still many Westerners on the left who think the post-9/11 interventions in the Middle East were noble). But, concurrently, we must be prepared to hold to account those who rightly condemn and fight colonial attitudes and policies and yet who devalue the lives and rights of their own citizens. We are at a historical junction where old colonialism, post-colonialism and neo-colonialism are laying their claims on the world. Morality itself has become instrumentalised. Internet traffic creates much sound and fury and makes us all feel the world is meaner and more conflicted. These are challenges, not reasons for defeatism. We must think beyond the usual paradigms.

There will be those who say that calling for an end to faith schools and making the case for immigration will simply turn off too many voters to be politically viable, but who says? There are some very progressive white, working-class people who don't think like that, but who is representing them? I was on the panel for the BBC's *Question Time* in Lincolnshire in January where there's supposed to be great hostility to immigration, yet the people in the audience were absolutely for refugees. Listening to our increasingly xenophobic national conversations, you would not expect that population to be so tolerant and empathetic. It is time to stop taking our cue from the rabid right.

I was also on a Channel 5 programme, *The Wright Stuff*, which talks to unemployed people, part-time workers, and many who by and large aren't engaged with politics. We were discussing ex-convicts and whether they should have to declare their convictions when applying for jobs. The most caring, generous calls came through from viewers, saying people must be given a second chance, they must be allowed to rehabilitate themselves. There are progressive populations willing to support progressive ideas, but they're being utterly failed by today's politicians (the reason many of them like Jeremy Corbyn is because they feel that at least he is listening to them, even if no one else is).

One other area the progressives will have to tackle is the idea that interest groups are islands, unable to relate to broader issues and concerns. Take women's equality and safety. This should be a concern for women of all ethnic backgrounds, but also for men. Men should fight for women, and women should fight for men. White, middle-class men may still have too much power in today's world, but they have to be part of the progressive project. I have no time for people who say men have no part in this, or people shouldn't meddle in other groups' affairs, and I reject the feminist movement's argument that men are not part of the solution to women's problems – they are! We must end this gender and race apartheid.

AN AWFUL LOT AT STAKE

We are at a very perilous point in human history. Across the world there's a rejection of enlightenment values and reason itself. Science, the arts, civil societies, intelligent political discourse, human rights, equality initiatives and laws, democracy itself are all under threat wherever you look, often thanks to the votes of the people. In India, you see a man elected to power who was banned from many countries because he's essentially a political gangster, but he offered the antidote to the secular, multi-racial, multi-ethnic India, which was 'Hinduism shall prevail' – and he won a thumping majority. We see it with Donald Trump in the USA, Nigel Farage in Britain, and various right-wing parties across Europe.

I have recently found aggressive and obnoxious demonstrators intimidating people entering a Marie Stopes clinic. When Salman Rushdie wrote *The Satanic Verses* and elicited a fatwa from Iran in 1988, it was global news. Now there are so many death threats against novelists in India as part of a clampdown on freedom of expression that they barely warrant a mention. And countries like Turkey, which used to be one of the most open societies in the world, are becoming increasingly closed and oppressive. I am not an absolutist on free speech – we all have lines on how far we can go before we hurt and insult people, but I am against all forms of state repression.

We need to find our nerve again. Under New Labour and the Tory–Lib Dem coalition, dissatisfaction with challenges to basic decency and freedom of expression was allowed to grow. Power is still held mostly by white, middle-class Oxbridge-educated men who are taking this nation to the right. Labour has, in the past, been complicit in this power grab and is now weak and disoriented. We must rise up against political/economic homogenisation and reinstate a progressive alternative. We owe that to the citizens of this country.

We have the basis of a template that can stand at the centre of a modern, decent, multi-racial and multi-ethnic society. We have an agreed set of principles for decency, dignity, equality, parity, and better outcomes for everyone, whoever they are. The Western parties need to stand up for, and live by, this very important set of standards. In this shared world, our common humanity should matter more than our differences. If we see a child being abused in an ethnic minority community and we choose not to interfere because we fear being racist or insufficiently respectful of religious practices, then we have to be clear that we are condemning that child to the abuse. When we interfere or criticise, it mustn't come from racism, but from a sense of social engagement.

This is an area for the progressives to seize – one that will resonate with all those who believe in a vibrant, diverse British society of the twenty-first century. There are barbarians and good people in every walk of life and every religion, race and community. A moral understanding of this duality would create new spaces and ways of thinking. A fair and universal set of standards would bring the divided nation together. Seizing this territory will not be easy, because it will be accompanied by deliberate misconstruing and accusations of racism. But needs must. The future must be better and more optimistic than the past has been. Humans, wherever they are, whoever they are, do generally bend towards light.

There was a time in the colonial and immediate post-colonial periods when you could divide the world into goodies and baddies, when we knew who the exploiters and the exploited were. That time has gone. The progressives in Britain need to update their view of post-colonialism and embrace this moral template if they are not to remain paralysed and deeply handicapped by a skewed view of doing the right thing.

Yasmin Alibhai-Brown is a writer and broadcaster on multicultural and social affairs. Born in Uganda of Shia Muslim Pakistani and Indian parentage, she came to Britain in the 1970s, completed a Master's degree in English literature from Oxford University, and was a teacher before becoming a journalist. She is a founder member of British Muslims for Secular Democracy.

IS THERE A PROGRESSIVE MAJORITY?

John Curtice

An initial glance at the outcome of the 2015 general election suggests a country that is divided down the middle so far as the level of support for and opposition to a 'progressive' outlook is concerned. On one side of the fence, the progressive parties, viz Labour, the Liberal Democrats and the Greens together with the nationalist parties in Scotland and Wales, between them won nearly 49 per cent of the vote. On the other side, the Conservatives and UKIP secured a little less than 51 per cent. The answer to the question 'Is there a progressive majority in Britain?' would appear to be that the forces on the two sides of the debate are more or less evenly matched.

Yet it is a mistake to try to infer the level of support for a particular policy or ideological stance from votes cast in a general election. True, the way in which people mark their ballots can be expected to reflect in part their values and their assessment of which party best represents their views. But there are also plenty of other considerations that voters can and sometimes do take on board.

Not least of these are evaluations of the competence of the parties – do they think that a party leader and his or her senior colleagues are up to the task of running the country, including, above all, managing the economy (Clarke et al., 2009)? Voters may also be concerned about whether a party appears united or divided, and thus whether or not its members are agreed on the merits of whatever promises it has made. Meanwhile, some may simply wish to express their disappointment with the record of the government in office. In short, elections are not just a battle of ideas but also an arena in which voters express a judgement about the abilities and capabilities of leaders and their parties.

If we are to form an accurate assessment of the extent to which the public back the progressive ideas that are the focus of this book, we need to look more directly at voters' views. This means examining the pattern of responses that people give when interviewed by a poll or social survey. Such information does of course need to be assessed critically; the answers that people give to survey questions depend on the way in which those questions are worded or phrased. Here we will for the most part use high-quality survey data that have been gathered after considerable effort has been expended on ensuring that the questions asked are both understood by respondents and are unbiased in character. But, at the same time, this approach does mean we do not have to regard 'progressivism' as a singular phenomenon that people either support or oppose; rather, we can look separately at its various constituent elements. Perhaps some progressive ideas are more popular than others.

Our survey evidence in this chapter comes from the British Social Attitudes (BSA) survey, an annual survey that interviews a random sample of British adults about their views on a wide range of social and political issues. Conducted by NatCen Social

Research, the survey has established itself as the key source of evidence on the key trends and patterns in British public opinion. Often the survey has the merit that it approaches a topic from a variety of perspectives, thereby enabling us to come to a rounded view about the balance of opinion on a subject. We make particular use of the most recently available survey, which was conducted in 2014, not long before the last general election at which the Conservatives won an overall majority (Ormston and Curtice, 2015). Fortuitously, this particular survey contains plenty of material of relevance to making an assessment of the level of support for progressivism as defined in the introduction to this book.

So far as that definition of progressivism is concerned, we focus on four key beliefs that it suggests constitute the key elements of a progressive outlook. These are as follows:

- A belief in social solidarity and economic equality.
- A belief in the importance of civil liberties.
- A concern to preserve and enhance the environment.
- A wish to see a more distributed structure of political power.

We shall now examine separately how much support there appears to be for each of these four beliefs.

SOCIAL SOLIDARITY AND ECONOMIC EQUALITY

Our first question, then, is to what extent is there support for greater economic equality and how far do people feel that they have a duty to help out their fellow citizens who are in need or adversity? In Table 1 we display people's responses in 2014 to a series of statements about, first, inequality and, second, one of the principal mechanisms for reducing inequality and implementing social solidarity: the welfare state. It suggests that while there might be quite widespread support for the principle of greater equality, this does not necessarily translate into support for some of the ways in which the government might try to achieve that objective.

Table 1: Attitudes to Inequality and the Welfare State

	Agree %	Neither %	Disagree %
Ordinary people do not get their fair share of the nation's wealth	60	25	13
The government should redistribute income from the better-off to the less well-off	40	26	33
Many people who get social security don't really deserve any help	32	35	32
If welfare benefits were not so generous people would learn to stand on their own two feet	53	23	23
The government should spend more money on welfare benefits for the poor even if it leads to higher taxes	30	30	39

Source: British Social Attitudes 2014

NB: Missing percentage points are a result of the 'Don't Knows' included in the denominator but not shown.

At the top of the table, we can see that no less than three fifths (60 per cent) agree that 'ordinary people do not get their fair share of the nation's wealth', a pattern of response that implies that the current level of inequality is unacceptable to most people in Britain. This interpretation is reinforced by the answers given when people are asked whether 'the gap between those with high incomes and those with low incomes is too large, about right or too small'. When this question was last posed – on the 2013 BSA survey – no less than 79 per cent said that the gap was too large, while just 17 per cent reckoned it was about right. Only 1 per cent felt it was too small! Moreover, when in 2012 people were asked whether or not it should be the government's responsibility to try to reduce income differences, as many as 41 per cent said it 'definitely' should be while another 29 per cent reckoned that it 'probably' should. In short, it seems that the extent of inequality in Britain is widely regarded as unacceptable, and that many believe it is the government's responsibility to try to do something about it.

However, when we look further down Table 1, we can see that this does not necessarily translate into support for some of the things that the government might do to reduce inequality. Redistributing income from the better-off to the less well-off is, for example, relatively controversial; while two-fifths (40 per cent) agree that the government should do this, as many as a third (33 per cent) actually disagree. Meanwhile, the provision of welfare benefits is not especially popular. Over half (53 per cent) feel that people would learn to stand on their own two feet if the system were not so generous. Just as many (32 per cent) agree that many of those on 'social security' do not deserve help as actively disagree (32 per cent). Meanwhile, rather more people (39 per cent) actually disagree with the idea of spending more on welfare benefits for the poor than support the idea (30 per cent).

To this evidence we can add some further examples of reluctance to embrace welfare provision in particular. Nearly three times as many (73 per cent) support the principle of a 'cap' on welfare benefits – that is that no household should receive more in benefits than the national average household income – as oppose the idea (25 per cent). Meanwhile, nearly twice as many (52 per cent) believe that 'benefits for unemployed people are too high and discourage them from finding jobs' as take the view that 'benefits for unemployed people are too low and cause hardship' (27 per cent). Indeed, one of the key findings of the British Social Attitudes survey in recent years has been a clear trend towards a more critical outlook on welfare, at least so far as those of working age are concerned (Taylor and Taylor-Gooby, 2015).

Yet this does not mean that social solidarity is simply noticeable by its absence. It certainly seems to be in plentiful supply when it comes to the health service. No less than 61 per cent think that it is 'very important' in a democracy that 'healthcare be provided for everyone'. Only 32 per cent agree that the NHS should only be available to those with lower incomes with everybody else expected to take out health insurance, thereby potentially paving the way to reduce taxes. At least half (51 per cent) are opposed to the idea. One key difference, of course, is that most people of working age are not (and never have been) reliant on welfare, whereas most people make some use of the health service, albeit that use is greater among older people than younger people. Ill health is something from which we all suffer periodically and thus is something on which most are happy for their taxes to be spent. Poverty, in contrast, is regarded as the preserve of a minority who perhaps are thought to bear some responsibility for the predicament in which they find themselves.

So, while concern about inequality is widespread, securing majority support for any particular action to reduce it may well be more difficult. Certainly, mechanisms that transfer resources directly from the better-off to the less well-off do not necessarily secure public support. That, perhaps, suggests that what progressives need to do is to focus on policies such as widening educational opportunities or setting a living wage that might help to reduce the extent of income and wealth inequality that arises in the first place, rather than looking to use the 'sticking plaster' of money transfers to reverse inequality once it has arisen (see also Rowlingson et al., 2010). Such an approach would, of course, present any future progressive government with a considerable challenge.

CIVIL LIBERTIES

Arguably at the heart of any concern with civil liberties are two beliefs. The first is that the rights of minorities should be respected and protected. The second is that there should be clear limits to the coercive power of the state. And in the abstract at least, there seems to be plenty of support for these ideas. Asked to use a scale from one to seven to say how important it is in a democracy 'that government authorities respect and protect the right of minorities', two thirds (66 per cent) give the issue a mark of six or seven. Meanwhile, 55 per cent express the same view when asked how important it is 'that governments respect democratic rights whatever the circumstances'.

However, general sentiment and particular circumstance are not necessarily the same thing. No government likes to see its policies opposed, but it might be regarded as essential that people are able to do so. Yet, evidently, many voters feel there are limits to how far protest should be taken. For example, just 22 per cent give a mark of six or seven when asked how important it is 'that citizens may engage in acts of civil disobedience when they oppose government actions'. Rather more (27 per cent) actually give this ability a score of only one or two. Acts of 'civil disobedience' may, of course, involve breaking the law, and two-fifths (40 per cent) believe that, 'the law should always be obeyed, even if a particular law is wrong'. Only 25 per cent expressly disagree with that sentiment. Regard for civil liberties has to be set alongside respect for the law in the eyes of many people.

Meanwhile, the way in which some choose to exercise their rights may be thought to infringe the rights of others, such as for example in exposing them to language and ideas that they find offensive. It seems clear that in these circumstances the rights of the latter group are widely regarded as the more important. Just 22 per cent think that 'religious extremists' should 'definitely' or 'probably' be allowed to hold a public meeting, only 20 per cent say the same of 'people prejudiced against any racial or ethnic group', while in the case of 'people who want to overthrow the government by force' the equivalent figure stands at 18 per cent.

We thus should, perhaps, be cautious when it comes to public support for civil liberties. While there is widespread support for the principle, there are clearly limits to how far the public think those rights can and should be exercised. That might, of course, be regarded as a judicious viewpoint given that in any particular instance there are often competing principles, such as the rights of minorities, at stake. Still, perhaps progressives should be aware that there are limits to the extent to which people feel that individuals should be able to exercise a 'right' to challenge the law and the state that stands behind that law.

PRESERVING AND ENHANCING THE ENVIRONMENT

Voters are certainly not insensitive to the argument that action needs to be taken to preserve the environment. For example, as many as three in five (60 per cent) agree that, 'for the sake of the environment, everyone should reduce how much they use their cars'. Only 13 per cent actually disagree. Indeed, as many as 74 per cent agree that 'next time I buy a car, I would be willing to buy a car with lower CO_2 emissions'. Voters are not averse, either, to the idea that the government might provide incentives to help reduce the environmental impact of transport. Nearly two-thirds (65 per cent) believe that 'people who drive cars that are better for the environment should pay less to use the roads than people whose cars are more harmful to the environment', while, again, just 13 per cent disagree. Certainly, relatively few believe that people have the right to use their car come what may. Only just over a quarter (26 per cent) agree that 'people should be allowed to use their cars as much as they like, even if it causes damage to the environment'. Opinion is very similar in respect of air travel. Only around a fifth (21 per cent) feel that 'people should be able to travel by plane as much as they like, even if this harms the environment'.

However, support for the principle of environmentally responsible behaviour does not necessarily translate into a willingness to do something in practice, and especially if it might involve a financial penalty. Certainly, no less than 62 per cent disagree that 'for the sake of the environment, car users should pay higher taxes'. Equally, while 40 per cent agree they would be willing to reduce the amount they travel by car 'to help reduce the impact of climate change', 42 per cent disagree. Meanwhile, although at 41 per cent the proportion who agree that 'the price of a plane ticket should reflect the environmental damage that flying causes, even if this makes air travel much more expensive' is markedly bigger than the proportion who disagree (24 per cent), support for the proposition is still well below 50 per cent. At the same time, while 28 per cent agree they are willing to cut down on flying to help reduce climate change, 34 per cent disagree.

There is, then, a widespread public acknowledgement of the merits of reducing activities such as driving and flying that can be injurious to the environment. There is also apparent widespread support for the introduction of incentives to persuade us to change our environmentally damaging habits. But at the same time many people evidently like being able to get around by car and having the ability to fly further afield, and thus any attempt to penalise our ability to do so might meet rather greater resistance. Progressives probably need to focus on ways in which we might be nudged and cajoled towards the path of environmental responsibility rather than approaches that might be regarded by voters as 'punitive'.

DISTRIBUTING POLITICAL POWER

The final aspect of the progressive vision is 'a wish to see a more distributed structure of political power'. There are, of course, many ways in which political power could be redistributed, but we will take it that what is meant is that power should not be primarily vested in a single-party majority government located in Whitehall, and that instead should be shared more broadly, including not least with 'the people' themselves.

Indeed, the idea that voters themselves should have a greater say in government decisions is in itself a good place to start. After all, voters are none too sure that they have sufficient influence over what government does. In the most recent BSA survey, as many as 44 per cent agreed that 'people like me don't have any say over what government does', while just 28 per cent disagreed. Meanwhile, when asked to give a mark out of seven as a way of saying how important it is that 'people be given more opportunities to participate in public decision-making', no less than 62 per cent gave the proposition a score of six or seven. It would seem that there is a considerable appetite among voters for having a bigger say.

The most direct way, of course, in which voters can have a say in public policy decisions is through referendums. Holding these is certainly relatively popular. Asked in general whether 'referendums are a good way to decide important political decisions', as many as 53 per cent agree while just 11 per cent actually disagree. Referendums appear to be even more popular when voters are asked how particular key decisions should be made. In the 2013 BSA, for example, just 15 per cent reckoned that MPs should make the decision as to whether or not the UK should remain a member of the European Union, while around two-thirds (68 per cent) said the decision should be made by voters in a referendum. Much the same picture emerged – 66 per cent felt that voters should make the decision – when respondents were asked about who should decide how MPs are elected.

There also appears to be some willingness to accept that, in so far as decisions are made by politicians, those politicians need not necessarily be located in London. As measured at least by attitudes towards how Scotland should be governed, it appears that there is widespread support throughout Britain for the principle of devolution to the smaller nations of the UK. In the 2013 BSA, for example, just 17 per cent opposed the idea of having any kind of Scottish Parliament (albeit, equally, only one in five – 20 per cent – supported Scottish independence). However, it is less clear how much enthusiasm there is for devolution in England. Certainly, the BSA has persistently found that rather more than half think that England 'should be governed as it is now, with its laws made by the UK government'. Most recently in 2013, 55 per cent backed that view. In contrast, just 20 per cent supported the idea of an English Parliament (itself a proposition that does not necessarily imply devolution within England), and only 14 per cent a system of regional assemblies.

In truth, the views that people express about devolution for England depend heavily on how the question is posed. For example, when people in England were simply asked by ComRes in October 2014 whether they supported or opposed 'giving more powers on issues such as tax, education, policing to local areas', no less than 82 per cent said they supported the idea. Yet when Survation asked just a few months later, whether in England powers should be devolved from 'the UK government to regions and communities across England', thereby (according to the question) mimicking the position in Scotland and in Wales, just 44 per cent said they were in favour. As many as 28 per cent said 'Don't Know', suggesting that the issue is not a salient one for many English voters. That perhaps is one reason that the wording of questions can make such a substantial difference to attitudes towards this topic.

Meanwhile, the current government has added to the mix of possible ways in which devolution might be pursued within England by advocating and beginning to implement a network of 'city regions', units (such as Greater Manchester) that are in effect smaller than regions (such as the north-west). Yet these appear to be no more popular than regional assemblies. When, in September 2015, Opinium asked a question not dissimilar to that previously posed on the BSA, but also including city regions among the possible options, just 12 per cent backed city regions, while 15 per cent said they preferred regional assemblies and 28 per cent an English Parliament.

Along with the notion of city regions there has been yet another attempt to revive the idea of directly elected mayors, even though the electorate have often expressed little enthusiasm for the idea when given the chance to vote on the idea in local referendums. While the introduction of such mayors can be regarded as an attempt to strengthen the voice and autonomy of England's cities, it also implies a concentration of power within local government itself. This perhaps helps explain the public's ambivalence about the idea. Thus, on the one hand, the 2011 BSA found that 61 per cent agreed that 'having an elected mayor means that there is always someone who can speak up for the area', while just 16 per cent disagreed. On the other hand, rather more people (36 per cent) agreed that 'having an elected mayor gives too much power to one person' than disagreed (28 per cent).

Not that this means that the public are necessarily unhappy with an electoral system that tends to concentrate power in the hands of one party at Westminster. This too is a subject where the answers that people give to survey questions depend heavily on how the question is asked. For example, the 2010 BSA asked the same group of respondents two different questions about the electoral system used to elect MPs to the House of Commons. First, they were asked whether they agreed or disagreed 'that Britain should introduce proportional representation, so that the number of MPs in the House of Commons each party gets, matches more closely the number of votes each party gets'. While 49 per cent said that they agreed with this proposition, just 16 per cent disagreed. At the same time, however, they were also invited to state with which of two possible propositions about how MPs are elected they agreed. They were asked:

> Some people say we should change the voting system for general elections to the (UK) House of Commons to allow smaller political parties to get a fairer share of MPs. Others say we should keep the voting system for the House of Commons as it is, to produce effective government. Which view comes closer to your own?

At that point, slightly more people (49 per cent) said that we should keep the system as it is as felt it should be changed (41 per cent). Meanwhile, when twelve months later – in the wake of the referendum on the Alternative Vote at which people voted by two to one against the proposed change – the BSA asked the question again, just 27 per cent wanted to change the system while 66 per cent said we should keep the system as it is. The experience of the Alternative Vote referendum should certainly serve as a reminder to progressives that the barriers to electoral reform are not necessarily confined to existing vested interests in the House of Commons.

DOES THIS CONSTITUTE A PROGRESSIVE MAJORITY?

Our examination has revealed that there is no simple answer to the question, 'Is there a progressive majority in Britain?' Sometimes progressive ideas have appeared popular, sometimes not. Nevertheless, a common theme has emerged across the four key elements of progressivism examined in this chapter. In each case we found that there did appear to be majority support for what we might consider to be the 'sentiment' of progressivism. A majority feel that Britain is too unequal, that civil liberties should be respected, that changes do need to be made in order to protect the environment, and that ordinary citizens do not have enough say in government decisions. At the same time, however, this sentiment did not necessarily translate into support for specific measures. There is, for example, a reluctance to embrace redistribution, protest that breaks the law, or increasing the cost of environmentally damaging behaviours, while voters sometimes seem inclined to stick with the constitutional status quo.

Thus the challenge facing progressives is not simply to find a way of mobilising an existing progressive majority. It is also to develop policy ideas and stances that the public regard as acceptable ways of turning their progressive inclinations into practice. There would seem to be a need, for example, to identify ways of avoiding the generation of inequality in the first place, of balancing the protection of civil liberties with regard for the rights of minorities, of finding incentives to promote environmentally sustainable behaviour, and thought about the greater use of referendums and other forms of direct democracy than has been the case hitherto. If they are to realise their ambitions, progressives not only need to come together, but to do some hard thinking about policy when they do.

John Curtice is professor of politics at the University of Strathclyde and senior research fellow at NatCen Social Research. He has been co-editor of the annual British Social Attitudes reports series since 1994, and has written widely on social and political attitudes in the UK. He is currently president of the British Polling Council, and is a regular media commentator on British and Scottish politics.

FURTHER READING

Clarke, H., D. Sanders, M. Stewart and P. Whiteley, *Performance Politics and the British Voter*, Cambridge: Cambridge University Press, 2009.

Ormston, R. and J. Curtice (eds), *British Social Attitudes: the 32nd report*, London: NatCen Social Research, 2015. Available online: http://www.bsa.natcen.ac.uk/latest-report/british-social-attitudes-32/key-findings/introduction.aspx

Rowlingson, K., M. Orton and E. Taylor, 'Do we still care about inequality?', in Park, A., J. Curtice, E. Clery and C. Bryson (eds), *British Social Attitudes: the 27th report*, London: Sage, 2010.

Taylor, E. and P. Taylor-Gooby, 'Benefits and welfare: long-term trends or short-term benefits', in Ormston, R. and J. Curtice (eds), *British Social Attitudes: the 32nd report*, London: NatCen Social Research, 2015. Available online: http://www.bsa.natcen.ac.uk/latest-report/british-social-attitudes-32/welfare.aspx

LESSONS FROM THE ASHDOWN–BLAIR 'PROJECT'

Duncan Brack

On 9 April 1992, the Conservative Party won their fourth general election victory in a row. After an election campaign that had seen the two main parties more or less tied in the opinion polls, Labour had entertained real hopes of emerging as the largest party, and the Liberal Democrats of holding the balance of power. The result, a Tory lead of 7.5 per cent over Labour, and a Tory majority in the Commons of twenty-one over all other parties, came as a crushing blow to Labour; the party's leader, Neil Kinnock, resigned a week later. The Liberal Democrats, too, were disappointed, though at least they had succeeded in recovering from their post-merger nadir of 1988–90. (The polls' consistent over-estimation of Labour's support reflected the pollsters' failure to pick up the speed with which Britain's electorate was changing; their sampling was wrong. *Plus ça change.*)

Political discussion after the election focused on the seemingly never-ending Conservative hegemony. Commentators seriously considered whether Labour could ever win another election. Echoing Mark Abrams's and Richard Rose's *Must Labour Lose?* of 1960 (which had followed three Tory victories, from 1951 to 1959), the Fabian Society published a series of pamphlets under the heading 'Southern Discomfort', focusing on Labour's loss of support in southern England. And, yet, the combined Labour and Liberal Democrat vote in 1992 clearly exceeded the Conservative level of support, so there was also speculation about whether there might be some grounds for collaboration between the two opposition parties.

In fact, the potential for cooperation between the non-Tory parties, or a realignment of them, had been a common theme of leaders of the Liberal Party for the previous thirty years – including Jo Grimond's call for a realignment of the left in the 1960s, the formation of the Lib–Lab Pact in the 1970s, and the alliance between the Liberals and the new Social Democratic Party in the 1980s. With the sole exception of 1955, the combined Liberal and Labour vote had exceeded Conservative support in every election since 1945 (and has continued to do so in every election since 1992). It was only the division between the two progressive parties, it was argued, that had allowed the Tories to hold power for so long. The most radical version of this argument ascribed Conservative success throughout the twentieth century to the disintegration of the pre-First World War Liberal Party, which had divided progressive politicians between the rising Labour Party and the surviving Liberals and had allowed the Tories to win power for most of the century on a minority vote.

Paddy Ashdown, the first leader of the Liberal Democrats, had been interested in exploring the possibility of cooperation with Labour since his election in 1988. Just five days after becoming leader, he met representatives of the newly formed Labour-friendly Institute for Public Policy Research (IPPR) to talk about think-tank cooperation, and the following April he and his lieutenant Richard Holme were talking about some sort of Lib–Lab 'Programme for Britain'. The 1992 election seemed to make the case even stronger. The day after polling day, he held a strategy meeting at which it was decided that the Liberal Democrats should not attack Labour too strenuously; he recorded in his diary that 'we must make use of this opportunity to realign the left'.

Exactly a month after the election, on 9 May, Ashdown delivered what became known as the 'Chard speech', given to an audience of only forty or fifty in a small town in his constituency; he said later that he believed it was the most important speech of his leadership. Arguing that the Liberal Democrats needed to 'work with others to assemble the ideas around which a non-socialist alternative to the Conservatives can be constructed', he called for a national electoral reform commission and for Labour to be more open to constitutional reform and a market economy, more pluralist and less a creature of the trade unions.

The speech was deeply unpopular with Liberal Democrat MPs (one took to referring to it as a 'burnt offering'), partly because at the time Labour seemed finished and about to descend, in the wake of Kinnock's resignation, into another bout of infighting. The Liberal Democrat peers were more supportive, but only last-minute wrangling prevented a strategy debate at the autumn conference placing severe restrictions on Ashdown's freedom of manoeuvre. However, there was very little response from Labour. Although some of the party's leadership, including Robin Cook and Peter Mandelson, were open to approaches from the Liberal Democrats, the new leader elected in July, John Smith, was determined to maintain his independence and believed that Labour was still capable of winning on its own. Events over the next twelve months seemed to suggest that he might be right – in September 1992, 'Black Wednesday', which saw the pound forced out of the European Exchange Rate Mechanism, destroyed the Conservatives' reputation for economic competence, and the party then started to tear itself apart over British accession to the Maastricht Treaty of European Union in 1992–93.

The Conservatives became so unpopular that between mid-1994 and the start of the 1997 election campaign the Labour share of the vote in opinion polls never dropped below 50 per cent. But many Labour politicians, and commentators, could not bring themselves to believe that the Tories would not win again; they had been too scarred by the experience of 1992. In the phrase of Neal Lawson (adviser to Gordon Brown 1992–94), Labour felt like gatecrashers at a party – they might be having a great time, but eventually someone would turn up and kick them out. So the possibility of cooperation remained alive, and it gained new impetus with the sudden death of John Smith in May 1994, and his replacement as Labour leader by Tony Blair in July.

Blair, influenced partly by Peter Mandelson, was far more open to some form of cooperation with the Liberal Democrats than Smith had been. Indeed, Ashdown had discussed the topic with him as early as July 1993 at a dinner organised by Anthony Lester (special adviser to Roy Jenkins in the 1970s, founder member of the SDP and, from October 1993, a Liberal Democrat peer). Blair, following Jenkins (whom he regarded as a mentor), recognised the strength of the argument that the historic split in the British left had handed power to the Conservatives; as he put it later, 'The twentieth century had been a Tory century precisely because good and talented people who should have been together were instead in separate parties fighting each other.' Two months after his election as Labour leader, he and Ashdown began what was to become a five-year series of meetings and discussions about how to get rid of the Tories and how best to work together both before and after a potential election victory – what became known as 'the Project'.

The details of the process can be followed in Ashdown's diaries and other sources. What this essay focuses on is what in practical terms the two parties did, and what lessons can be learned from the Project for cooperation in today's very different political environment.

Assuming that the Tory vote was likely to recover before an election in 1996 or 1997, some kind of cooperation certainly seemed to make sense; and even if Labour did win, it seemed quite possible it would be with only a small majority, and might thus need additional Liberal Democrat support in the Commons. By 1993–94, the Liberal Democrats were also benefiting from the collapse in Tory support, in local elections and by-elections – in many areas, particularly south-west England, they seemed better placed than Labour to dislodge the Conservatives. In July 1995, they fought off a strong Labour challenge to win the Littleborough and Saddleworth by-election from the Conservatives, suggesting that they would not simply be swept aside by the rising tide of support for Labour.

But what kind of cooperation? One possibility was an electoral pact, where Labour and the Liberal Democrats would field common candidates. Blair suggested this in talks with Ashdown in November 1995, at least for seats in the south-west. But, as Ashdown retorted, this was 'totally impossible'. He added, 'And we would waste a lot of time dividing our parties if we tried to do it. It would also look like a grubby plan designed to gain power and votes for ourselves, instead of one based round principles and what was best for the country.' The Liberal Party had been through a process of seat allocation with the SDP, and it was a divisive, time-consuming and exhausting exercise even between two parties with very few policy differences.

What Ashdown preferred was to lay out a small number of key positions on which Labour and the Liberal Democrats agreed and make it clear that they would cooperate on them in the next government. This would enable the parties to retain their distinctiveness in other areas while at the same time promoting an atmosphere of cooperation that should encourage tactical voting among the electorate. Many of the discussions between Blair and Ashdown over the following twelve months explored these possibilities. This was assisted by the formal abandonment of 'equidistance' by the Liberal Democrat conference in 1995. Although many of the party's activists and MPs were highly sceptical of Ashdown's approach, and resisted any attempt to more publicly align their party with Labour, the reality was that Liberal Democrat policy positions were, with a few exceptions, much closer to Labour's than to the Tories', and the government was so unpopular by 1995 that it was ludicrous to pretend that the Liberal Democrats were indifferent, or 'equidistant', between them and the official opposition.

Discreet cooperation began to develop between the two parliamentary parties. Archy Kirkwood and Donald Dewar, the Liberal Democrat and Labour Chief Whips, began to talk more frequently, developing what Kirkwood called a 'doctrine of no surprises'. They tried to avoid major rows between their own parties and on occasion coordinated their MPs' attacks on the Tories, helping to reinforce the impression that the government was an increasingly beleaguered minority. This approach paid dividends when

Kirkwood and Dewar discovered that the Conservative whips were 'pairing' the same Tory MPs against both Liberal Democrat and Labour members, effectively reducing opposition numbers. Blair and Ashdown also sometimes coordinated their attacks on the government at Prime Minister's Questions.

Talks, generally over dinners, between small groups from both parties helped each side understand each other's positions, explore the possibilities for cooperation in Parliament (short of a coalition) should the Conservatives lose power, and paved the way for cooperation over policy in the form of a series of talks on constitutional reform led by Robin Cook for Labour and Robert Maclennan for the Liberal Democrats. Starting in March 1996, a year later the group reached agreement on a package of proposals including incorporation of the European Convention on Human Rights into UK law, freedom of information legislation, devolution to Scotland and Wales (and elections by proportional representation to their Parliaments), an elected authority for London, removal of the hereditary peers from the House of Lords, proportional representation for the European elections, and a referendum on voting reform for Westminster elections, comprising a choice between the existing first-past-the-post system and a proportional alternative, to be agreed by a commission on voting systems. Most of this had been Liberal Democrat policy for years (or was a watered-down version of it), but some was new for Labour. Blair saw it as part of his programme of modernising the Labour Party, and the position of the constitutional modernisers within Labour, such as Robin Cook, was thus strengthened.

The Cook–Maclennan process was public. What was discussed in secret, however, was something much more dramatic, what Ashdown called 'the big thing', an agreement to fight the election on a common platform on at least two or three major issues. Ashdown went so far as to draft successive versions of a 'Partnership for Britain's Future', covering constitutional reform along the Cook–Maclennan lines, cleaning up politics (after several examples of corruption and dishonest conduct among MPs), the reform of welfare systems and economic policy reform, including investing in education, awarding independence to the Bank of England, and adherence to the criteria for entry into the single European currency. From July 1996, Blair and Ashdown started to talk about Liberal Democrat participation in a Labour government; Peter Mandelson later claimed that this would have involved including two Liberal Democrat MPs, Alan Beith and Menzies Campbell, in Blair's first Cabinet.

In the end, the 'big thing' was too big a step. What worried Ashdown and his colleagues was Blair's refusal to commit firmly to the introduction of proportional representation for Westminster elections – the absolute bottom line for the Liberal Democrats, who could not be expected to tie themselves to a much bigger partner without being able to survive its eventual fall. Ashdown's diaries record in painstaking detail a long series of meetings in which Blair was first educated about what PR meant and the different systems through which it could be introduced, and then prevaricated, hinting at his own possible conversion to it (or maybe to something weaker, such as the Alternative Vote), but stressing the opposition he would face in the Parliamentary Labour Party. In the end, policy cooperation extended only as far as the Cook–Maclennan agreement.

The approach of the general election raised the question of how far the parties should cooperate – and be seen to be cooperating – during the campaign. Ashdown argued for overt collaboration, campaigning together to get rid of the Tories, even to the extent of appearing at joint rallies with Tony Blair. But polling in the party's target seats conducted by Chris Rennard, the Liberal Democrats' experienced director of campaigns and elections, showed that while those who had voted Conservative in 1992 were open to the proposition that the Liberal Democrats could participate in government with Labour should the Conservatives lose, they strongly disliked the idea that the Liberal Democrats should actively campaign for a Labour–Lib Dem coalition, and any hint of this would drive them back to the Conservatives. Furthermore, the prospect of a coalition did not help with those who had voted Labour in 1992; they preferred the Liberal Democrats to the Tories anyway, and the evidence suggested that not many of them really understood tactical voting, believing that they had to vote Labour to bring down the Tories, even when their candidate was in a poor third place in their own seat. These findings were unwelcome news to Ashdown, but the polling evidence was so clear that he had to accept it; and it recalled what had happened in the last week of the 1992 campaign, when it was felt that speculation about the possibility of a hung parliament had driven voters back to the Tories. Holme also shared the figures with Mandelson.

So overt cooperation would be counterproductive. But what about covert cooperation? In January 1997, Neal Lawson and Neil Sherlock (a member of Ashdown's speech-writing team) – both supporters of cooperation – organised a dinner in the Goring Hotel in Victoria to bring together key individuals from the election campaigns on both sides, some of whom had not before been involved in the Project. Chris Rennard raised the idea of the *Mirror* (the main Labour-supporting tabloid) endorsing Liberal Democrat candidates where Labour had no chance. Mandelson agreed this could be done, and smoothed the way with the *Mirror*'s staff. Originally supposed to cover just ten seats, on the eve of poll the paper published a list of twenty-two seats where, if Labour voters backed the Liberal Democrats, the Conservatives would be defeated. In the event, the Liberal Democrats won twenty of them.

Mandelson also requested a list of Liberal Democrat target seats so that Labour knew where to restrict its campaigning efforts. Rennard supplied a list of twenty-eight seats to Labour deputy leader John Prescott's office, disguised (in case of leaks) as an academic paper identifying constituencies where the Liberal Democrats could win and Labour could not. It is not clear to what extent either party really held back in their campaigning – and the extent to which campaign managers can direct their activists to go to seats other than the ones they live in is probably less than the managers like to think – but it helped that in many of the targets it was obvious that the Liberal Democrats were better placed to win than Labour. The number of seats where both opposition parties were in contention with each other was very small, though there was certainly no let-up on either side in those constituencies; in the end, Labour gained two seats from the Liberal Democrats.

The parties also collaborated, in a fairly low-key way, during the 1997 election. Blair and Ashdown stayed in touch both before and during the campaign, discussed using a common language to attack the Tories, generally avoided criticising each other's parties, and focused on much the same issues in campaigning – health, education and crime (they would probably have done this anyway; these were the leading issues). The fact that the two parties' policies were different – Labour had promised to stick to Tory spending plans; the Liberal Democrats to raise income tax to invest in education – also helped, marking out a distinctive case for the Liberal

Democrats and making it clear that cooperation did not mean a Labour takeover. The most obvious example of cooperation came in the decision to withdraw each party's candidate in Tatton, to give a clear run to the former BBC journalist Martin Bell, standing as an independent 'anti-sleaze' candidate against Neil Hamilton, a Tory MP (now UKIP's leader in the Welsh Assembly) deeply embroiled in the cash-for-questions scandal; Bell, assisted by activists from both parties, won convincingly.

The 1997 general election saw the Conservatives go down to their worst result in a century and a half, losing a quarter of their vote and half their seats. Their losses were exaggerated by tactical voting; as the psephologists John Curtice and Michael Steed concluded, 'The scale and impact of tactical voting in the 1997 election was unprecedented.' They estimated that Labour gained between fifteen and twenty-one seats, and the Liberal Democrats between ten and fourteen, as a result of tactical switching to defeat Tory MPs. Supporting one of the findings of Chris Rennard's target seat polling (see above), Liberal Democrat voters proved more willing to switch to Labour than Labour voters to the Liberal Democrats – the surge in support for Labour was so great that often the best that Liberal Democrat candidates could hope for was to keep the Labour vote at its 1992 level (which was often enough to win, given the collapse in the Conservative vote). Tactical voting was more widespread in areas where the Liberal Democrats had done well in local government over the preceding five years, which had established the party as a credible contender in the eyes of the local electorate. Effective targeting of resources throughout the Parliament also clearly helped.

In a close election, tactical voting on this scale would have made a major difference to the outcome. But the 1997 result was not close:

Labour won 419 seats, for an overall majority over all other parties of 179. Nevertheless, as late as election day, Blair and Ashdown were still talking about whether they could entertain any form of cooperation. Blair declared that he was 'absolutely determined to mend the schism that occurred in the progressive forces in British politics at the start of this century'. He hinted at a coalition, though Ashdown pointed out that it would be unacceptable for Liberal Democrat ministers simply to implement a Labour programme. By the next day, however, Blair had changed his tone, talking merely of a 'framework for cooperation'. Robin Cook later confirmed that Gordon Brown and John Prescott had both made clear to Blair overnight their virulent opposition to any role for Ashdown or his colleagues in government. In any case, the size of Labour's majority destroyed any argument for it.

The rest of the story of the Project can be followed elsewhere. In place of a coalition, a Joint Consultative Committee was created between the two parties to discuss issues where there was already agreement in principle, such as devolution or first-stage reform of the House of Lords; it was later extended to European issues. It is difficult to judge what, if anything, the Committee achieved, and it was largely abandoned by Charles Kennedy in the run-up to the 2001 election. The key stumbling block to further cooperation was Blair's continued refusal to commit to proportional representation. In December 1997, the government finally announced the establishment of an independent commission on voting reform, to be chaired by Roy Jenkins – but when his report was published in October 1998, advocating an additional member system of PR, Blair's response was entirely neutral, with no commitment to a referendum. Later that day, Jack Straw, the Home Secretary, rubbished it publicly, and did so again in a Commons debate the following week. Effectively this was the end of the Project, and Ashdown decided that it would also mark the end of his period as Liberal Democrat leader; he announced his resignation three months later.

No comprehensive and objective assessment of the Project has yet been carried out. However, it seems clear that it made a difference in at least two respects. The Cook–Maclennan agreement had a direct impact in the shape of the constitutional reforms Blair implemented after 1997. Probably Labour would have devolved power to Scotland without any prompting from the Liberal Democrats, but Labour's attachment to issues such as Welsh devolution, proportional representation for the European elections or freedom of information was much weaker, and these policies may not have been implemented in the absence of the agreement – or their introduction may have been delayed and perhaps eventually dropped. Second, the atmosphere of cooperation that Ashdown and Blair built between them in the run-up to the 1997 election, and specific instances such as the *Mirror* list of winnable seats, made a difference to the election result, encouraging supporters of each party to switch to each other to defeat the Conservatives and thereby exaggerating their losses.

What lessons can we draw for the future from the experience of the Project? There are (at least) six:

First, don't talk about coalition, even if that's what you have in mind. The target seat polling from 1997 showed that those who had voted Tory in 1992 would be frightened back to their original party if they thought Labour and the Liberal Democrats were ganging up in advance of the election. This is strongly reinforced by the experience of the 2015 election, when the prospect of a Labour government in coalition with, or supported by, the SNP proved deeply unpopular (though not quite as unpopular as the Liberal

Democrats' apparent willingness to join a coalition with almost anyone).

Second, it is nevertheless worth exploring the potential for pre-election cooperation over specific areas of policy. The most obvious is constitutional reform, along the lines of the Cook–Maclennan agreement or, more ambitiously, the Scottish Constitutional Convention of 1989–95. The gross distortions of the 2015 election result, where it took, on average, 34,000 votes to elect a Conservative MP, 302,000 to elect a Liberal Democrat and 3.9 million to elect a UKIP MP, makes a strong case for electoral reform in particular. Voters do not tend to get excited about these kind of issues, however, so the state of public services, particularly the NHS, could be another possible topic – the evidence suggests that voters like the idea of politicians setting aside party differences to work together (though the fact that that's what coalitions do seems to have eluded them).

Third, do everything you can to maximise tactical voting, which is a rational response to the distortions of the first-past-the-post electoral system. This will probably be more effective if it is promoted from outside the parties, as in the *Mirror* piece in 1997. In 2020, there should be extensive potential for arranging vote swapping via social media. Parties' campaigning resources – which, with the much greater use of telephone canvassing, are now more centralised than in 1997 – can also be deployed to avoid attacking each other, at least up to a point.

Fourth, either keep it all as quiet as you can – or be as open as you can. Some party activists are open to cooperation – and it is of course widespread in local government – but many are not. Journalists often like to look down on party members as 'tribal', but another way to put this is that they are loyal, to their beliefs and their colleagues. Most party activists will spend their entire political careers delivering leaflets, raising money and knocking on doors without ever being elected to anything, and without realising any personal financial benefit. Belief in the cause is what keeps them going, and naturally they will not be well disposed to giving up their efforts to see another party's candidate elected. So, either don't tell them, or as be as open as you can, explaining what's going on and what the benefits are. The Ashdown–Blair Project is an example of the former approach; in retrospect it is remarkable how little of what was going on leaked to the outside world. The overwhelming vote at the Liberal Democrat special conference in May 2010 to enter coalition with the Conservatives is an example of the latter, showing that reasoned argument can convince activists to work with other parties in the national interest.

Fifth, none of this will work unless the personal relationships between the key individuals involved are very good – they have to trust each other to work together and stick to their side of the deal. The Project would never have happened without the rapport that Ashdown and Blair built up over several years of dinners and discussions.

Finally, be clear what you want the outcome to be: a coalition, a confidence and supply arrangement, an agreement to reform the voting system and then call another election, or something else. And, despite all the difficulties, never forget the reason: to avoid the twenty-first century seeing another succession of Tory victories on ever-diminishing shares of the vote.

Duncan Brack was the Liberal Democrats' first policy director (1988–94), chair of the party's Conference Committee 2003–10, and special adviser to Chris Huhne at the Department of Energy and Climate Change 2010–12. He is currently vice-chair of the party's Policy Committee. Professionally he is an independent environmental policy analyst and adviser.

FURTHER READING

Ashdown, Paddy, *The Ashdown Diaries: Volume One, 1988–1997*, London: Penguin, 2000, and *Volume Two, 1997–1999*, London: Penguin, 2001.

Ashdown, Paddy, 'A broader movement dedicated to winning the battle of ideas', 9 May 1992 [the Chard speech], in Duncan Brack and Tony Little (eds), *Great Liberal Speeches*, London: Politico's, 2001.

Interview with Paddy Ashdown, *Journal of Liberal History*, 30, spring 2001.

Blair, Tony, *A Journey*, London: Hutchinson, 2010.

Lawson, Neal and Neil Sherlock (eds), *The Progressive Century: The Future of the Centre-Left in Britain*, London: Palgrave Macmillan, 2001.

Leaman, Alan, 'Notes on a Political Relationship: Blair and Ashdown', *Journal of Liberal History*, 67, summer 2010.

Meeting report, 'The Progressive Coalition that never was: lessons from the Ashdown–Blair 'project', *Journal of Liberal History*, 83, summer 2014.

I am grateful to Archy Kirkwood, Neal Lawson, Roger Liddle, Chris Rennard and Neil Sherlock for agreeing to be interviewed for this essay. Any errors or omissions are of course my own. – DB

EXAMPLES OF PROGRESSIVES WORKING TOGETHER

Chris Bowers, Caroline Lucas & Lisa Nandy

The concept of parties working together is hardly revolutionary. In fact, it happens all the time on the European mainland. It also happens in Britain at council level, often forced by inconclusive election results that leave councils with 'no overall control'. So what are the lessons that can be learned and the pitfalls to be avoided from experience of the progressives working together at council level?

We have selected three councils that have had formal coalitions made up of Labour and the Liberal Democrats: one from the present, one from the recent past, and one from twenty years ago. We asked the leaders of the Labour and Lib Dem groups on all three councils (in one case an alternative senior councillor) to give their views of how their arrangement worked or didn't work, what problems they encountered, and what lessons they might draw for cooperation at national level. None of them saw their opposite number's contribution until it was in print.

Here are the views of the six councillors in their own words, with our interpretation after each one.

CUMBRIA COUNTY COUNCIL

The shire county of Cumbria elects its eighty-four councillors every four years. After the 2013 elections, it remained – as it had been since 2001 – with no overall control; Labour had thirty-five seats, the Conservatives had twenty-six, Liberal Democrats sixteen, and seven others. An administration was formed with Labour and the Liberal Democrats sharing all the executive positions, an arrangement that is due to last until May 2017. The Labour leader is Stewart Young; the Lib Dem leader is Patricia Bell.

Stewart Young (Labour)

> We clearly had some negotiating to do at the start, but we expected that. After all, Cumbria has had one-party control only twice since it came into existence as a council in 1974. Knowing the Lib Dem members of the council, and knowing that we had more in common with enough of them than the Tories, meant that establishing an administration was fairly easy.
>
> Geographically it's worked because it is a natural fit. We had very few head-to-head battles for seats between Labour and the Lib Dems – Labour support is strongest in the urban fringes along the coast, while the Lib Dems are strong in

South Lakeland, so we complemented each other well both geographically and politically.

The Lib Dems had been in coalition with the Conservatives for much of the previous eight years, and after the 2013 elections there were three-way discussions in which we talked to the Lib Dems, the Lib Dems talked to the Conservatives, and we even talked to the Conservatives. The big breakthrough came when the Lib Dem group elected Jo Stephenson as leader in place of Ian Stewart – Ian had been much more comfortable with the Conservatives, whereas Jo was more of a social liberal with a lot in common with us, so that freed the way for us to form a joint administration. [Jo Stephenson subsequently died suddenly, and was replaced as Lib Dem leader by Patricia Bell.]

The arrangement has worked surprisingly well. We've certainly had no serious fallouts, at least none I can recall. We've faced the same challenges, and we've had to balance the budget by making huge cuts, many of them controversial.

As deputy leader, Patricia [Bell] has the finance portfolio, and it's been very difficult at times. For example, we proposed closing some of the retained fire stations, but it's easy to launch a campaign to save fire stations because firefighters are rightly highly respected, and when the campaign gets the support of the district councils and the MPs it creates a lot of pressure. The Lib Dem MP Tim Farron was particularly vocal, which made it difficult for the Lib Dem group.

Of course there have been divisions, but there are divisions within groups. In fact, there are as many divisions within groups as between groups – ultimately we're all coalitions.

When I was first elected to the council, the main decisions

were made by a network of committees made up of councillors in proportion to how the parties had done at the last elections. I think that's a better system, because it reflected the reality of Cumbria, and no doubt other places too. If we're going to have the Cabinet system that has been forced upon us, my preferred system would be for the council to elect the leader, and for the leader to appoint Cabinet members proportionate to the make-up of the council. I'm not sure whether having a Cabinet – of a council or a national government – made up of people all from the same party is necessarily the best option.

The problem is that the national political parties don't like us working together locally, even though local people want us to. National politics has an impact on local politics, and our coalition could yet break up before May 2017 if either party feels it can gain more by going it alone, even though the arrangement is working well.

Our model in Cumbria could work nationally, but the parties would have to try to identify what they have in common rather than what their differences are. In this respect it's easier locally than nationally. But the public is hugely switched off by confrontational party-based politics, which is reflected in poor turnout at elections and general disillusionment. The majority want politicians to work together to solve problems, and if we could respond to that in our political system, we'd create a healthier democracy.

Patricia Bell (Liberal Democrat)

I feel the arrangement has worked brilliantly, and has done since the moment the 2013 elections delivered a result that suggested the only viable arrangement for the council would be a Labour–Lib Dem coalition. That doesn't mean there have been no problems, but it felt like a very natural thing to do.

In fairness, I fall on the more social liberal wing of the party, closer to Labour than the Conservatives, and there were others who felt it was not so natural. We did have one councillor who left the party in protest at our arrangement with Labour and went independent, but his local Lib Dem party has handled the matter with great sensitivity, so we have kept on good terms and there's a possibility he may come back. I feel it shows how broad a church the Liberal Democrats are.

Our current partnership with Labour feels very different from the joint administration between the Conservatives and the Liberal Democrats that was in progress when I was first elected, and which ran until August 2008 when the partnership broke down. My memory is of a falling out with the Conservative leader and of being treated as very much the subsidiary partner.

One of the big things we found in 2013 was that the Cumbria Conservatives were not interested in a partnership based on setting out what we could achieve, whereas Labour was. A deal with the Tories might just have worked numerically – between us we'd have had exactly half the council seats – but Labour was much more constructive.

We worked out a partnership agreement, which sets out what we want to achieve over the four-year term of the council. It wasn't particularly difficult to do, perhaps because what Labour wanted and what we wanted were fairly similar – we probably just used different words and different emphases.

And we have kept lines of communication open. We now have a number of joint briefings involving councillors of both parties, which gives us a sense of coherence – in fact there are times when you wouldn't know who was Labour and who was Lib Dem if you saw us discussing issues. We also have a 'quad' of the chair and leader and deputy leader of both parties who meet annually to review how the partnership agreement is going.

A significant feature has been the generosity of spirit inherent in the arrangement. Based on our number of councillors, Labour could quite reasonably have argued that we should only have three of the executive portfolios, but they offered us four. There has also been a willingness on both sides to recognise that we run our parties differently – by comparison with Labour, we are much more consultative within the Lib Dems. But the important thing to recognise is that neither method is right or wrong, it's just how it happens, and we work with it. The fact that Stewart Young [the Labour leader] isn't a headline-chaser makes sharing the credit among the two parties easier.

It probably also helps our partnership that we are not really fighting each other geographically. The areas where we are strong are not areas where Labour has much hope of winning seats, while its core areas aren't great hunting grounds for us. That might change, but for now our spread of seats means many parts of the country are represented in the Cabinet.

And there's almost a sense that we are into an easier phase now there is no national coalition. When we were in government with the Tories, Labour was quite measured in its attacks, but since the Tories have been in government on their own, Labour has felt freer to say what it really thinks about what Cameron and Co. are doing, and in fact we have been able to do this together.

The way we have worked together in Cumbria suggests the same could work at national level, but I believe two things are crucial. Firstly, the relationships are very important, not just at leader level but at all levels. We need to understand and recognise our differences, but also to value what we're striving to achieve. Secondly, there needs to be a partnership agreement that both sides are happy with, that is constantly monitored, and which is based on achieving specific goals within the timeframe of the administration.

The strongest message from the Cumbrian experience is the importance of good personal relationships and the accompanying generosity of spirit – on both sides, but in particular from the larger party. Based on these two accounts, it appears the desire to genuinely achieve something over the four years of the council has taken precedence over the aversion among some councillors to working with another party. This may be partly to do with the numbers of councillors from different wings of each party – if the Lib Dem group were made up of more people who were closer to the Conservatives than to Labour, the coalition might not have been a success; equally if the Labour group had comprised more traditional left-wing councillors, there may have been more tension. That's why changing minds is as important as finding common ground. In addition, political realities can never be overlooked: some councillors, for example, might be personally happy to work with another party, yet fear punishment at the ballot box if they do.

EAST SUSSEX COUNTY COUNCIL

The shire county of East Sussex elects all its councillors every four years. After the 1993 elections, the Conservatives, who had controlled the council for many years, lost their majority, and the Liberal Democrats and Labour teamed up to form an administration sharing all the executive positions. The arrangement lasted until the 1997 elections when another council under no overall control was elected. The Conservatives formed a minority administration for one year, but in 1998 a second Lib-Lab administration was formed which lasted until the 2001 elections. The following contributions relate to both the 1993–97 and 1998–2001 arrangements. The Lib Dem leader – and leader of the council – in both administrations was David Rogers. The Labour leader in 1993–97 was Ken Bodfish and in 1998–2001 it was Keith Bridger. Keith Bridger has since left the Labour Party and Ken Bodfish is now in a role that requires him to be non-party-political – therefore the Labour contribution here is written by Godfrey Daniel, who was chair of planning in the 1998–2001 administration.

David Rogers (Liberal Democrat)

It was fourteen long years into the 1979–97 Conservative government, most of it with Margaret Thatcher as Prime Minister, but by then John Major. In local elections, opposition parties were making gains every year. East Sussex County Council had always been run by the Tories, until that first Thursday in May 1993. As the results came in, it was clear that change was in the air, and the final numbers showed that the Liberal Democrats had won thirty seats, the Conservatives twenty-two, and Labour eighteen. Of all the English counties, only Buckinghamshire remained with a Conservative majority.

From discussions prior to the elections, I knew that my own colleagues would be keen to form a non-Tory administration, and this was confirmed by an early group meeting. We drew up a paper setting out our thoughts on how this might be achieved, with a view to approaching the Labour group for their take on it, and whether or not they would wish to become part of a shared administration. I then spoke to the Labour group leader, Ken Bodfish from Brighton.

I was aware that Liberal Democrat colleagues in other local authority areas had advocated similar power-sharing arrangements at various times over the preceding decade – and that on this occasion, results in the English counties meant that many others would be seeking to do so now. But I knew the Labour Party nationally was not so keen, and therefore Ken would have to tread carefully to make it viable. Locally, however, the background was more positive, in that across East Sussex there were very few county divisions where the real contest had been between Liberal Democrat and Labour. The Labour group came largely from Brighton, with a few from Hastings (where all three parties had councillors). The Liberal Democrats had been elected mainly from Eastbourne, Lewes, Rother and Wealden – the four districts in the centre of the county consisting of small- to medium-sized towns and villages.

In less than two weeks, the agreement was refined and the potentially thorny questions of which individuals would take up which positions were all resolved. I became elected chair of the Policy and Resources Committee, and Ken became vice-chair; in effect we were leader and deputy leader of the council, although it would be some years before the leader and Cabinet system was introduced widely in local government. Where a committee had a chair from one party, the vice-chair came from the other, and we instituted joint briefings from the relevant chief officers to determine agendas.

Many county services are statutory, with limited room for local decision-making. But where local issues were concerned (and for the geographical reasons suggested above), the Labour group were able to support our concerns, and vice-versa. An example of where we shared the objective of promoting environmental policies was in the economic development brief of Norman Baker (then a councillor, not yet MP for Lewes), who advocated working with businesses on energy and waste issues. Looking beyond East Sussex itself, Ken Bodfish was a member of the EU's Committee of the Regions, so we agreed to set up a Europe Office, including staff based in Brussels, and signed an accord with our immediate French partners. Ken's interests often took him abroad, sometimes to the bemusement of his own colleagues when matters he and I had agreed had not been adequately communicated!

In hindsight, one issue dominated much of that four-year term, to the detriment of more significant policy development, and that was the government's decision to impose reorganisation on local government. Brighton (and eventually Hove too) wanted unitary status, and many other variations and combinations had their supporters and opponents in all county groups, and among political colleagues across the districts. The energy of both elected members and officers was sapped by this process, which eventually resulted in the creation of Brighton and Hove unitary council in April 1997; East Sussex County Council continued, with one-third fewer citizens but only about 5 per cent less land area, as did the remaining five district councils. (For a few weeks in April, with councillors for divisions in Brighton and Hove effectively barred from acting, the Liberal Democrats technically had an overall majority, though it was of little effect.)

The 1997 county elections were held on the same day that Labour won a large parliamentary majority and Tony Blair became Prime Minister. The combination meant that, in those East Sussex constituencies which remained very Tory even on that day, the higher turnout meant that we lost council seats: the result was Conservatives twenty-one, Liberal Democrats sixteen and Labour seven. Terry Randall from Hastings led the Labour group, and made it clear he did not wish to work with us, so a minority Conservative administration was formed. A year later, under a new Labour group leader, Keith Bridger, there was a change of heart and once again we embarked on a shared administration – for the remaining three years of that council.

Godfrey Daniel (Labour)

The Labour county councillors who were elected in 1997 were a very different bunch to the ones we'd had in 1993–97. In 1997, Brighton and Hove went unitary, so we lost Brighton's and Hove's councillors from East Sussex County Council, and the Labour county councillors were elected from Hastings borough with one from Bexhill, so all from one end of the county. Apart from Jeremy Birch, we were all new and had no experience of working with the Liberals, at least not at county level – they had taken over Hastings Borough Council from us shortly before, so there was a lot of tension between us.

The first year of the 1997–2001 council saw a Tory minority administration, but they kept getting defeated on important votes, so it was a pragmatic decision for us to form an administration with the Lib Dems. In those days, the council was still run by the committee system, not the Cabinet system, so Labour were given the chairs of three committees (education, planning and legal and community services) while the Liberals chaired the other committees. It never really worked because the committee chairs apparently didn't talk with each other, at least not formally – there may have been some informal chats. If it was going to work as a cooperative venture, some sort of real communication between the committee chairs needed to happen.

I think there was a lack of personal chemistry among the leading people – there was at least one of the Liberals whom I liked and respected, but David Rogers as leader never engendered any warmth as far as I was concerned.

It worked after a fashion. We kept it going until the 2001 elections, and it did give Labour some say in aspects of East Sussex. But there was a lot of antagonism between the parties. Speaking personally, I distrust the Liberals more than the Tories, and I think that also goes for some of my colleagues. The Liberals seemed to change their positions whenever a petition suggested they were on the wrong side of public opinion, they ran slogans like 'Labour can't win here' to try to get our voters to vote for their candidates, and I felt many Liberals were like Conservatives. I feel we and the Liberal Democrats are very different parties.

If there were a hung parliament after the 2020 election, I can't see more than a minority government. Politics throws up some strange bedfellows; sometimes you have to work with people you never expected to, so I'd never say 'never'. But I think it's in our interest to wipe out the Lib Dems. I detest the Tories but at least what they stand for is quite straightforward, while I feel the Liberals are a moving feast and lack principles.

Well, we never said it would be easy! The visceral dislike of the Liberal Democrats by the Labour councillor demonstrates how deeply tribal loyalties are felt. One might overlook his use of the term 'Liberals' for a party that has been the 'Liberal Democrats' since 1987 – after all, Peter Mandelson had to upbraid Gordon Brown for referring to 'the Liberals' in 2010 when Brown was courting Lib Dem support for a possible coalition. But Godfrey Daniel is clearly more at home with the old certainties of a Labour–Tory battleground than working with a party that contains some people he likes but others he feels are closet Conservatives. Despite this, cooperation between Labour and Liberal Democrats clearly worked well for geographical reasons – like in Cumbria – because by and large the two parties were not fighting each other but the Conservatives in most of their divisions. This suggests that cooperation between the progressives is likely to work best where one party is clearly the main challenger to the Conservatives, and less well in areas where there is no clear-cut anti-Tory challenger.

CALDERDALE COUNCIL

The metropolitan borough council of Calderdale in West Yorkshire elects its councillors in thirds. After the 2010 elections, it was left with no overall control for the ninth year running. An administration was formed with Labour and the Liberal Democrats sharing all the executive positions, an arrangement that lasted until 2013. The Labour leader was Tim Swift; the Lib Dem leader was Janet Battye.

Tim Swift (Labour)

From 2000 to 2010, the Conservatives were the largest party in Calderdale, usually close to but not quite achieving an overall majority. Both Labour and Liberal Democrats were fed up with their arrogant and out-of-touch leadership – but most of all with the sense of drift and lack of ambition for the community.

That's why, after the 2010 local elections, despite what was happening nationally, we agreed to form a coalition to replace the Conservatives, with the Liberal Democrats leading as largest party from 2010 to 2012 and Labour taking over the leadership of the coalition in 2012. In May 2013, the Labour group took the decision not to continue with the arrangement and formed a minority administration.

There were some great strengths in the original agreement, and both parties should be proud of what they achieved. We made major changes to how the council was run, opening up the Cabinet to public questions and scrutiny, and despite having to cope with huge cuts in local spending, we were able to protect front-line services substantially while achieving real savings in back office costs and efficiency.

Most importantly, at a time when many councils were reeling from cuts, we gave the council a sense of ambition and direction which has continued today. We were also able to take forward several major investment projects that had largely stalled under the previous administration, and started to secure significant funds and influence through West Yorkshire collaboration.

Working together in a Cabinet system under difficult circumstances is inevitably not just about politics, but also requires workable personal relationships. These got more difficult as time went on. It wouldn't be appropriate to talk about the reasons, suffice to say there are some things I would organise differently if a similar arrangement came up in future.

The change of leadership in 2012, as Labour became the largest group and the Liberal Democrats lost seats, inevitably caused increasing tension. It was difficult – and I do not intend this as a criticism, but a statement of reality – for the Liberal Democrat leader to adapt from being leader of the council to deputy.

But I also believe that both groups were changing politically. There was a growing faction in the Labour group who were opposed to working with the Liberal Democrats locally while they were part of the coalition nationally, and this became a tougher issue as the cuts continued and policies such as the bedroom tax were rolled out. This was a touchstone issue for many Labour councillors in a way that the Liberal Democrats never understood.

Local politics also played a part. A hard-fought by-election contest in a Lib Dem ward just after the May 2012 elections led to a lot of bad blood, particularly as Labour believed that the Lib Dems used confidential information from discussions between the two parties in their campaign, as well as some extremely unpleasant attacks on the Labour candidate. The new Liberal Democrat councillor, who quickly became a significant figure in their group, was inevitably seen as basically anti-Labour and his influence was viewed with considerable doubt by Labour colleagues.

Each year, we discussed and agreed a set of priorities and principles, and this was an important part in shaping our work for the year. This wasn't a detailed manifesto, but underpinned the way we approached issues as they arose.

We trusted lead members from separate parties to act responsibly in line with these, and to bring issues back to Cabinet for collective decisions. But we never completely clarified potentially conflicting loyalties from Cabinet member to council leader (regardless of party) versus Cabinet member to group leader. In any future arrangement, I would build in regular three-way discussions between the two group leaders and individual Cabinet members.

Is there is an automatic 'progressive alliance' between Labour and the Liberal Democrats? I don't feel able to answer that. While there are strong areas of common ground, there is a clear split between those who see 'progressive' politics largely in economic terms and those who see it through a social and libertarian lens. Both parties nationally and locally move their positions on this spectrum.

I believe, however, that the biggest problem in Calderdale was the role of the Liberal Democrats in the coalition government. Had there been a majority Conservative government throughout, then I suspect that the arrangement would have continued for longer.

Janet Battye (Liberal Democrat)

There is a long record of no overall political control on Calderdale Council, so we had been working with Labour before 2010 during a lengthy period of minority Conservative control. When we did well in the 2010 elections, we went into shared control with Labour with ourselves as the bigger group, but the balance changed and we lost a lot of seats in the two subsequent elections. The arrangement was ended in 2013 by Labour.

It wasn't easy working with Labour (or the Conservatives, as we subsequently did). Even though we had a written agreement with them, which was honoured, we always felt that what they were really wanting was to gain more power and take control for themselves, so it was easy to see their cooperation with us as part of a long-term aim to kill us off.

While cooperation and collaboration have to be important principles, it's hard work. It's very difficult to trust a different party, and I often felt there were different agendas at work. We had built our strength locally on the basis of hard-working councillors who knew their patch and had personal votes as much as they had people voting for the party name, whereas Labour were campaigning very much under the Labour name. That caused tensions because we had the impression that we cared more for the locality than they did, and when we teamed up with the Conservatives to oust Labour in 2014, it was because we felt Labour hadn't listened to local people over a couple of big issues.

My reservation about us developing a close relationship with Labour at a national level is that I think they'd do the

> same to us as the Conservatives have just done. My experience in Calderdale and with the national coalition has caused me to want to limit any cooperation to specific issues which are important to us and on which agreement can be reached. I could see national cooperation working if, for example, it was for the sole purpose of getting a proportional voting system, but formal cooperation on an ongoing basis worries me.

The theme running through both accounts of the Calderdale coalition – of mistrust creating tension and requiring a lot of hard work to overcome – holds important lessons for cooperation among progressives. In particular, there is clearly a need for an explicit framework to be set out, so that both/all parties in a cooperation arrangement know exactly where the lines of responsibility lie, disagreements are dealt with appropriately so they don't become resentments, and the potential gains and achievements are set out so all those involved in the arrangement understand the tangible benefits of cooperating with another party.

A point missing from all three case studies is how the coalition worked for local residents. We have focused on the difficulties between the parties, because that is the subject matter of this book, but there is anecdotal evidence to suggest that the public might quite like joint administrations (in as much as they are aware of council politics; sadly, most people have no idea which party runs their local council). There is a parallel in the non-governmental organisation or campaigning sector. Many a campaign has been fought by a temporary coalition of NGOs, which takes a considerable toll on the individual NGOs but which strikes a chord with those it seeks to help by uniting various campaign groups behind one single aim. Similarly, where cooperation at council level leads to a more effective administration, we believe the public are likely to welcome it, and that the majority of politicians would be prepared to put joint working ahead of the tactical interests of their own party.

LESSONS FROM ABROAD: THERE IS ALWAYS AN ALTERNATIVE

Uffe Elbæk

Let us put it bluntly: the political establishment is failing to such a degree that democracy itself is under threat. This is true for the United Kingdom, but you are not alone. We have a similar situation in Denmark, and movements such as Podemos in Spain, Syriza in Greece and others are born as a reaction to the same syndrome. But, out of the depths of political despair, we have created a movement in Denmark that has caught the imagination of the people, and there's no reason it can't be replicated across the developed world.

The background to our story will be depressingly familiar. Inequality is on the rise throughout Europe, reaching heights we thought were reserved for the USA. It is rising even in a country as proud of its welfare system as Denmark. From 2001 to 2011, we could blame it on our centre-right libertarian government, but even after a centre-left government made up of the Social Democrats

(Socialdemokraterne), Social Liberals (Det Radikale Venstre) and Socialist People's Party (Socialistisk Folkeparti) took over in 2011, nothing happened to stem the rising inequality – in fact, trends continued. People without money were left behind, while people with money continued to stride further ahead.

Like the rest of the Western world, we have also seen a rise of the nationalist right, which places the bulk of the blame for rising inequality on refugees and migrants. I see this particular development as the recurrence of a threat we have faced many times before: when people feel insecure and afraid they take comfort in the most straightforward answers, often resulting in a 'them and us' rhetoric that leads to scapegoating. Despite the European Union's success at keeping the peace for the past sixty years, we still seem unable to consign such nationalism and scapegoating to the dustbin of history.

As we have seen throughout history, the blame game will get us nowhere. The analysis is simply wrong. The problem is not refugees and migrants, so the answer is not nationalism. The heart of the problem is a political and financial establishment so inept at evolving and integrating new answers that no one in their right mind still trusts that they will. The problem is a political and financial establishment unable to solve the global challenges we face. Both in Denmark and across the world, we have a serious lack of political courage and creativity, and the result is that the political establishments seem satisfied with just maintaining what historical ambitions have afforded them. Politicians, many of whom undoubtedly have dreams and aspirations, have let these dreams and aspirations become submerged in the battle to keep their status and power. As a result, politics has become a competition about who is the best administrator of the current system, and political ambitions have been reduced to a desperate effort to maintain society just as we know it today for as long as possible.

'DEAD MAN WALKING' MAKES A COMEBACK

In Denmark, a voice is rising that dares to challenge politics to mean something. It started with a question I posed to myself a few years ago: why do so many people seem convinced that what we have today is as good as it gets? Why blindly fight to maintain the status quo, instead of looking for something that could serve society better?

I will never find satisfaction in an ambition to maintain what we already have. Rather, I would venture to suggest that now is the time to dare to be creative, to think outside the box, to seek that something that is better. To me, it is clear that we have to begin devising ways to revitalise democracy and our political systems. In a Danish context, this means a move from the representative democracy to a far more engaging and involving democracy.

Had I written this contribution three years ago, it might have been my epitaph – that I felt there was something better, but I was never able to unleash the brave and creative forces needed to realise it. Fortunately, I'm writing this essay in early 2016, and we have already made considerable progress. Not that this seemed likely in early 2013, when political colleagues, pundits and journalists dubbed me 'the dead man walking of Danish politics'.

Before I came to be the 'dead man walking', I was a city councillor in Aarhus, the second largest city in Denmark. I had served as the CEO of the World Outgames, and I had founded the Kaospilot International School of New Business Design and Social

Innovation, of which I was the principal for fifteen years. Before this, I was one of the initiators of Frontløberne, a business environment for cultural entrepreneurs. I had built a career by founding and nurturing creative, entrepreneurial and successful institutions and environments.

In 2011, I was elected to the Danish Parliament. I ran for the Danish Social Liberal Party (De Radikale), of which I had been a member for most of my adult life. Our 'side' won the election and, together with the Social Democrats and the Socialist Party (Socialistisk Folkeparti), we formed the first left-wing government since 2001. I served as Minister of Culture in the government of Helle Thorning-Schmidt, until I resigned in December 2012, having become disillusioned about how much national politics had become stripped of its ideals, left as little more than a game – or, should I say, a war – of power. It was after I resigned that the 'dead man walking' tag followed. But, in reality, I felt free again. Free to be creative, to think outside the box, and to dream big.

Being the old anarchist that I am, I have always liked a good challenge. So, drawing on my entrepreneurial background and my experiences with politics-as-usual, I began preparing for a risk-it-all comeback. I knew how the political system worked, and how it malfunctions too. I knew too well how the media shapes and misshapes the democratic discussions and the decision processes, and I knew their immense power. I had a personal ambition of proving that even a political system so set in its ways can be changed, and I knew it could only be achieved by building participation, social innovation and enterprise. With a handful of good people around me who were as tired of politics-as-usual as I was, we began designing an alternative – in every way we could imagine. And that became our name: The Alternative.

First of all, we set out with an ambition to come up with answers to three crises we identified as the most serious of our time: the environmental crisis, the empathy crisis, and the crisis of our systems – be it the political system, the institutional system or the system of management.

We decided that all of our politics should be measured on how well it creates a surplus on the financial, the social, and the environmental bottom line. The days when we ran huge deficits on the social and the environmental bottom line to secure a surplus on the financial should be well behind us.

In our view, these challenges are so daunting that traditional politics cannot solve them. Politics-as-usual involves pitching ideas that are constricted by more or less preset ideologies into a dirty, no-holds-barred contest with similarly constricted ideas from the other side. This simply reinforces the old and the outdated: 'socialism versus liberalism', 'capitalism versus communism', 'class war', 'businesses versus the public sector', 'left versus right', etc. These divisions of thought restrict action in ways that are no longer helpful or even meaningful. The challenges we face are new, and thus the old political divisions should be rendered obsolete.

Some issues that could and should gather broad political support have been taken hostage by one or the other of these old political factions. The collection of problems we face – for example, rising inequality, climate change and the political crisis – must be a uniting issue in the future. We can disagree on how, but not on if. The ambition of creating a sustainable society is not a threat to individual freedom or the free market. It is an ambition of a society in movement, not lacking in dynamics. At least that was our analysis, and we decided to give ourselves the freedom to use what works best without having to consider if it was 'proper socialism' or 'proper libertarianism', without having to confer with some sort of ideological 'bible'.

A ONE-PAGE MANIFESTO AND NO POLITICAL PROGRAMME

Instead, we identified six core, guiding values that characterise our internal and external working processes as well as our politics and political proposals. The values are courage, generosity, transparency, humility, humour and empathy.

Courage to confront the problems we face head on. Generosity to share everything that can be shared with anyone who is interested. Transparency in the way we work so that everybody can monitor what we're doing – on good days and on bad days. Humility about the task we have given ourselves and humility towards those whose shoulders we stand on and to those who will follow us. Humour because it is the prerequisite for creativity that leads to good ideas. And, finally, empathy, to allow us to put ourselves in other people's shoes and see the world from their point of view and create win-win solutions for everyone.

These goals and measures became a one-page political manifesto accompanied by the following headlines:

The Alternative is a political idea
The Alternative is a wake-up call
The Alternative is a positive countermeasure
The Alternative is curiosity
The Alternative is collaboration
The Alternative is openness

The Alternative is courage
The Alternative is already a reality
The Alternative is for you

That was it! Our analysis, our six core values and our manifesto was all we had when, at a press conference on 27 November 2013, we launched The Alternative as a political platform consisting of a movement and a political party. We didn't even have a political programme. We dared to say – as we still do – that we do not have answers to everything, that we do not know everything, and that we never will. Instead, we had put dreaming into a formula by creating an arena where it is easier, encouraged, and appreciated when you dream out loud with your eyes and ears open. We call that space 'political laboratories', and we presented a plan to launch a series of these where everyone – irrespective of age, background, political persuasions and party membership – was invited, invited to dream out loud, to help form a new political vision, to take part in creating our political programme.

The same day, an in-depth feature on The Alternative was released by the Danish media *Zetland* (*Zetland* is an entirely new and so far very successful media platform offering in-depth features of around fifteen to twenty pages at a cost of a couple of pounds a month). The journalist had had full access to meetings and all internal emails leading up to the announcement of the movement. We put all our cards on the table, and, although the article didn't really pass judgement on our possibilities, it gave us credit for our openness.

According to media pundits, we had no future and no chance whatsoever to be elected to the Danish Parliament. The general judgement seemed to be that we were a political joke thought up by idealistic amateurs. That didn't surprise us; in fact we took it as another sign of how internalised the idea of politics-as-usual had become.

In 2014, we presented what – to the best of our knowledge – is the first 100 per cent crowd-sourced political programme: sixty pages, all dreamed up by those who had shown a willingness to partake. Our political programme is also 100 per cent dynamic in the sense that we have hosted and will continue to host political laboratories. The political laboratories are both a means and an end. They are a means to creating an ever-evolving political programme, and an end towards revitalising democracy by making politics engaging and inclusive.

A key part of our political programme is the chapter on changing the political culture. The fact is that trust towards politicians has for too long been dwindling and is now at an all-time low; politicians are at the bottom of the list – below even used-car sellers and journalists. Neglecting the role of journalism in the matter would be wrong, and thus we do not, but instead of fighting the media, we have chosen to change the 'game' from within – by showing the alternative to spin, catchy and aggressive one-liners, and lobbying that benefits special interests.

In all our communications, we have thus pledged to uphold six basic tenets:

1. We have pledged to draw attention to both the advantages and disadvantages of what we suggest;
2. We have pledged to listen more than we talk and to meet our political opponents where they are;
3. We have pledged to highlight the values that lie behind our arguments;

4. We have pledged to openly admit when we cannot answer and admit if we have been wrong;
5. We have pledged to be curious towards those with whom we debate;
6. We have pledged to openly and impartially argue how our vision can be achieved.

Upholding these six tenets is as hard as it is revolutionary in the political culture in Denmark today. Most of the time we succeed, but to ensure we do not start slipping, we have formed our own Ombudsman Council, which has the task of looking over our shoulders and formulating any criticisms in a thorough report twice a year.

REACTIONS TO THE ALTERNATIVE

So, how did my erstwhile political colleagues, Danish political pundits and journalists react to all this? With ridicule. Although we were no longer without a political programme, the framing of The Alternative as a naive project run by amateurs with no flair for politics persisted. In a now-famous news show in January 2015, five of Denmark's most experienced political pundits rated the chances of The Alternative breaking through the 2 per cent threshold of votes necessary to be represented in Parliament. The comment that stands out came from the pundit Jarl Cordua: '0.1 per cent chance of them getting in [to Parliament]. They are not getting in. It is an amateur project.'

Nothing had changed predictions when, only four short months later, in May 2015, Helle Thorning-Schmidt called an election.

However, during the three-week election campaign something did change. To everyone's astonishment – and surpassing even our own expectations of breaking the 2 per cent barrier – we began to surge in the opinion polls. Each one was better than the last, and pundits and media alike were scrambling to make their predictions come true by continually framing us as naive amateurs. On this, entire books could be written.

In the end, though, our ideas and our radically different approach to politics resonated with the public. The Alternative got 4.8 per cent of the popular vote and won nine of the 179 seats in Parliament.

Not in any way to diminish the accomplishment of being elected to Parliament and the great opportunities afforded us through the political system, I believe that change can happen more rapidly through broad movements than through politics as it is practised today. While mainstream politics continues to avoid it, we continue to insist that a sustainable transition is an absolute imperative. We have a saying: 'When the system is not responding, we the people have to rise up to pave a way forward.' Ours is a loving revolution in which everyone takes their authority and capacity to act seriously. We – meaning each and every one of us – *will* find a way!

In that regard, I am optimistic. After only ten months in Parliament, the number of paid-up members of The Alternative had quintupled. Around 40 per cent of our members have never been active in politics before. We have also made good on our ambition to be an international movement. In January 2016, we welcomed our first sister party, The Alternative Norway, founded by like-minded Norwegians who felt that our manifesto and values resonated in Norway. They now aim to do what we have done in Denmark. I hope they surpass us.

We now have MPs, and though this essay has been written in the offices of Christiansborg Palace, the Danish Parliament, it is important to stress that The Alternative is not based in Parliament: it is a political platform for the whole of Denmark on which we have built the political party and the movement. We plan to build many other entities on the same platform; entities that should be sustainable and can still succeed, even if others do not. It could be publishers, solar panel projects, educational programmes, think tanks, creative design, shops, etc. Everything is possible as long as any new entity is based on our values and manifesto.

In fact, from the beginning The Alternative was conceptualised as a fourth-sector corporation. Fourth-sector corporations are not-for-profit initiatives that take the best from the three traditional sectors: the private (business) sector, the public (government) sector, and the social (non-profit) sector and combine them into one. From the private sector, they draw on their experience creating and distributing goods and services that enhance our quality of life, promote growth, and generate prosperity. From the public sector, fourth-sector corporations draw on their protection of public interest while at the same time ensuring a level playing field of opportunity, and the protection and expansion of democratic freedom for both individuals and communities. From the social sector, they draw on their efforts to build and protect human values, share wealth and resources equitably, and ensure all people have access to adequate necessities of life, including clean air, water, food and shelter. Fourth-sector enterprises also have a strong environmental element, working to sustain and support, not systemically alter, degrade or destroy the earth, its diversity of life or the ecological systems that support life, and to promote the idea that the many species that share this planet must work together for the benefit of the entire world.

Fourth-sector corporations draw on all these experiences and dedicate more resources to delivering social and environmental benefits.

Many of them operate with a triple bottom line in the sense that they have to run a surplus on the financial, the social and the environmental. Indeed, The Alternative has adapted the thought of the triple bottom line and strives to make it a defining factor of all we do.

I am certain that fourth-sector corporations will be a driving element of the next societal leap forward. From all corners of the world, we are beginning to see the contours of something almost revolutionary: more and more people are choosing to work in jobs that are meaningful to them. Not just jobs that pay the most money. This demand for meaning as something more than just a monthly pay cheque will be a defining feature of the future. Adding to that, it is becoming more and more obvious that the world as a whole is facing problems of such a magnitude that neither the private sector nor the public sector can solve them by themselves. The problems we are facing are calling for an entirely new way of organising our efforts, and I believe this is to be found in the fourth sector.

We have another saying in The Alternative: that we are striving not for Denmark to be the best country in the world, but the best country *for* the world. One tangent of this ambition is to launch the next wave of political and societal innovation, to take control of the future, and in doing so – hopefully – be the inspiration to the rest of the world we once were. I am certain we can deliver on this ambition, because, after all, we have done it before – we did it with the cooperative movement.

CROSS-POLLINATION OF THE NEW POLITICS

Just as The Alternative has been inspired by social movements and political ideas from around the world, I hope that our ideas will be used in the rest of the world. I hope our ideas will cross-pollinate. In recent years we have seen many progressives who think and do politics differently making great strides around the world.

One of these, and one that bears many resemblances to The Alternative, is Podemos of Spain. The party was officially launched on 16 January 2014, and is headed by a professor of political science turned television presenter, Pablo Iglesias. Like The Alternative, Podemos is strongly anti-establishment, and its main objectives are to end rampant corruption and inequality, and to reform the European Union from within – ending the EU's adherence to the politics of austerity. Podemos's political programme is the result of a collaborative effort and includes the introduction of a basic income for everyone, lobbying controls and punitive measures for tax avoidance by large corporations. The programme also includes an ambitious set of initiatives regarding climate change, such as reducing fossil fuel consumption, promoting public transport and renewable energy initiatives, reducing industrial crop agriculture, and instead stimulating local food production by smaller corporations. All political aspirations we agree wholly with.

The parallels between The Alternative and Podemos are indeed many, but perhaps one of the most important is Pablo Iglesias's thoughts on political ideologies. He has argued that leftist organisations need to 'put away old flags', and that the dichotomy of left and right is not always useful. I would call Podemos's political aspirations entirely progressive (as I would our own), and I find them aspirations that are becoming increasingly difficult to reject. Someone has yet to argue that a fossil-fuel-based society is better than one based on renewable energy. Some forcefully argue that the green revolution will be difficult, but few, very few, argue that a green society based on clean, renewable energy sources is not a better society. The case is the same for equality – evidence continues to mount showing that equal societies are better societies. Such ambitions should be shared by everyone, but for some reason they are not at the moment. And in my view, progressives must reflect upon their own role in taking ownership of these issues. If the goal is a better world, as it is for me, we must share ownership of the progressive political agenda.

Syriza of Greece, the Five Star Movement of Italy, the Pirate Party in Iceland, and Bernie Sanders in the US presidential election are other examples of progressive thinkers, parties and movements with ambitions of shedding the shackles of strict adherence to any one old ideology. They aim for a radically different future and to change the path we are on. All of these have gained much more support and recognition than The Alternative. That is great to see, because they are challenging the political establishment and politics-as-usual, and thus are an open challenge to the rise of an extreme right seen in so many countries in Europe and the US. All of them are an inspiration to start doing things differently, creating a much more involved and inclusive democracy, bridging the widening gap between the electorate and the political elite. By their mere existence, they are changing the political landscape for the better.

What we also share with these parties is the fact that our rise and current existence is based on an electoral system able to accommodate new political parties and thus the innovation they bring. The Danish voting system is based on proportional representation, meaning that our number of seats in Parliament almost exactly reflects the share of citizens who voted for us: 4.8 per cent voted for us and we hold 4.8 per cent of the 179 seats in Parliament. Thus our electoral system welcomes challenges to the existing politics-as-usual rather than the opposite, and this is very different from the British system, which – in my opinion – has an undemocratic built-in flaw in the Westminster model, popularly called first-past-the-post. A good example of why I think the Westminster model is undemocratic was the 2005 election where Tony Blair won a majority of sixty-four seats in Parliament with only 35 per cent of the popular vote. Another example was the most recent election, in which the Green Party of England and Wales received 3.8 per cent of the vote but was awarded only one of the 650 seats in Parliament – equivalent to 0.15 per cent of the parliamentary representation. The system favours strong one-party rule while very effectively deterring and impairing challenges by free-thinking, progressive movements. Thus, progressive British movements face a tough first challenge: changing the electoral system. However difficult, I believe this can be achieved by formulating a serious, progressive agenda able to mobilise the public – perhaps centred on progressive initiatives and movements such as Compass, the Green Party, and Scotland's independence movement.

I believe it is key for all progressive initiatives in Europe to stand together, learn from each other and collaborate on formulating a political agenda based on the premise that we cannot solve the crises facing us by perpetuating what created the crises in the first place. When national politics fails to provide the results the world so desperately calls for, others have to step up. We have to find another way, and we have to do it together to build a critical mass that demands an end to politics-as-usual.

When national Parliaments fail to act, there is hope in the many progressive solutions that come from local communities, municipalities and cities. Some great examples stem from the UK. From initiatives like Transition Towns, across local currencies like the Lewes and Brixton pounds, communities across the UK have shown that positive action does not have to wait for top-down politics. This is mirrored across the globe, and it is an essential counterweight to the slow-moving, often conservative national Parliaments. In the face of politics-as-usual, I believe it is the responsibility of all progressives to pave the way for these. We should all strive to connect these progressive dots and support cooperation across local and national borders, so best practices can pave a way forward for all of us.

The recent mayoral election in London also testifies that there is hope in local politics. Not least thanks to the participatory model of London's citizens, that stands as an admirable testament to the fantastic power and creativity that can be unleashed when you give the democratic authority back to the citizens themselves.

I am hopeful because, just like the examples above, The Alternative and I are living proof that it can be done. But it is also true that, however fast we may be growing, The Alternative is still a small political platform in a small country, so we need others to dream up new futures as well. At least here in Denmark, The Alternative has been able to break out of the hypnosis that allowed us to forget that there is always an alternative. I will continue to do my utmost to ensure that we never forget it again.

Uffe Elbæk is the political leader of The Alternative, Denmark. As well as his political work, he has been a social worker, an author, an entrepreneur and a trainer of entrepreneurs. He was also chief executive of the World Outgames, a global sporting and cultural festival sanctioned by the Gay and Lesbian International Sports Association.

The Alternative's political programme can be found at: http://en.alternativet.dk/political-program/

IS THE PARTY OVER?

Indra Adnan

During a particularly difficult moment in the general election campaign last year, I opened an urgent email from the Labour Party. There was Ed Balls, declining to make a comment about the news, but urging me to grab a cartooned tea towel while stocks last. I didn't get another email that day. I wondered then who they thought their members were.

It's no news to any of us that membership of the major political parties is in long-term decline. Even with the surge under Jeremy Corbyn's leadership in the autumn of 2015, membership of the Conservatives, Labour and the Liberal Democrats is at a historic low. Meanwhile, membership of other parties has increased markedly in recent years. In June 2015, Green Party membership (England and Wales) was around 61,000, compared to 13,800 in December 2013, while in June 2015 SNP membership was around 110,000, compared to 25,000 in December 2013. UKIP's membership increased by around 10,000 over the same period, from 32,000 in December 2013 to around 42,000 in January 2016, though it is reported to have dipped to 30,000 since then.

Yet, even if you add them all together, the total number of people who are signed up anywhere comes to less than 1 per cent of the population. Can the political party as we have known it for most of our lives be an effective tool of democracy if it commands the attention of so very few of us?

Janan Ganesh, political columnist for the *Financial Times*, regularly taunts the left with the charge that British people don't care enough about politics to get involved. They vote Conservative because they like their lives – oblivious to the political or economic settlement – and expect David Cameron to maintain their equilibrium, no more. That's not the same, incidentally, as saying the Tories won the economic argument: it's closer to Galbraith's 'Culture of Contentment'.

Yet, looking at political activism in the wider sense – the rise of socio-political movements, online advocacy, petitioning, campaigning – one might say Janan is asleep at his desk. The internet campaigner 38 Degrees has 2.5 million members, increasing numbers of whom not only click on petitions, but start campaigns of their own. Half a million people are regularly working to save the NHS – many times more than knocked on doors at the general election.

Membership of grass roots activist groups, now too many to mention (though I will later on), has only grown steadily. Civil society organisations, including charities, NGOs and social enterprises, not only grow but significantly increase their attention share with Facebook, Twitter and YouTube presence. According to the American business magazine *Fast Company*, social media has overtaken pornography as the number one activity on the web: today those with desk jobs are more likely to find a cause that prompts them to take action amidst the cute cat videos on Facebook than at the local party meeting in a community hall.

But are we talking about a straight shift of energy from the established parties to the new forms of activism in which the latter take over from the former as the main vehicles of public agency? Clearly not. While activists are skilled in creating spectacle, generating discussion and building advocacy, their numbers and impact are still hard to measure. And the resources for major and sustained change remain in the hands of those in power. In the recent EU referendum, the failure of the left to connect with 'the people' who voted Leave was painful.

Instead, we have a very fragmented field of different forms of action, new and emergent cultures of behaviour and leadership in a diverse set of conditions across the UK, Europe and the world – all of which bear upon each other in ways that are not easy to control. And they are not working together: grass roots initiatives attack NGOs for their funding from corporates; local community groups challenge local government for their austerity narrative; fledgling anti-government parties compete aggressively with each other for a share of the political market. How can those hungry for change make any sense of it and know how best to invest their passions? And how can they, in turn, reach those oblivious to the inequality and injustice they are unknowingly complicit in?

THE PARTY IN THE INTERNET AGE

In 2015, Compass published two papers that set the complex scene we are now negotiating. Neal Lawson and Uffe Elbæk's *The Bridge* described the revolutionary impact of the internet in the early years of the twenty-first century, which suddenly made it much easier for people to share information – peer to peer rather than boss to subordinate – and then mobilise. In a subsequent paper, entitled *New Times*, Neal and I explored the multiple shifts that this revolution – it is no less – gives rise to, amounting to a radically altered experience of living in the world; not simply because of more time spent in the relational world of Twitter, Facebook and online shopping (still a relatively privileged notion), but due to public space itself becoming largely virtual and the onus on citizens and customers to access their own services, create their own media, name their own social agendas. (If you missed David Bowie anticipating this with a sceptical Jeremy Paxman, find it on YouTube.)

Where does the party, until recently the caretaker of political power, stand as citizens begin to explore and exercise their individual and collective agency in unprecedented ways, or watch others doing so? In 2008, the Carnegie Trust wrote about the need for greater power literacy in *Power Moves: Exploring Power and Influence in the UK*. Echoing the shifts in geopolitical terms, the authors made a distinction between the hard power that parties exercise in enacting policy and husbanding resources and the soft power of creating the context within which decisions are taken. While the state – specifically the ruling party – has the money, the non-state actors have a growing influence over whether the party can spend that money freely.

The sociologist and political activist Hilary Wainwright goes further in questioning the traditional idea that the only way to make change happen is for parties to win power and control all the instruments of state ('power over'). In her chapter 'Beyond Social-Democratic and Communist Parties' (for *Capitalism's Crisis: Class struggles in South Africa and the World*, Wits University Press), she says effective operation of the state comes before the needs of the people in the traditional political framework. Parties appeal to voters to help them (the parties) become managers of the state rather than representatives of the people, which means parties effectively serve the state and expect the support of their members in putting them into the position of power to do so. Within this culture, governments effectively become 'cartels', more concerned with serving business and industry than responding to citizens' needs.

In contrast, when the parties see their job as representing the people to the state, they find themselves dealing in the 'power to' transform. Their audience is both business and society. Forging relationships, creating consensus and the conditions for change, mobilising opinion – all this can be done even from opposition and allows a far more open conversation with party members and the broader public. In a sense, party activity of this kind could be modelling the kind of behaviour and building the relationships that will give rise to the society we want, rather than waiting for us to win power before we can enforce it.

At this moment, UK parties – even in Scotland – err on the former relationship to power but are surrounded throughout Europe by live experiments with the latter, more on which below. At the same time, we might say, the UK world of activism – especially in Scotland – is burgeoning. Is there a way to bring the two worlds into a healthy relationship, to create what Compass likes to call 'politics at 45 degrees' between the vertical and the horizontal? Or should we expect the growth of activism to develop into forms that eclipse old-style political parties altogether?

FOUR LENSES ON THE FUTURE OF THE POLITICAL PARTY

There are four lenses through which we can map the changes in plural forms of political agency that, together, can begin to tell us a useful story about the future of the party.

1. User experience: what are people prepared to do as activists, citizens, party members? In what kind of spaces can parties meet citizens, with what purpose?
2. Structure: what kind of party structure allows a productive connection between the vertical and horizontal distributions of power? Where should the initiative arise? Who manages the polity?
3. Leadership: what skills and capacities are required to both attract and sustain momentum? The pros and cons of charisma.
4. Political culture: what is the political culture that prefigures the good society? What values must be upheld among activists and party members? What behaviour is good?

1. User experience

When Yanis Varoufakis, the former minister of finance for Syriza, in his *Manifesto for Democratising Europe* describes the cartel government of Europe as anti-democratic, he is calling for a vigorous response – a rising up against the governments of today. But can an uprising ever deliver lasting change? What happens when the moment of confrontation is over? How do the relationships between different levels of responsibility settle?

Here's a story from a friend who was – and remains – a fervent Yes voter on the Scottish independence referendum. During the run-up to the referendum, he joined the SNP and was tireless in attending rallies, local events and gatherings, Facebooking and generally making noise for Scottish independence. Failure was a kick in the stomach, but not terminal, and he settled in for the long haul towards an eventual victory he feels will come. But, less than a year on, he has stepped back from front-line activism because local politics has regressed to business as usual: the elections for the Scottish Parliament pitched colleagues against each other and narrowed the focus of politics to minor differences. Guidelines on what is permissible in social media come down from on high. In local meetings he feels recruited and managed: the shared vision and inspiration has all but gone.

A Compass survey looking at how Labour members experienced their party revealed a long list of similar complaints, typically: lack of democracy, too much focus on short-term survival, extreme partisanship, overly commanding local leaders and – most tellingly – that it was boring. Although the range was broad (explored further in the 2016 Compass paper 'The 21st Century Political Party: Are You Being Served?') an overarching problem could be described as a lack of MPs' engagement with the party members themselves and a tendency to see them as the indiscriminate fuel for the PLP engine, rather than as the engine itself.

Is this the fault of the politicians, more focused on the 'cartel' – the business and industry members they need resources from? Or the fault of the electoral system that demands wins on a first-past-the-post basis every four or five years? Or is it the sheer weight and number of issues an MP is expected to deal with on a daily basis, sending them into a trance of box-ticking and presenteeism soon after being elected? Undoubtedly it is all of those reasons and more.

But is it also a failing of the members – and potential members

– having no way to express and articulate their needs and capacities better?

Maybe the loss of interest in party membership alongside the growth of activism in civil society is exactly the non-aligned autonomy a healthy democracy depends upon? The experiences of activists working on single-issue campaigns, local community enrichment, cross-party questions about diversity, power and privilege, report ongoing energy and commitment. On this scale, groups offer belonging and a sense of ongoing purpose in ways parties are failing to.

Yet, unless something connects them, harnessing their passions, Janan Ganesh's analysis of an apathetic society, however inaccurate, will continue to be borne out.

Maybe the interregnum between elections – and most particularly now, post the failure over Europe – is the time to do the patient work of separating out the many ways in which people are prepared to engage politically, and drawing up a map of politics that would see party and non-party political activity working together? Some think of this as a network analysis, and, indeed, it is vital and enlightening to sketch out the networks each of us are working in. But soft power – the ability to influence without coercion – is not something you can control easily, as every diplomat knows (see my submission to the House of Lords Select Committee on Soft Power, http://tinyurl.com/zng6t9u).

Movement for Change, founded by David Miliband, was a possible vehicle for the space between party and people as long ago as 2010, and Momentum could be that for the Corbyn-led party. However, if the modus operandi is predetermined, even by a subset of the party, and leaves little space for the people to define their own contribution, the gap between party and people will persist. Both could usefully draw on research conducted by Sarah Allan and others at Involve detailing the multiple conditions and motivations that shape participation – from economic resources (the bus fare to get to a meeting) to the emotional triggers (from natural disasters to becoming a parent). Unless parties start from the perspective of participants' needs and capacities, says Allan, they won't be able to count on their support in the future.

Another vehicle that could give rise to a new relationship between party and people is the proposed Constitutional Convention currently being championed by Labour's John Trickett. While the UK does not have a written constitution, 'conventions' invite people to come together to agree what the laws and structures we already live by should mean for the way we govern our country: its intention is democratic renewal. Unlike the Constitutional Convention that was convened in the 1990s and is credited with leading to devolution for Scotland in 1999, this convention is likely to occur without a predefined outcome – in that case the 'Claim of Right of the Scottish People' – and would acknowledge the complex nature of British society. Such a project, if it were cross-party and time-limited, should reveal the vast range of citizens' actions that contribute to a healthy democracy. And rather than harness them indiscriminately – as the Big Society threatened to do – a constitutional convention could find distinct places for them according to their relevance in the governance of the country.

Prospects of a simple e-democracy similar to that trialled by the Pirate Party in Germany frighten some people, largely because of the wildly varying degrees of attention or personal autonomy we are able to exercise in our pressed lives. But, when looking for more public participation, should we be jumping straight for the easy and quick responses when there is so much citizens' engagement that already goes unacknowledged by politicians and society?

Consider for example the broad range of time, attention and capacity required to do each of the following:

- sign a petition/share on Facebook/tweet
- go on a protest march
- volunteer as an 'ambassador' for your country, e.g. Olympics, Commonwealth Games
- attend regular meetings of a community project, e.g. with Frome's 'Flat Pack Democracy'
- commit to regular activism
- run a local community project
- volunteer with a church, mosque or ashram, e.g. Brent daily homework club
- volunteer regularly for a charity or NGO, e.g. part-time job at the Oxfam shop
- volunteer for a Citizens' Jury

Would a Citizens' Assembly, for example, be able to witness, monitor or even process the diverse offerings available across society in a way that enriches our democracy on a longer-term basis? Could it work as a third House, or replace the House of Lords – or should it exist well outside established power structures? And would this in turn give rise to a medium through which parties could engage more effectively with the people? The tension between the virtues of institutionalisation and the call to fluidity in a more meaningful democracy are right here.

2. Structure

Few would disagree that political parties have become more

disciplined operations aimed primarily at fighting and winning elections, with less time for discussion on issues. The result is that meaningful engagement between the government and the people through political parties has been lost entirely. This is not unique to political parties and for the left is understood as the product of neoliberal marketisation. A market approach to services, allowing efficiency to dictate practice, ends up disconnecting people. Witness the ways in which public services have reduced the role of their workers from interlocutors to providers of services to 'customers'. Just as care workers have switched from meals on wheels delivered personally to the elderly to meals by post, eliminating any time-wasting chat, so we the citizens are expected to turn up and tick the correct boxes just once every five years. No engagement required.

Of course, this is not the lived experience for individual MPs who are caught in the middle between Westminster and their constituencies. Most experience a sharp contrast between the ever-better-articulated frustration of their members – emails, petitions, tweets, on top of regular surgery appointments – and a lack of capacity to represent their needs and views in Parliament. It doesn't help that many of the bodies that might have acted as intermediaries – job centres, Citizens Advice Bureaux, legal aid centres – have been shut down, often with their complicity.

Maybe politics, then, could learn from the breakthrough work in public services such as that of nursing organisation Buurtzorg, investigated by Frederic Laloux in his popular book *Reinventing Organisations*. In it he describes how, when nationwide services are run by electronic timetables, clients suffer and regularly die for want of attention: even the coldest-hearted bureaucrat understands this is neither efficient nor effective. Buurtzorg understood that patients' needs could best be met when nurses self-organise neighbourhood by neighbourhood. These horizontal, peer-to-peer networks, which meet to share understanding and information about clients, allowed relationships and trust back into the system. A higher tier of management accepts the findings of these self-organised groups, using the information they bring to plan the future for the organisation as a whole. What started as a local initiative has become a nationwide network of 6,500 nurses who are transforming healthcare in the Netherlands.

Strangely, this model sounds like the representative democracy we are already supposed to have: local networks of people tackling their needs with their MP, whose job it is to feed those findings up to a fully interested government. How have the parties drifted so far from being the respondents to their constituents' needs, to being the hard-to-reach Honourable Gentlemen and Ladies with their own agendas, expecting support from the people? Putting all the issues of self-interest aside, is it because they themselves cannot manage the size and scope of the problems they are tasked with solving on a daily basis, i.e. our globalised world?

If we were to draw a diagram of the possible relationship between Westminster and the people it purports to serve, the 1990s and 2000s model would look like a pyramid, with global business and industry at the top, the MPs below them, civil society below that and the people stretched along the bottom. Not all, but too many MPs were looking up in thrall and attention drips intermittently downwards. That was easy to maintain as long as those in authority could control the information flowing downwards; power is most easily protected through selective access to information.

But that has changed. The old model is bust and in flux.

Today, as described above, the free access to information and the ability to tell new stories and open conversations about the state of democracy is in the hands of the people. What is generated are not simply demands – as in the old model – but much of the research and new thinking that government needs to answer our socioeconomic problems. The context for MPs to act in ignorance of the people – and the resources they bring – has gone as the non-state actors increasingly reshape the public space.

How long has it been since we looked to Westminster for cutting-edge thinking or problem-solving? Whether it is work on a Citizen's Income, local currencies, relational welfare, community organising or green energy, we are pleasantly surprised when MPs appear up to speed with innovation. We are not there yet, but the logic of an upside down pyramid is growing.

For inspiration – though not imitation – we might look at how the Spanish party Podemos arose from the grass roots to hold the balance of power in government in less than a single electoral cycle. The party structure is made up of concentric circles. The most important body is a Citizens' Assembly made up of the 350,000 members currently registered, who have an equal vote on everything from leadership to policy and strategy. It is served by an outer ring of small circles – meeting locally or sectorally – to discuss issues in preparation for the vote. Within is an inner council of leaders who 'serve' the membership and stand for office. The circular structure emphasises the democratic intent, giving voice to all, irrespective of status. Of course it is early days, the conditions in Spain are ripe for radical change and the leaders are charismatic and media savvy: even so, it is easy to see how the structure feels natural, human and inviting.

While this will be discussed in other essays, the prospects of grass roots movements developing on a municipal level around a popular mayor – the British equivalents of Ada Colau in Barcelona or Manuela Carmena in Madrid – should prompt MPs not to waste any time in opening their closed doors and encouraging change. A healthy, networked relationship between these levels can only be good for democracy: the alternative is that similar municipal movements may become parties themselves to begin a whole new chapter in our political history.

3. Leadership

In the run-up to the 2015 general election, opinion polls regularly suggested that Labour would win, or at least be in a position to form a government with the support of others, but Ed Miliband never once went ahead of David Cameron in the personal ratings. The fact that Labour lost the election begs the question as to whether Miliband was the right leader. But that question needs to be answered not simply on the basis of personal popularity but in a more nuanced way.

In his report *Anti Hero*, Richard Wilson argues that 'the modern challenges we face have fundamentally changed what we need from our leaders, requiring a shift from Heroic to Antiheroic leadership'. On examination, that doesn't simply imply the servant leader but, in a more complex fashion, the capacity to display all the familiar traits of strong leadership at one moment, and the ability to step aside the next. Why is this important?

In the world of one-, two- or three-party politics that we are now seeing discredited all over Europe, the polity was divided largely between the left, right and the centre. Ideology and class did a big job of speaking for the people and authority was largely placed in the Prime Minister and the Leader of Her Majesty's Opposition to represent the nation. Personality mattered because the people were quite invisible.

Today the people are much more visible; they don't fall into simple class divides any more but report themselves as more fragmented, diverse, pluralistic. Within the Labour Party there are two or three quite different, often competing groups, and the same goes for the Conservatives. The first-past-the-post system is increasingly discredited, with huge anomalies in the number of seats relative to the votes cast. Young people are uninterested in membership of a single party but otherwise sign up to multiple interest groups. When the Women's Equality Party allowed dual membership, it became the fourth party – larger than UKIP – by recruiting 45,000 members within three months of its launch. All these facts suggest political activity, but decreasing possibility for single-party dominance or control of the political landscape.

If this book generates waves in the British political scene, at least four parties will begin to consider how to work better together to challenge the Tories. Within an alliance, leadership has to be distributed and more fluid; party leaders will have to take turns to represent issues and give way to MPs that are otherwise their competitors. This aspect of letting go of overall control is closer to what Richard Wilson describes as 'post-egoic leadership' – less about the self and one's own party, more about the whole: winning for the people.

The leadership style of Podemos's Pablo Iglesias and his appeal to the electorate beyond the left and right divide must take some of the credit. Even so, the anti-government conditions in which he has been successful have also given rise to the Madrid-based popular movement Ciudadanos (meaning 'Citizens'), led by Albert Rivera, and the success of the activist Ada Colau in Barcelona at a time when the call for an independent Catalonia is at fever pitch. But will this combined challenge to the two-party state be able to find agreement among themselves to change the political destiny of Spain? The capacity of these three charismatic leaders to rise and give way to each other will be tested.

From the perspective of leadership culture, the progress of The Alternative in Denmark will be instructive. Before the party leader Uffe Elbæk went into politics, he ran a business academy called Kaospilot for twenty years. With branches all over the world, he taught the next generation of leaders how to be able to surf the increasingly complex landscape of global innovation. Today his party is marked by its emphasis on attractive politics, youthful support and its fluid leadership style (see pages 237–52).

4. *Political culture*

As social movements thrive and political parties shrink, how important is the political culture as an attractor? Paul Hilder, a key figure in the launch of Avaaz (now with 45 million members), vice-president of global campaigns at Change.org (80 million users) and most recently co-founder of online voting platform Crowdpac, cites three key aspects for a successful people's organisation. First, there should be a commitment to serving the members and their participatory experience. Second, that being a member of the organisation – party or movement – should be transformational: it should change your life. Third, that the issues the organisation takes on should be intersectional – crossing boundaries, creating new vistas, opening up possibilities.

The power that such organisations generate is more soft than hard, generating influence and creating the conditions for change while prefiguring the good society. Can a political party afford to invest so much in building what Hilary Wainwright describes as transformative capacity rather than pursuit of dominance? It is certainly hard to achieve from the benches of Her Majesty's Opposition in a Westminster culture that is brutally competitive.

The persistence of inequality, rigid hierarchies and puerile behaviour from all parties on the floor of the House of Commons is now giving rise to more direct critique. The New Economic Organisers Network (Neon) wrote a paper, *Power and Privilege*, that puts all forms of historic and cultural dominance under the spotlight. Not only does it articulate an ideal of equal opportunity to speak, act and be heard, but it offers concrete practice and training for how to get there. This includes how to run meetings, what kind of venues are conducive to democratic practice, and how to check yourself for selective deafness.

But what are the equivalent calls on the right, and how do we, in the interests of democracy, accommodate the needs of people who vote differently from us, most recently the Leave voters in the EU referendum? While it is tempting to shrug those questions off – we can't do everything! – it is notable that many of the new political parties arising in Europe are prepared to do just that. Rather than left versus right, Podemos frames its political stance as the people against the elite and is committed to listening to all the complaints of the less privileged – including the whole package of fears arising from globalisation. While this doesn't imply an injunction to agree with the policies of the right, it does demand an openness to the emotional needs driving them. While a healthy political space already embraces that culture, party-specific spaces often don't.

In the UK, Labour often attempts to describe an open space, willing to take on the worries about migration or the desires expressed by 'aspiration' normally associated with the right. But, rather than stay open-minded and invite a public debate, it has a tendency to triangulate from the centre, to find a middle way on behalf of its members so that one 'party line' prevails. In contrast, the Green Party allow their members to discuss and formulate policy, and to vote in a freer, less 'whipped' way. In Scotland, proportional representation gives members the chance keep all debates open – with two votes you can vote for a party leader but you can also limit their power by using your second vote for a different party. The progressives need to create a political culture that understands and respects the emotions behind non-progressive opinions, like anti-immigration and Euroscepticism, even if the progressive movement disagrees with such opinions.

WHAT CAN BE DONE STARTING NOW?

Looking at the possibilities for change through the four lenses set out in this essay – user experience, leadership, structure and political culture – Westminster seems a long way off giving rise to a 21st-century party that is distinct from the twentieth-century model. Maybe because we are overly attached to an image of the Mother of Parliaments with a duelling chamber at the heart of government, we can't imagine something open and fluid being effective. Yet the call is getting louder day by day, and the publication of this book suggests there are enough MPs in the building who are willing to experiment.

As the cliché has it, change can begin in the heart and mind of any single MP; why not move on from seeing every other party, particularly those on the left with you, as competition? If your intention is to serve the British people – and the numbers are not there – why not look for the ways that can be achieved through cooperation? This is particularly important for Labour, who would most likely be the leader of any progressive movement, but only if it is willing to put some of its historic tribalism towards Liberals and Greens aside.

For constituent MPs, the best opportunities must lie in becoming immersed in local networks, irrespective of party membership. Finding time to get involved with people whether they vote for you or not is crucial in developing the post-egoic leadership that Richard Wilson describes. Encouraging the development of open groups – like Podemos's circles – on the fringes of the party that can be run without guidelines from the centre, avoiding the language and culture already dominant in the party, is vital. Movement for Change, for example, was an early example of Labour's capacity to reinvent itself (Momentum less so).

To shift the thinking out of its current malaise, what about reading groups focused on books about the future? Jeremy Rifkin's *The Zero Marginal Cost Society*, Paul Mason's *Postcapitalism* and Nick Srnicek and Alex Williams's *Inventing the Future* are all guaranteed to rewire the reader and tune them into the currents of change happening outside the bubble.

If and when new parties arise – as they will, should proportional representation ever be introduced, and maybe before – it will be the capacity for openness, relationship and vision for the future that will guarantee the survival of those that currently hold sway. And if any of us reading this are that new party, the challenge is barely different. Buzzwords like distributed leadership, self-management, peer-to-peer networks and servant leadership are mere platitudes until we develop the capacity individually and collectively to introduce them and sustain them. We will not implement the change, we can only be the change – it's a journey of personal and collective transformation that cannot be underestimated. But, in so doing, we lay the foundations for the good society.

Indra Adnan is a futurist and founder director of the Soft Power Network. She consults to government bodies including in Brazil, Mexico, Denmark and the UK. She is also a socio-psychotherapist consulting to schools, civil society organisations and leadership, and a Compass Associate.

EMBRACING ELECTORAL REFORM

Katie Ghose

The term 'electoral reform' has come to be largely a synonym for proportional representation (PR), a system of voting – of which there are several viable variations – for making the number of MPs, councillors or other representatives consistent with the number of votes cast for each party. For progressives seeking common ground, PR is clearly a massive issue, perhaps the biggest one as smaller parties are increasingly making a more proportional voting system a red-line issue for cooperation in government. Historically, however, electoral reform has encompassed a wider set of democratic reforms, rooted in the idea of widening the franchise, opening up democratic participation and placing power with people rather than party or parliamentary elites. These ideas have been at the heart of many battles, of which the Chartists' campaigns of the 1840s and 1850s and the campaign for votes for women are the highest-profile examples. In the last century, the Labour government's scrapping of additional franchise for business owners and graduates in 1948 to achieve 'one person one vote' and lowering the voting age from twenty-one to eighteen for the 1970 general election are also notable examples.

In the last two decades, the principles of devolution and decentralisation of power have driven fundamental changes to where power lies within and between the nations of the UK and constantly challenge us to consider how a healthy democracy should be conceived – and work day-to-day. Devolution was started in earnest by the Labour government in 1997, with the transfer of significant powers from Westminster to new institutions in Scotland and Wales, and since then a broad cross-party consensus has formed around the general principle of more powers – including fiscal controls – being held closer to people in their communities, even if differences remain on precisely how this should be achieved. The electoral system has always been part of a democratic jigsaw, involving core ideas of voice, representation and mandate. Now, as the march of devolution continues, with more powers moving to Wales, Scotland and to English localities – and with increasing political diversity putting strains on a system designed for another age, the interplay of voting reform with other electoral rules and wider political culture cannot be ignored.

The UK has become a multi-party, multi-national democracy in which first-past-the-post elections to Westminster produce a distorted electoral map, exaggerating political differences between and within the four nations, and making it impossible for any party to be truly 'one nation'. This essay focuses on the incentives for change, alternatives and how reform might be achieved.

INCENTIVES FOR A PROPORTIONAL VOTING SYSTEM

For all the complexities of the electoral map following the 2015 general election (the most disproportionate in British history), one thing is simple – Labour holds the trump card on electoral reform. Smaller parties favour electoral reform at Westminster, but with the Conservatives implacably opposed, it is Labour that will determine the prospects for change. This section therefore inevitably focuses largely on what Labour stands to gain by embracing PR.

The Labour Party faces a huge electoral challenge to win in the next election, which makes the case for a proportional voting system attractive to it, but the case for reform cannot be founded on the party's current fortunes alone. Labour memories go back to 1992, when disappointment at a fourth successive electoral defeat made the party look seriously at PR, only for it to romp to a massive election victory in 1997. It may be tempting to hope that voters will return to old two-party voting patterns and propel Labour to a similar emphatic victory at the next election, or perhaps the one after. But leaving aside the fact that the circumstances at the next two elections are likely to be very different from those in 1997, there are more fundamental reasons why Labour should embrace electoral reform.

If Labour wants to convince the public that it is a party serious about doing politics differently, it must surely embrace the possibilities of electoral change to reconnect with voters in every corner of the country. First-past-the-post squanders Labour support in safe seats, and constricts elections to being decided by fewer than 200,000 floating voters in marginal seats. This in turn concentrates government investment in competitive constituencies instead of areas in most need. Such a situation acts as a brake on the party's ambition to generate fresh ideas, reconnect with disaffected voters and create a new politics.

In Scotland, first-past-the-post has hastened Labour's decline. For many years, Labour's majority seemed unassailable, yet the dominance that first-past-the-post afforded ultimately prevented the party from getting ahead of social and political changes, including the development of devolution that started with the creation of the Scottish Parliament in 1998. A culture of safe seats, a common feature under winner-takes-all systems, kept Labour representatives focused on Westminster, with no incentive for the party to cultivate voters beyond its base. This helped to feed a belief that Labour was part of a Westminster establishment rather than 'on the side of Scottish voters'. That in turn boosted the independence movement, and the extent of defeat leaves Labour now having to rebuild from just one Westminster seat in Scotland, which will almost certainly deprive it of a majority at Westminster in the next election. Yet Labour was short-changed at the 2015 general election – its one seat was scant reward for having secured one quarter of Scottish votes. By contrast, at Holyrood, the proportional system means Labour currently holds twenty-four out of 129 seats on around a 19 per cent vote share.

It's not just in Scotland. If Labour is to revive its connections with voters in every part of the UK, as well as tackling its decimation in Scotland, it needs a more proportional voting system. Combined with an ambitious package of democratic modernisation encompassing an elected second chamber, boundaries drawn on population not voters, sixteen-year-olds getting the vote combined with political education and truly democratic devolution – where new powers are matched with increased public accountability – electoral reform could become part of the answer to 'What is Labour for?', and a recipe for renewal and modernity.

First-past-the-post has masked a long-term trend of decline in support for both Labour and Conservatives, with each party able to form majority governments on under 40 per cent of the vote, raising questions of legitimacy. In 2015, the Conservatives secured a twelve-seat majority with 37 per cent of the votes while in 2005 Labour's 66-seat majority was achieved on 35 per cent of the votes.

Now that legitimacy to govern is being called into question by slim majorities, the full impact of the electoral system can no longer be ignored. This is especially so in the electoral deserts in the south of England and in rural areas where Labour voters are denied a fair share of MPs or councillors, activist bases are weak and unable to campaign effectively in national or local elections, further diminishing the party's ability to organise to attract support.

First-past-the-post also fosters a tribal approach that sits uneasily with the desire for cooperation and common endeavour that attracts many to Labour in the first place. Greens, Liberal Democrats, SNP and Plaid Cymru are all enemy parties to be squeezed out of power, regardless of any shared policy ground. Party members go through contortions when a pressing local issue – a failing school or day centre closure – cries out for a cross-party campaign, as they prepare another round of leaflets damning their opponents and claiming 'only Labour can win here'. It should be noted that the smaller parties are guilty of this too, especially when they see the chance of winning in places where they can 'squeeze' the Labour vote – this is a natural compensation under first-past-the-post.

Many recent grass roots innovations in the Labour Party stem from an appreciation that few voters now are tribal. Such innovations include creating new supporter categories, enabling local parties to contact trade union members directly, community organising that encourages local collaboration across party lines, and more. This implicitly recognises that the modern voter's route into party politics is more likely to follow involvement locally in a campaign or passion for a cause than to come as a ready-formed attachment to a party rosette. Yet the system insists that parties adopt a monolithic stance of being right on all issues. All parties are affected, but for Labour striving to make a new, kinder, more collaborative politics part of its broad appeal, propping up a system that demands the opposite has a jarring effect.

And Labour must surely see a proportional voting system as a logical step in its proud tradition of supporting electoral reform in the broader sense. Its pioneering accomplishments range from championing women's suffrage, finally achieved in 1928; achieving 'one person one vote' by scrapping the additional franchise for business owners and graduates in 1948; to extending the franchise from twenty-one to eighteen for the 1970 general election. These were not always easy to achieve, but they were both the right things to do, and brought many more potential voters to the Labour cause. At its heart, voting reform is about opening up democracy to ensure everyone's voice is heard; the fair translation of votes into parliamentary seats and a different model of government where power-sharing is the norm. Surely this is more in tune with the Labour community's mantle as democratic reformers than adhering to a system that is out of step with the party's interests and ethos, simply because it might just bring a single-party parliamentary majority? Surely a pledge to bring electoral reform into the heart of an ambitious agenda of democratic rejuvenation would sit more comfortably with what Labour stands for?

OPTIONS FOR PROPORTIONAL REPRESENTATION

If first-past-the-post is wanting, where is the evidence of a better alternative? Opponents of electoral reform often point to other countries to signify that proportional systems bring chaotic outcomes and foster extreme elements. Italy, Israel and Belgium are frequent culprits, despite the fact they have politically distinct cultures and their specific systems need form no basis for a British solution. More useful comparisons are to be found in the mainstream of international reform, where systems combining first-past-the-post with an element of proportionality are more common.

Closer to home, the UK has become an electoral system laboratory in recent years, with five different systems in use. First-past-the-post has not been adopted for any new institution or office since 1997 and is now used only at Westminster elections and for council elections in England and Wales. MEPs are chosen by a closed party list system, Scotland and Wales both use the Additional Member System (AMS) to elect MSPs and Assembly Members, Scotland adopted the Single Transferable Vote (STV) in 2007 for Scottish local council elections, and elections for single office-holders (mayors; police and crime commissioners) use the Supplementary Vote.

The **closed party list** system chosen to elect Britain's MEPs is unpopular, even among advocates of proportional representation, as it gives party elites all the control, is bad for turnout, and is more restrictive than the systems used in most European countries, which allow voters to express a vote for an individual candidate. Very large constituencies reinforce distance between voters and candidates, few of whom can name one let alone all their MEPs. Where **open lists** are used, enabling voters to choose individuals from a list provided by the party, evidence suggests voters are more likely to be contacted by candidates and more likely to feel well informed. In legislation to reform the House of Lords in 2012, the Single Transferable Vote and open lists were the two credible alternatives, with open lists making it into the final draft. The importance of enabling voters to choose independent-minded candidates with and without a party badge – achievable under STV – was well understood.

Scotland and Wales both use the **Additional Member System** (AMS) to elect Members of the Scottish Parliament and Assembly Members, similar to **Mixed Member Proportional** systems used in Germany and New Zealand. Each voter has two votes – one for their constituency, which returns a single MSP or AM in the style of first-past-the-post, the other for a party list. The votes for the party list candidates are then allocated to 'top up' the number of seats won by each party to represent their share of the votes proportionally; these are the 'additional members'. Issues have arisen from the existence of two mandates: in Wales, the low ratio of list to constituency members favours the party (traditionally Labour) that maximises its success in constituencies; and perceptions in some quarters that list members are inferior, have a lesser mandate, or fail to share the casework load.

Having two different types of MSPs was an issue in the first Scottish Parliament, but with hindsight it appears this stemmed in part from the idea prevalent at the time that only first-past-the-post elections provide democratic legitimacy. As support for devolution and the Scottish Parliament have grown, and with Scotland's adoption of STV for local government in 2007, people have begun to accept that electoral mandates can come from a wider range of systems. Now that the main parties have both held a reasonable number of constituency and list MSPs, and many members have experience of both mandates, the idea of differing status is diminishing.

In elections for single office-holders (mayors; police and crime commissioners), the **Supplementary Vote** gives voters two preferences. If no candidate receives a majority, the top two candidates continue to a second round and all other candidates are eliminated.

The second-choice votes of everyone whose first choice has been eliminated are then put towards the first-round totals for the remaining candidates to determine the winner. Supplementary Vote does allow for some limited cooperation between parties – for instance, in the first London mayoral elections, Ken Livingstone and the Greens recommended each other as their second preference. However, with only two preferences indicated, it is still reasonably easy to win with less than half the votes, as large numbers of voters will not preference one of the top two candidates. Until the election of Sadiq Khan in 2016 by securing 50.4 per cent of first and second preferences (57 per cent to Zac Goldsmith's 43 per cent in the final tally), no London mayor had won more than half of all votes cast on the day.

Finally, in Scotland, voters have used the **Single Transferable Vote** (STV) for local elections since 2007, a proportional system allowing voters to number candidates in order of preference, with '1' as their preferred, '2' as their second choice and so on. Used in wards of three to four councillors, a quota system ensures no wasted votes, and the election of a cross-party local team is commonplace, broadly reflecting the spread of local residents' political views.

The change has stimulated competition (there are now no uncontested seats) and the steady increase in voters using second, third and fourth preferences suggests growing familiarity with the system – accompanied by the clear incentive for candidates to reach out across the community in order to gain second or third preferences.

One of the biggest concerns expressed about a move to a proportional voting system is that it would lose the link between voters and a constituency. This is a misconception. All UK systems, except for the closed lists used in European elections, are constituency-based, and the idea of a closed list party PR system attracts virtually no support at all.

Both AMS and STV have constituency-based seats; the difference is that constituencies are significantly larger, but voters have more than one representative whom they can approach either for practical help or to raise a policy issue. Under STV, seats might cover a city, or in some cases a county. But voters would have a choice of representatives to go to, with some evidence showing that representatives compete to provide the best constituency service or develop specialisms. Voters are more likely to have a representative from a party they voted for. Additionally, when a party wins multiple seats in an STV district, it is often the case that they will divide the constituency up into smaller units to share the casework load. So while the constituency link is changed by proportional representation, it is not eliminated, and by having multiple representatives, a more sophisticated form of constituency link may appear.

Opponents of proportional representation often claim it gives fringe elements too much power, leading to a range of smaller parties represented in Parliament, which in elections with a tight result between the major parties can make forming a government into a complex patchwork operation. In reality, thresholds are a common feature of PR systems. Typically the rules specify that a party cannot win seats unless it secures a minimum percentage of the vote, say 4 or 5 per cent. In addition, the size of a PR constituency can be set to act as an effective threshold and barrier to entry – for example, ten constituencies with five seats is a higher barrier to entry for smaller parties than one fifty-seat PR constituency. But, ultimately, above a certain level parties should get the representation that reflects their popular support. Moreover, once parties have the parliamentary spotlight on them, their policies are more readily scrutinised and arguably more likely to be 'proofed' against becoming too extreme.

The Single Transferable Vote is a tried and tested system that would work well for electing MPs and councillors, as it does already in Scotland in local elections and in Northern Ireland for all elections aside from the House of Commons. A preferential system designed to maximise voter choice, it is well designed for a modern, multi-party era in which voters want to support a more diverse group of parties. It preserves, but adapts, the constituency link, by introducing a team of around three to five MPs (often from different parties), working in constituencies larger than now to represent everyone in the local area. Candidates can be put forward who reflect different wings of a party – challenging the dominance of any one faction – and there are no 'off-limits' areas when it comes to campaigning. Most profoundly, it would shake up the model of government, giving parties seats in Parliament that broadly reflect their popular support and thus enabling parties to form governing alliances unthinkable under first-past-the-post, as the next section shows by examining Welsh and Scottish experiences under alternative systems.

GOVERNMENTS CREATED UNDER PR

Proportional systems create different forms of government where power-sharing rather than power-hoarding becomes the norm, and seeking consensus is integral to the conduct of politics. Such power-sharing does not have to mean a formal coalition, though the first seventeen years of devolved governments in Scotland and Wales have seen enough coalitions for the idea not to be alien to British politics.

In Wales, a Labour-led coalition government from 2000 to 2003 (with the Liberal Democrats) was followed by majority government until 2007 and then further coalition, this time with Plaid Cymru in 2007–09. The 'One Wales' agreement forged by both parties straight after the 2007 election was instrumental in clarifying joint positions on most issues likely to arise. A commitment to a referendum on further powers towards the end of the term (2011) worked as further 'glue' to hold the administration together. Rhodri Morgan, the former First Minister of Wales, writes: 'Coalition is not abhorrent, and it doesn't make a country ungovernable. Nor does it render the smack of firm government impossible. You can make coalitions work, though they are harder than running majority governments.'

Labour led the first Scottish government from 1999–2007 with the Liberal Democrats, largely based on full implementation of Labour's manifesto, with a few key Lib Dem election pledges added in, including switching to proportional voting for local elections. The close election of 2007 saw the SNP form a minority government on forty-seven seats (Labour had forty-six) and achieve informal support from the Conservative Party (and Greens) until 2011.

Jack McConnell, Labour's First Minister in the 2001–07 period, gives a glimpse into the mechanics of successful negotiation, from achieving party members' buy-ins to advance planning and relationship building: 'Labour wanted far-reaching legislation on crime and antisocial behaviour and an agreement that economic growth was Scotland's top priority. The Liberal Democrats secured proportional representation for local government. Only with both could either have agreed.' Following the 2016 elections in both Scotland and Wales, minority governments have taken shape, with the SNP and Labour respectively having to reach agreements with other parties to pursue their manifesto commitments.

Internationally, centre-left coalitions have held power and implemented progressive programmes without relying on winner-takes-all systems. Scandinavia has several examples of long-running centre-left governments with policy programmes that achieved results. Most famously, Sweden's Social Democrats ruled from 1936 until 1976, usually in minority, from where it worked with parties both to its left and right to create what is still one of the world's most admired welfare states. West Germany saw the pioneering government of Willy Brandt from 1969 to 1974, made up of Social Democrats and Free Democrats (economic liberals), which massively expanded the German welfare state. The Netherlands saw the Kok Cabinets in the 1990s, which, by bringing together social democrats and liberals, made great strides forward in social policy, such as being the first country to legalise same-sex marriage – it is from this period that much of the Dutch reputation for progressive social norms originates.

In New Zealand, Labour governed for three terms as the leading party in power-sharing administrations, including coalition, confidence-and-supply, and a cooperation agreement. Formally in a minority government with the Progressives, Labour adapted to bring in four other parties, who agreed to support the government in key areas in return for policy concessions. Ministers were appointed from these parties who did not become Members of the government but were bound by Cabinet collective responsibility for the portfolios they held. Constitutional creativity thus enabled a different kind of government, and a highly successful one if measured by policy implementation, longevity and popularity.

IMPLEMENTING ELECTORAL REFORM

Under first-past-the-post, a progressive governing alliance is hard to achieve. It would rely on a hung parliament in which the only viable government were one in which Labour with other parties secures at least 326 seats (301 following the reduction from 650 to 600 MPs to be introduced after the proposed boundary review) and can agree a joint programme of government. If such a government became possible after the next election, there would be two obvious ways of achieving electoral reform: either the progressive parties would have to pledge electoral reform before the election in their manifestos and could then enact it without a referendum, or they would commit to holding a referendum.

That the Scottish Parliament was able to reform Scotland's council elections stemmed from a mix of principled belief and practical politics. While Labour's First Minister Jack McConnell was a convinced reformer, the wider Scottish Labour Party was on the whole strongly against. The Lib Dems, who had a long standing pro-PR policy (although in reality it proved to give them little party advantage in Scottish councils), provided cover for McConnell within his own party by making sure it was presented as a major condition for the coalition deal. It took two parliaments and two commissions and reports to get to the change. That meant both Lib Dems and Labour had some degree of manifesto commitment to reform in the election prior to the relevant Bill being passed.

There is no legal requirement for a referendum to change the voting system, although doubters will argue that the 2011 referendum on the Alternative Vote created a precedent for any future change to how MPs are elected. Clear manifesto commitments, backed up by consistent evidence of public support for reform, would obviate the need for a referendum, although a progressive initiative without a public vote would require proper public consultation in its place. Otherwise, reform could be vulnerable to a future government switching back again or insisting on a referendum.

In this context, New Zealand's 'two-stage' experience merits consideration. In 1992, a non-binding referendum was held on whether or not first-past-the-post should be replaced by a new, more proportional voting system. Voters were asked two questions: whether or not to replace first-past-the-post with a new voting system; and which of four different alternative systems should be adopted instead. An electoral reform coalition campaigned actively in favour of the Mixed Member Proportional system originally recommended by a royal commission. People voted overwhelmingly (84.7 per cent) for reform and a clear majority (70.5 per cent) supported moving to Mixed Member Proportional (MMP) voting. A year later, a second, binding referendum was held in which voters supported the move to MMP.

In New Zealand, therefore, a discussion – and vote – was held on the status quo, a dimension missing from the 2011 UK referendum on AV which gave opponents ample opportunity to reject reform by picking holes in the system on offer, deflecting attention from the flaws of first-past-the-post. Progressive parties could make an electoral pact with manifesto commitments to abolish first-past-the-post and hold a two-question referendum preceded by a citizen-led convention to examine the issues and foster public information and debate. Or a constitutional convention could be tasked with consulting widely before recommending an alternative system to Parliament to be legislated for without a public vote. Canada's current situation could prove instructive on a parliamentary route to reform without a referendum, with Prime Minister Justin Trudeau promising before the 2015 election to make it the last federal election conducted under first-past-the-post. His government has convened an All-Party Parliamentary Committee to review a wide variety of reforms, such as ranked ballots, proportional representation, mandatory voting, and online voting, with nationwide public consultation to be followed by legislation in 2017.

Regardless of the precise route to reform, building public awareness is vital. When the Electoral Reform Society asked voters in April 2015 what they thought of current arrangements for electing MPs, the biggest surprise was the number who thought a proportional system already existed. Why wouldn't seats match votes cast? A fortnight later we had the most disproportionate election result in British history, with a fractured, multi-party vote shoehorned into a single-party majority by first-past-the-post. Stark numbers: one MP each for the 5 million votes for Greens and UKIP; fifty-six out of fifty-nine MPs for the SNP on half the Scottish vote; and huge regional imbalances. It all helped to strike a chord with many as being 'not fair'. Yet sustaining awareness about voting systems outside of a general election campaign every five years is a major challenge.

As we have seen, change can come without a referendum and would be perfectly legitimate with demonstrable public and party support. But, in the event of a full public vote – or whole-hearted public consultation – awareness cannot be stimulated overnight: the issue may be about democratic fundamentals, but to many people, even informed citizens, it can feel technical and remote. Reformers must build a stronger awareness of how first-past-the-post is short-changing the public to equip them to take part in the next stage: what should replace it? A constitutional convention, composed of randomly selected citizens who convene to deliberate and make recommendations on the future shape of our democracy has a crucial role to play, and Labour's plans, led by Jon Trickett, shadow Minister for the Constitutional Convention, to launch such an initiative with full support from several other parties has real potential. A convention that successfully tackles pressing issues about where power should lie within and between the nations of the UK could also cover electoral systems – or form an excellent foundation for a subsequent phase that tackles voting reform specifics and forges strong recommendation for a replacement to first-past-the-post. Conventions in Canada, Iceland, Ireland and the Netherlands as well as two pilot assemblies in Southampton and Sheffield organised by Democracy Matters (a consortium of academics with the Electoral Reform Society) in 2015 all provide a wealth of evidence on how to involve people in constitution-making.

The path to reform is far from straightforward, but it's worth taking. Winner-takes-all systems only work for parties when there's a big prize – a decent spell in majority government. When the days of a comfortably secure majority – for any party – are long gone, the system becomes a brake on new ideas and alliances that can confront the challenges of modernity. It is in this space that arguments – and forging a realistic route to reform – need to happen. Progressive parties need to reclaim and renew an ambitious package of democratic reform in which changing the electoral system is a catalyst to forging a truly representative and modern democracy.

Katie Ghose is the chief executive of the Electoral Reform Society. She chaired the 'Yes to Fairer Votes' campaign for the Alternative Vote in the 2011 referendum. Previously, she was director of the British Institute of Human Rights, where she was awarded Pro Bono Lawyer of the Year in 2009 by the Asian Lawyers' Association, and a barrister representing refugees and asylum seekers. She has worked for Age Concern and Citizens Advice in parliamentary and public affairs. Her book *Beyond the Courtroom: A Lawyer's Guide to Campaigning* was published by Legal Action Group in 2005. She is a council member at the University of Sussex. She is a Labour Party member.

CREATING THE SPACE FOR CHANGE

Zoe Williams

Sometimes this looks like a uniquely inopportune moment to expect parties to cooperate with one another, when they have never been more divided among themselves. And yet, the internecine battles are the latest and surest sign that the old parliamentary truisms are no longer true.

In the past, politics came in two blocs, and 'the people' sat somewhere in the middle. Whichever bloc gave the best account of itself to the people would smash the other bloc. Traditionally, a successful right gave an account that appealed to sound economic sense, and a successful left appealed to something a bit more hopeful and nebulous, working together to build a better society. Smaller parties existed mainly to force some difference in the larger ones, rather than for any direct influence of their own. This approach actively excludes party members: when both sides are fighting for the centre, their own members are by definition, since most people do not join parties, atypical, unrepresentative, useful for leafleting but fundamentally not to be taken seriously. So a crucial – perhaps *the* crucial – democratic pathway has been closed off. The way to get your voice heard, by this rationale, is not to engage but to disengage. This drives people away from parties, which then lose legitimacy. But it also creates these implacable tensions within the major parties – Corbynites versus Blairites in the Labour Party, Remainers versus Brexiteers in the Conservative Party – as they all try to enforce their vision of what 'the people' want by bare assertion. The adversarialism allows no input from any actual people, let alone any other parties, and the debates are shorn of meaning. In order for grass roots politics to re-enter the conversation, that understanding of politics as warfare must change.

I have been in many meetings about vertical versus horizontal politics, and have never until this moment taken the time to figure out exactly what those terms mean. There is a fluidity to these ideas that is sometimes useful and sometimes obstructive.

'Vertical' often means 'the kind of politics I don't like'. I know that's how I use it. Top-down, hierarchical command structures, in which ideas are brokered and manicured rather than fought over and fought for, participants are from a political class and not the 'real world', and the institutions exist to do the exact opposite of what a parliamentary democracy was conceived to do: represent the state to the people rather than the people to the state. There is, however, a lot to be said for vertical politics; it has solid institutions, it is extremely organised. It understands the structures that surround it, where they are porous and where they aren't. It is disciplined and knows how to create concrete actions from discussion, or at least move through or past the discursive phase so that action can be taken. There is something dispiriting about listing the advantages, since they are so conspicuously absent from horizontal politics, and on a dark day, everyone involved in grass roots anything must have thought that only vertical politics can achieve those things; the very act of inviting infinite participation itself militates against the practical business of making stuff happen.

Which brings us to the definition of horizontal politics. It is a more spontaneous affair, arising out of an issue or belief, rather than defining itself as 'politics' and then deciding where to position itself on an issue-by-issue basis. It is inclusive and non-hierarchical. It prides itself (or should) on its openness, and on treating all its participants equally. This means taking active measures to ensure that everyone feels equally able to speak, rather than simply asserting that they may if they wish. Many of the practices people mock about progressive grass roots politics spring from the attempt to create a genuinely warm and inclusive discursive space; waving your hands about rather than actively opposing, saying 'yes, and' rather than 'no, but', trying at all times to observe and be sensitive to the constellations of disadvantage that might silence people.

A lot of procedural detail has changed between, say, the Greenham Common CND camp of the early 1980s and the Balcombe anti-fracking protests of 2013; an inclusive and warm space sometimes used to mean 'no men', and it would be unlikely to mean that now. Yet the kinds of practices that earn horizontal politics a reputation for being faintly ridiculous, while at the same time orthodox to the point of being alienating – even an aerobics class becomes exclusive when there are too many unspoken rules – are rooted in meaningful and essential desires: to forge a movement in which everybody believes they have the power to change things; are heeded; are valuable; and are in the business of real solidarity, not just a talking shop in which a handful of the garrulous need a (diverse!) roomful of the silent in order to feel legitimate.

THE RECENT FAILURE OF HORIZONTAL POLITICS

Too often, those beliefs just don't stand up, and people start to trickle away. Thinking of the 1980s, there was a huge amount of passionate, meaningful community politics, from the miners' strike to CND, from local Labour Party activism to LGBT rights campaigning. Only the last could be counted as a success, and there is a separate discussion we could have – probably quite briskly – about why identity politics was so much more successful than industrial and class-based power struggles. The fact is, if you were a kid in that era as I was, the 1990s came as a phenomenal relief. The problem with socialism, as the saying goes, is that it takes a lot of evenings. Activism took a lot of time, and the most concrete, indeed, the only concrete success of it was in raising money, which could then be spent on more activism, or funnelled towards other activists, who weren't winning either.

The fundamental weakness was twofold: there was a lack of diversity, but I don't mean that in the way people mean it now, to strangle activism in its crib because it doesn't meet the strict criteria of perfect demographic representation that no fledging movement could ever meet. Rather, people were distanced from the issues they were fighting for, so you would have middle-class Londoners meeting to fulminate about the industrial north, or affluent Home Counties sort-of hippies talking about poverty in Wales. There was no lack of sincerity, but there was, of course, a lack of fundamental emotional connection. It lacked the immersive quality of the early trade union movement for the very good reason that people were battling for rights and conditions in which they had no stake. Consequently, it lacked confidence – it was relatively easy to persuade people that they were irrelevant, they were dreamers, they believed things the rest of the country didn't believe.

Secondly, there was often a very profound sense of separation between the individual and the locus of power and decision-making. This was particularly marked in discussions about nuclear power, nuclear disarmament, globalisation and the environment (acid rain and the ozone layer were much more talked about than climate change, but the root sense – that profit and nature were vying in a cost–benefit analysis that nature would always lose – was established). It was extremely hard to believe that you could make a difference against these issues that towered like the Wall in *Game of Thrones*. I remember going to Greenham and seeing the barbed wire, the soldiers, that unapproachable, inaccessible greyness that characterises military bases the world over, and thinking: this is just extravagantly pointless. What threat could we ever pose to those people or the order they defend? They are carrying actual working weapons, and most of us aren't even wearing clean underwear.

It's in that diagnosis that I find my optimism about horizontal activism this century. On the matter of diversity, it is still a problem, indeed, it's a greater problem than ever. Even if you had a broad racial cross-section in a movement, which is extremely rare, and perfect parity between women and men, also still rare, you would instantly abut the fact that time is a luxury. You will not see those who are truly struggling with low wages, insecure work and eroded workplace rights in a town hall on a Tuesday night. The chances are they are at work, or they are waiting for a call about work, or they are tired. You will not see the ultimate victims of the corroded welfare state because their disability living allowance has been cut and they can no longer run a car. And so on. The system is still –

if anything, more than ever – stacked against the civic engagement of the dispossessed, and then the failure of any given town hall to contain sufficient members of the underclass is taken as proof of its irrelevance. But, at root, that is just rhetorical bad faith.

Because underneath, something real has changed. Conditions have changed for everybody. All under-25s, excepting those from extremely wealthy families, emerge from education with a life-altering amount of debt. All under-forties, including those who have done everything right, from their hard educational graft to their excellent life choices, are facing housing insecurity and attendant financial pressure. A group like Generation Rent will include people from every class – though probably not every generation – not speaking on behalf of one another, but facing the same fundamental problem, viz that when one set of people wants to live off rents, that is, unavoidably, living off the labour of others. Economic rent is defined by Josh Ryan Collins from the New Economics Foundation as any unearned and untaxed profit above and beyond that which is necessary to maintain the upkeep of a property due to demand for the limited resources that are available. The key distinction between this and what we might term classic capitalist investment is that it produces nothing. No wealth is created, no tangible goods result. The upshot is merely one person living off the labour of another. There is room for many stances on whether this is ethical or not, but one thing is undeniable: practically speaking it means the second person is going to have to work much harder than the first, to end up with less. The second person will never own that house, will never have anything to show for their years of rent. As the relative inequality grows between the landlord and the tenant, the power balance shifts in favour of the landlord. We can see this already, with the rise in practices like revenge evictions.

What you see in Generation Rent is not just a spontaneous grass roots group, in which everyone has skin in the game; it is also a discursive space in which people have different ideas. It can work and meld quite easily with smaller, more proximal housing movements like New Era 4 All and Focus E15 because it is not a manufactured group looking for a problem to solve. It is a problem that has brought together large segments of different people, who are de facto invited to find creative solutions. Some people believe in rent caps, some believe in increasing housing supply, some think the answer is in community housing projects, some in compulsory purchase orders so that the state retakes its role as landlord, some want to join forces with environmentalists so that responses to the housing crisis simultaneously answer the energy crisis. It's perfectly plausible that an affordable housing movement in Sussex could work with its anti-fracking group, who themselves – in real life and not just my *Pollyanna* imagination – had already joined forces with a solar energy campaign.

Successful movements are born when conditions, injustices, exigencies emerge that feed into one another and affect, if not everyone, sufficient people at least that the engagement is both communal and personal, not distant and by proxy. I believe that moment has arrived; not everybody uses a food bank or is on the minimum wage; but food poverty activists have enough in common with fuel poverty activists, who have enough in common with housing activists, who have enough in common with environmental activists, that they all start to look not diffuse but complementary.

On the second issue, then – the weakness of horizontal politics caused by activists being too far removed from the people or entities making the decisions – the forces of real power haven't become any less faceless. You don't look at shadow finance or the globalised energy market or the Troika or the drivers of TTIP and think, these are easy targets, always open and reactive to the demands of the citizen. But we are starting to tell a different story in the way we approach apparently omnipotent foes and immutable situations. It's hard to describe except by example.

THE LESSON OF POSITIVE MONEY

Positive Money was established as a campaigning movement 'to democratise money and banking so that it works for society and not against it'. It was set up to ask questions about how money is created, on the basis that most people didn't know. This turned out to be correct; nine out of ten MPs surveyed didn't know how money came into being. Since it is a democratic resource, and they are our democratic representatives, this is a pretty serious shortcoming. Yet more important still would be if they were typical of the level of understanding among the general population, and there's no reason to suppose they aren't.

Money is created by private banks, in the form of debt. Every time GDP goes up by £100, that is because £100 worth of credit has been extended by a bank. It doesn't exist in any real sense, but I have no problem with that; the problem is that debt has to be a two-way street. The creditor must take a risk on the debtor going bankrupt. If the creditor bears no risk, and the debt simply becomes more and more onerous until some other – probably indebted – citizen has to step in, in the form of a bail-out, then that isn't a debt so much as a racket.

Even that isn't the most destabilising thing about the way money is created. Eighty-five per cent of it is extended in loans on existing residential property; in other words, it doesn't generate new property, still less ferment innovation, manufacture, creativity or anything you could hold or use. It simply increases the price of property. Indeed, house prices become theoretically limitless, as they are not related, except very indirectly, to wages, and are governed instead by the interests of a banking cadre that bears very little risk. Even if some natural restraint were in place that meant this hadn't affected house prices very much – which there isn't, and it has – it would still be undemocratic.

If we accept that money is merely credit and has no material value, there is no reason for its creation to be in the sole care of a very small number, acting in their own interest. It's a social resource and needs to be decided by society; we might well decide that banks are the best people to do it, because they're numerate and regulated and perhaps, in dialogue with the wider society, could do it more creatively. But these are discussions we all need to be in, and we can't be in until we understand. Hence Positive Money.

Now, it seems slightly preposterous, to have a local group, meeting like a book group or a basketball circle, in about the same numbers, to talk about the creation of money. It takes a long time to make an impact that way, and longer still to demonstrate your impact. Yet I started to look at it from the counter-factual: what if no one ever set up this group? What if no one ever met in a pub to discuss money? What if no more than 10 per cent of people ever understood how it worked? What if nobody ever talked about the way it affects society? We know what that looks like, because we live in it. The point of grass roots activism is not what change it can instantly bring about, but that, without it, nothing ever changes: or, rather, things do change, but not in the interests of the grass roots.

As Positive Money gained traction, it garnered some allies that you might call the internal critics of the status quo – Martin Wolf, on the *Financial Times*, and Adair Turner, former chair of the Financial Services Authority. And as they variously supported and critiqued its agenda, another thing revealed itself: there are many people, perhaps a majority of people, who work to create the system as it is without necessarily fully supporting it. There is a huge amount of anxiety, within very establishment sectors, like banking, about social purpose, not just for reputational reasons – though these are stronger than ever – but because a vanishingly small number of people actively want a world in which we're all, to quote Thomas Piketty, 'paying rent to the Emir of Qatar'. But doing things differently involves more than ceaselessly castigating the way they're currently being done. In order for institutional changes to come about, informal groups demanding change must create the pathways of possibility. Otherwise the way things are done takes on a quality of inevitability; it must be the right way to do it, because that's what we do.

Finally, and crucially, I believe in a kind of Keynesianism of human energy. The exchange of ideas, hope, vision and ambition generates them afresh since, like money, they have no concrete value – they are merely promises of trust in one another so that we can get on and build. Activism as nourishment is the second footfall, irrespective of the issue that drove the first: to be in a room with people who share not your views but your optimism.

If we believe in a new progressive politics, it has to integrate horizontal politics where it makes sense to do so. It's easy to dismiss the horizontal politics of the past as unsuitable for today, but then the politics of the past is unsuitable for today. There must be space created for those who seek genuine change based on their own experiences, not just because they have chosen to engage with the party political process.

Zoe Williams is a writer, reviewer and political commentator, mainly for *The Guardian* and *New Statesman*. A graduate in modern history from Lincoln College, Oxford, she has written a number of books, notably *Get it Together: Why We Deserve Better Politics* (Hutchinson, 2015). She is a supporter of the British Humanist Association, and lives with her husband and two children in London.

THE APPETITE AND MECHANICS FOR COOPERATION

Andrew George

The so-called 'shy Tory' remains an enigma to opinion pollsters. Neither properly understood nor easy to quantify, these Conservative voters prefer to feign neutrality, not just when faced with centre-left party doorstep canvassers but even when interviewed confidentially for an opinion poll. Failure to fully fathom the 'shy Tory' at the 2015 general election didn't just leave egg on the faces of opinion pollsters, but produced shock waves across the political spectrum, from a delirious Conservative Party to Paddy Ashdown's exasperated milliner.

Of course psephologists are not really suggesting that a significant proportion of Tory voters are bashful by nature, nor that their shyness is provoked by the ebullience of less bashful centre-lefties. Pollsters prefer to tactfully describe as 'shy' what others may consider is a sense of 'shame'. And it helps if we better understand why some who support the Conservatives might be less forthcoming about their predisposition.

It is generally accepted that part of the political spectrum appeals to self-interest. This partly justifies its outlook with 'the poor have only themselves to blame' perspectives, and it comforts those who anticipate a large inheritance or who might seek to maximise 'tax efficiency' (lawfully, of course). If only through artful 'dog whistles', they offer an acceptable platform to blame others (foreigners, migrants, 'scroungers', Europe, gypsies etc.) rather than themselves for the ills of the world.

It is of course human to be susceptible to the frailties of avarice and self-absorption. But those who seek to appeal to our better instincts – for a better country, a society that supports those less able to fend for themselves, mutual security and benefit, an environment and society we would be proud to bequeath to our children – appear to have less reason to be shy (or shameful) about the politics they choose to support. As John Curtice demonstrates (page 186), we cannot be confident that those who share this perspective – the 'progressives' of this book – are necessarily a majority. The fact that progressives are often more forthcoming, dominating much of political debate, from social media to those who are most keen to turn out to form the audience for mainstream political discussion panels, makes it easy to think they form a majority, when in reality they are currently on the back foot, and with the Tories in the ascendency.

As a Liberal Democrat who has spent much of his life resisting a two-party politics, I'm not advocating that the two poles of the spectrum should coalesce into a new two-party system. But in view of the political reality that Curtice lays bare, it makes sense that those who share a broadly progressive political perspective should recognise when there's a shared interest and seek common cause, especially if the risk of a long-term political shift to the right is crying out for a firm counterbalance.

This essay reviews the prospects and, to an extent, the appetite for cooperation among progressives. In doing so I have taken an agnostic view on the relative merits or otherwise of the current or potential future party leaders. It concludes that those with a broadly centre-left/green/liberal or just plain anti-Conservative perspective should do more to work together, because:

- what generally divides them from each other is less pronounced than what divides them from Conservatives;
- the Conservatives are currently quietly rigging and gerrymandering the system to grant themselves an unassailable stranglehold on power for decades to come;
- an electoral system that permits – as it does now – Conservatives to have effectively dominant power when 76 per cent of electors didn't vote for them needs to be reformed, and it won't be reformed so long as they have power;
- the majority of non- or anti-Tory voters who are not members of the party they vote for don't understand why politicians who share a broadly progressive perspective seem to spend more time rehearsing their disagreements than identifying where they agree;
- if the parties carry on as they are, they will fight each other to a standstill in enough marginal constituencies at the next general election to comfortably grant victory to David Cameron's successor.

This reasoning requires further explanation before we consider how progressives can cut through the visceral tribalism of our party political system to forge a degree of cooperation in time to contest the inevitability of the Conservatives securing a greater majority at the next general election, and the one after that, and with it a greater stranglehold on power.

WHERE AND WHY HAVE PARTIES COOPERATED?

Cooperation isn't and hasn't been a slippery slope towards the merger of parties and the loss of the values that importantly distinguish parties from each other. There are many ways in which parties can cooperate without losing control, ownership and identity. Notwithstanding the example of pre- (and post-) election cooperation described by Duncan Brack (page 202), there are many useful examples of how parties in other countries have worked to create pre-election alliances or cooperation to improve their success at an election, in both first-past-the-post and proportional electoral systems.

It is, of course, difficult to accurately and objectively assess the impact of pre-electoral alliances on political parties' electoral performance, whether that effort is overt or covert. It is hard to prove that it was this 'alliance' that caused a particular election outcome, and not some other aspect of a campaign strategy, voters' preferences, or other factors.

In her book *The Logic of Pre-electoral Coalition Formation*, Professor Sona N. Golder of Pennsylvania State University examined 'pre-electoral coalitions' between 1946 and 2002: why and how they are formed, what they are, and how they interact with different electoral systems. She defined pre-electoral coalitions as 'a collection of parties that do not compete independently in an election, either because they publicly agree to coordinate their campaigns, run joint candidates or joint lists, or enter government together following the election'.

Perhaps contrary to expectations, Golder found that pre-election coalitions are more likely in majoritarian (i.e. first-past-the-post) systems like ours than they are in proportional representation systems, but only where a sufficiently large number of political parties exist. She highlights the case of France, where elections take place under a majoritarian voting system, but in two rounds. She found it common for pre-election coalitions to form both on the left and the right prior to the second round of voting, and somewhat less common (yet still frequent) for coalitions to form prior to the first round. Indeed, the most recent French regional elections in December 2015 saw the very effective result of cooperation among parties to successfully frustrate the progress of Marine Le Pen's far-right Front National.

As well as France, she discovered that pre-electoral coalitions were relatively common in mature democracies, including European countries with proportional voting systems such as Austria, Denmark, Germany (mixed voting system), Ireland and Belgium.

There has also been some revealing analysis by Karen Cox (University of Nottingham) and Leonard Schoppa (University of Virginia) into how political parties coordinate their strategies in mixed member voting systems (published in Comparative Political Studies, 2002). These systems 'feature electoral rules where seats in separate tiers are allocated both nominally and by party list. Voters cast votes that determine which names win seats, usually under plurality rules, while also casting separate votes that determine which parties win seats under PR [proportional representation] rules.'

Their article considers the activities and interaction between political parties in Japan, Germany and Italy. Cox and Schoppa found that the system produces certain 'interaction' effects. If the tier elected by proportional representation is used to compensate the results of the tier elected by majoritarian procedure to make the overall result more proportionate (as is the case in Germany), small parties have incentives to run in as many constituencies as they can and to attract as large as possible a share of votes. However, if the proportional representation tier does not compensate the majoritarian one (as is the case in Japan and was in Italy pre-2006), small parties have incentives to enter into electoral alliances in order to win seats under majoritarian procedures. Since 2006, Italy has had a proportional representation electoral system, but electoral alliances still persist.

IS THERE AN APPETITE FOR COOPERATION?

There's still an assumption among many progressives that the 2015 general election represented a high water mark for the Tories; that, just as night follows day, the pendulum will inevitably swing back at the next election, and scores of Tory marginals will be comfortably picked off. A reality check is needed.

I recently completed a project – supported, like this book, by the Joseph Rowntree Reform Trust – to assess the desirability and feasibility of a 'progressive alliance'. The project gathered impressions and opinions across the centre-left political spectrum through conversations and meetings, albeit falling short of being a scientific, stratified or randomised gathering of opinions/impressions. It concluded that there is a widely shared (though privately expressed and therefore of necessity unattributable) agreement among politicians and party activists that if progressives do nothing to cooperate – or barring an improbable political miracle – the Tories are destined to strengthen their grip on power at the next election. The collated reasoning behind such a conclusion would require another chapter.

It also identified that the current electoral advantage to the Conservatives will be further reinforced by their proposed electoral changes, which I prefer to describe in more brutal but accurate language as rigging and gerrymandering the system to their advantage. They propose to do this through:

1. a redrawing of constituency boundaries that is estimated will benefit the Conservatives by at least twenty seats compared to the current boundaries;
2. changes to voter registration rules that have resulted and will continue to result in the removal of mostly non-Conservative electors;
3. laws to restrain trade unions from making financial contributions to political parties on behalf of their members, which would ensure the Conservatives have a massive funding advantage over their rivals;
4. the 'neutering' of anti-Conservative Scotland from the UK parliamentary arithmetic and other initiatives.

Furthermore, there appears to be a substantial acknowledgement among MPs and those whose political activism gives them a more than local perspective that the Conservatives' advantage will remain largely unassailable as long as anti-Conservative electors in Tory and opposition marginals are uncertain which of the progressive candidates has the best chance of defeating the Conservatives in their constituency. This effect will become more pronounced after the constituency boundary changes come into force.

The project inevitably unearthed some activists in all parties (mostly at constituency level) who believe that a 'politics as usual' approach should be maintained. But they were a minority. In contrast, most of those operating at a national level – especially opposition MPs – or working in academia and policy development had already concluded that the prospects for defeating the Conservatives are very slim. It was hard to avoid the conclusion that there is now a necessity as well as a desirability for an initiative or initiatives to foster and develop a degree of cooperation between progressive anti-Conservatives.

Electors who support centre-left parties rarely share the same sense of tribal party loyalty as party activists, and, indeed, today's party members may not necessarily share the same degree of devotion as party members have in decades past. This trend has been recognised. For example, recent opinion polling confirms that 'the public overwhelmingly (73 per cent) want the main political parties to be less tribal and less closed' (YouGov, June 2015 for Compass).

If the antipathy towards tribalism among the voting public isn't enough to encourage party tribalists to stop and think, then perhaps the likelihood of growing Tory dominance might persuade those party activists who remain driven by personal enmities and petty rivalries to reconsider. Progressives require parties of the centre-left to lay down their arms (even if they're only soft toys) and try constructive engagement.

The 2015 election was a disaster for both Labour and the Liberal Democrats, in fact with the exception of the SNP it wasn't a storming success for any of the parties that are home to progressives. However, all is not lost. If we take an 8 per cent swing as a reasonably plausible range for an ambitious, effective, campaigning challenger, 102 of the current 331 Tory-held seats are winnable. Of these, Labour are in second place in seventy-six, Liberal Democrats in twenty-two, the SNP one and UKIP three. There are no Green Party candidates in second place in any, though there are many seats where Green votes did and will continue to have an impact on the outcome, and they will therefore also be significant players in any pre-election arrangements. Of course, forthcoming boundary changes will muddy the waters to a certain extent, but it will be possible to extrapolate where the new 100 or so Tory marginals are likely to fall.

It is difficult at this stage to properly assess the impact of these changes on the prospects for cooperative progressives. We know the overall effect of the boundary changes will benefit the Conservatives more than any other party, but if centre-left parties cooperate this could more than nullify that advantage. The cultural challenge for the parties is to find reliable advocates to explore cooperation. Translating the favourable mood music detected at a national level to local constituencies – where effigies of long established rivalries and personalised enmities are sometimes jealously guarded – will be a significant challenge.

POLITICAL COOPERATION AND ELECTORAL REFORM

When the Conservatives secured their stunning victory on 7 May 2015, they in fact increased their vote by less than 1 per cent: from 36.05 to 36.9 per cent. The last time the Conservatives secured a marginal victory was in 1992 when John Major achieved 41.93 per cent. Of the 46,420,413 electors registered to vote in 2015, the Conservatives had secured just 24.4 per cent (11,334,576).

The argument for a fairer electoral system that produces

outcomes that more accurately reflect the proportion of support each party achieves in the election has become ever more persuasive. At the same time, the historic justification for first-past-the-post – that it supposedly produced strong and clear governments – is no longer valid in a political culture where several parties secure large numbers of votes. The Conservatives have been rewarded with a disproportionately advantageous share of MPs for pursuing an effective (some would say cynical) use of their overwhelming arsenal and wealth to target 'floating voters' in a small number of 'swing' seats. Or, to put it another way, their majority was built on less than 0.1 per cent of the electorate. We would never accept bribery in our electoral system, so why do we put up with a voting system that can easily be manipulated by the wealthy and determinedly cynical to secure disproportionate power, as first-past-the-post does? Any future government that respects democracy and wants a legitimate mandate from the electorate would be hard pressed to seek it without ditching first-past-the-post in favour of a more proportional system.

The question is: can the centre-left agree to deliver electoral reform? Sensible electoral reform cannot be achieved unless parties of the centre-left cooperate; and if electoral reform is achieved it seems inevitable that progressive parties will have to embrace a world of mutual accommodation and respect that will grow from a proportional electoral system. As Katie Ghose points out (page 273), the key player here is the Labour Party and whether it (or a sufficient proportion of its MPs) is prepared to adopt electoral reform as policy.

The particular position of the Green Party reinforces the argument for an early resolution of the present unfairness of first-past-the-post. With just one seat from their 1,156,149 votes in the 2015 election (3.8 per cent of the votes cast at an average of 4.7 per cent in the seats they contested), they have a distinct interest in any arrangements that would lead to electoral reform.

Whatever form future cooperation between progressives may take, on the face of it there would otherwise be little incentive for the Green Party to take part. As mentioned above, the Greens are not second in any of the potential target seats. However, their support and votes would and could make the difference in many of these seats, so it is clearly in the interests of the progressive community to make some practical concessions to the Greens. It would be unwise to see cooperation merely in terms of a cold, seat-by-seat arithmetic process – it needs to be cooperation that ensures that all parties have 'flesh in the game'. A firm pre-election commitment to electoral reform from all parties – especially from a still sceptical Labour – will become ever more essential.

A PROGRESSIVE ALLIANCE – PRACTICAL STEPS

Some but not all of the ingredients are in place for creating a progressive alliance. The potential for establishing a non-party Citizens' Convention with a limited set of policy asks – say, covering social and tax justice, public services and fair votes – would be a very welcome vehicle both to engender hope and to generate a wider public engagement. However, unless there were a genuine prospect of defeating the Tories at the next general election, it would lack the required passion of plausible expectation. Therefore, the creation of an effective progressive alliance would complement the work of a Citizens' Convention.

However, securing cross-party cooperation to present a credible challenge to the Conservatives at the next general election may be difficult to achieve. While it might not be necessary to establish an environment of pally personal chemistry as outlined in Duncan Brack's account of the pre-1997 Ashdown–Blair 'Project' (page 202), nevertheless, as he says, establishing trust between key players will be essential.

Below is a menu of potential initiatives that might be acted upon by a new progressive alliance. However, the menu should be read with Duncan Brack's health warning in mind: that the promoters should 'either keep it all as quiet as you can – or be as open as you can'. It is not exhaustive, but it ranges from overt, nationally coordinated campaigns advanced by party leaders to ad hoc covert accommodations at a constituency level. None are exclusive, so some options might work in tandem with others. In the current post-referendum climate, it's also likely that popular demands for centre-left cooperation might come from a wider community dismayed and traumatised by the rise of a right-wing, anti-migrant agenda. Of course, the approach adopted in one constituency may not necessarily be replicated in another. Localised arrangements could be supported in some circumstances, for example by non-partisan candidate endorsements, advocating 'vote swapping', and the promotion of candidates who sign up to a platform of cross-party policy pledges.

National initiatives:

- **'Official' party endorsement for local deals between centre-left parties and candidates**

  If the prospects for cross-party cooperation are perceived to be worthy of formal acknowledgement and approval, then senior party figures could be seen to recognise and either not disapprove of or actively endorse local deals that help to advance the defeat of incumbent Conservative candidates.

- **'Unofficial' cooperation**
  The example of Tatton in 1997 (where the independent Martin Bell took the safe Tory seat when Labour and Liberal Democrat candidates stood down) provides the template of how local 'arrangements' can be made that are neither endorsed nor especially criticised by the party hierarchy. Respecting local decisions while promoting the party's interests at a national level are presented as not incompatible.

- **'Non-aggression' arrangement**
  Whether overt or covert, a firm recognition of where fellow progressive party targets are and to adopt mutual 'non-aggression' to facilitate and allow for this.

- **Vote swapping**
  The practice of VoteSwap was established at the last election to encourage tactical voting by Labour and Green supporters. This apparently generated 21,500 VoteSwaps. Practical support and more public endorsement as voters become more IT savvy may mean that such an initiative could begin to make a difference, especially where parties endorse its use at local level. Clearly the promoters of VoteSwap would, by implication, encourage and support cooperation between all centre-left parties.

- **Candidate endorsement**
  Where a non-party campaign group, such as Common Decency

at the 2015 election, endorses the candidate most likely to defeat the Conservative in each seat. Parties cooperate in acknowledging 'main challenger' candidate recognition on a constituency basis.

- **Promotion of tactical voting**
  Whether through the more sophisticated VoteSwap or a strong message about tactical voting through a team of either non-partisan campaigners and/or cross-party representatives. The last example of this was GROT ('Get Rid of Them' – i.e. the Tories – in 1997, where Labour and Liberal Democrat activists promoted tactical voting in target seats).

- **Pre-election coalition agreement**
  Not recommended, but this would be based on a decision by key parties to commit to a shared agenda if the electoral arithmetic delivers a defeated Conservative Party and hung parliament.

Constituency-level initiatives:

- **Jointly selected candidates**
  In circumstances where centre-left parties at a constituency level commit to supporting the candidate from the party that stands the best chance of unseating the Conservatives, the parties standing down are given the opportunity to be involved and have influence in the final selection of the candidate. This will give parties the opportunity to clarify what the policy priorities are and a procedure for handling policies that are considered significant but where there is not a settled will.

- **Jointly endorsed/recognised candidates**
  Similar to jointly selected candidates (above) but with less formal second-/third-party involvement in selection and policy priority identification.

- **'Independent' candidates on the Tatton model**
  Where centre-left parties cannot agree, where there is no clear challenger, where there is a three-/four-way marginal, or where a strong independent candidate emerges, parties may agree to stand aside to make way for a strong independent who shares key values of the centre-left parties who stand down in her/his favour. (See second bullet under National Initiatives.)

- **Policy pledges**
  Where representatives (whether endorsed or not by their respective parties to perform this function) assist in identifying, say, eight to twelve key policy commitments covering our future relationship with the EU, social and tax justice, public service, environment, economy, fair votes, and other areas, and that could reasonably be endorsed by centre-left but not by Conservative candidates. This could be relatively straightforward where the incumbent Tory was a Brexit supporter. A similar initiative was advanced by Stephen Moss in *The Guardian* (12 August 2015; see page 332). The list of pledges would have to include a commitment to electoral reform, and possibly constitutional reform too. The purpose of this would be to give electors reassurance that the primary challenger to the Tory candidate shares many of the same priorities as other centre-left candidates they may otherwise have supported and promotes a sense that there is a shared interest in working together to effect change.

- **Non-aggression agreement**
  Where nearby constituencies with alternate (e.g. Labour and Liberal Democrat) primary challengers are unable to negotiate an agreement for their third-/fourth-place candidates to stand down. Instead they jointly agree to persuade their local members and supporters – and even their candidate – to help in the nearest winnable seat and to not make any (or much) effort in their own 'no hope' seat, thus leaving the main challenger a relatively free run at the sitting Tory.

- **Candidate endorsement**
  Where a non-party campaign group endorses the candidate most likely to defeat the Conservative in a particular seat. (Local constituency application of the principles of the fifth bullet under National Initiatives, above.)

- **Openly endorsed tactical voting and vote swapping**
  Active use of nationally arranged VoteSwap as referenced above and/or broad promotion of tactical voting and clear signals regarding how anti-Tory voters can most effectively influence the outcome.

The writing's on the wall. With the distinct possibility of the next general election coming before 2020, and with much soul-searching going on in the Labour Party, there's still a need for the centre-left to think strategically, if it can. There's a clear 'do or die' message here. If progressives don't cooperate, the chances are they can look forward to decades in the political wilderness as the Conservatives exert a stranglehold on power. However, there is hope for a better future. Not if the parties resume 'business as usual', reverting to internecine tribal rivalries and enmities, but instead seek purposeful (if limited) common cause to defeat the Conservatives through cooperation, better coordination and mutual accommodation.

Andrew George was Liberal Democrat MP for St Ives from 1997 to 2015. Though perhaps best known for his rebelliousness in Parliament, he led many successful national campaigns, including for housing reform and fair trade. Since 2015, he has forged research into the scope for cooperation among the progressives with support from the Joseph Rowntree Reform Trust. He is also director of the Cornwall Community Land Trust.

COMMUNICATING A NEW POLITICS

Carys Afoko

Ideas and arguments that convince us, or, better yet, change our minds are not necessarily the ones that are supported by the most facts and figures. Communicating political ideas means reaching people on an emotional level, connecting their values to your own.

If we want people to support progressive ideas and to vote for progressive parties, we need to do four things well. We need to tell people a consistent and coherent story about how the world works and how we want to change it. We need to frame issues on our own terms instead of accepting conservative language and imagery. We need to understand the attitudes and opinions of people in Britain today, to strike a chord with their experiences. And we need compelling messengers to bang the drum for progressive ideas, people who are credible and convincing to large numbers of people.

At the moment progressives of all parties fall short on each of these fronts much of the time. But where we most fall short is by making different cases for progressive values. To defeat

Conservative ideas and move the needle of public opinion we need shared stories and frames that pull in the same direction.

This essay looks at what makes for powerful political communications, how conservatives are communicating, and where progressives are getting it right and wrong. It offers some suggestions for what effective, cross-party communications could look like as well as some reflections on the challenges progressives face.

THE KEY TO POWERFUL COMMUNICATIONS

Psychologists, linguists and pollsters who analyse how we form political opinions agree that people rarely weigh up facts and statistics when forming their beliefs. We decide what politicians and parties we support based on an emotional reaction, and an assessment of who best speaks to our personal values. In other words, if you want to convince someone you're right, you are better off telling them a compelling story than reeling off a list of statistics.

Powerful political communications, whether they are progressive or Conservative, have four component parts:

- **They tell a consistent and coherent political story.** Stories are an incredibly powerful way to persuade people. Research suggests our minds process ideas communicated in stories differently. When we hear a good story we become more interested in issues that do not affect us, more likely to change our minds, and less sceptical – we can literally suspend disbelief. A good political story is a coherent explanation of how the world works and how we want things to be. It has heroes, villains, a plot, and a clear appeal to values.

- **They frame the issues in their story deliberately**. In the same way that our minds use stories to understand the world, they also think in frames. Frames are like cognitive shorthand – a quick way for us to understand the world based on existing preconceptions about it. Good framing is about being aware of the associations different words and images have and harnessing them. For example, the phrase 'tax burden' is a deliberate way to frame taxation – a burden is a heavy, unpleasant weight, so framed in this way taxes are something we should want to minimise. The American academic George Lakoff finds that once we hold a certain frame strongly enough, we will reject facts that do not fit with it. He argues that one of the biggest mistakes we can make is to accept the framing and language that our opponents use. If progressives use Conservative frames, for example talking about the 'tax burden', they are reinforcing ideas that contradict their own and ultimately undermine their own arguments.

- **They understand their audience.** To communicate well about politics you must connect to people emotionally, and convince them their values are the same as your own. That means knowing and understanding your audience, the people that you want to reach. Audience insight and message testing have become billion-dollar industries in their own right, and some progressives view polling research with scepticism. But whether you're drafting a manifesto or speaking at a town hall meeting, you need to find some way to put yourself in your audience's shoes, to understand what concerns them and what will resonate with their experience of the world.

- **They have a powerful messenger.** The messenger matters as much as the message. Whether we trust an argument is often determined by the person making it. What would you think if Jeremy Hunt told you the NHS was in good health? Would it be the same as if a respected academic told you? Or a friend who was a junior doctor? Having credible and convincing messengers is as important as developing a strong political story.

To understand these ideas in action, the rest of this chapter focuses on how progressives and Conservatives have communicated about the economy over the last few years. In particular the arguments and frames used to make the case for and against austerity.

HOW CONSERVATIVES ARE COMMUNICATING

Conservatives have been telling the same story about the economy for almost ten years. Their story, which makes the case for austerity, is an almost textbook example of a powerful political story. It offers an explanation of how the economy works now and how Conservatives would like it to work, with clear heroes and villains and powerful imagery. The story says Britain is dangerously indebted, the result of a decade of spending by a careless Labour government. This debt caused the financial crash and it must be paid off by cutting excessive public spending. Britain is a country with a maxed-out credit card, the story goes, where too many people live on welfare and handouts, and hard work is not rewarded. The Conservatives want to build an economy that works for the 'strivers', wealth-creating entrepreneurs and hard-working families who pay their taxes and play by the rules.

Most readers of this book will not agree with this story, but they are probably pretty familiar with it. It has been the consistent refrain of Conservatives and their supporters for years. For almost a decade in print and online, in TV and radio interviews, Conservative voices have made a clear and simple case for austerity economics again and again. And it's been very effective. In 2010 we saw a Conservative-led coalition elected, and in 2015 the Conservatives won a majority. In both elections the economy was one of the top issues that mattered to a majority of voters. And, in 2015, poll after poll found most voters were convinced the Conservatives were the best party to manage the economy.

Their story sets out powerful frames to shape how we think about the economy, in particular how we understand public finances, austerity and welfare. Conservatives deliberately frame the national economy in terms of personal finance – using images like the maxed-out national credit card. This is a particular way of understanding national debt, framed to make us feel anxious and insecure; who doesn't feel anxious at the thought of an unpaid loan? Austerity itself is also framed very cleverly. Conservatives consistently present it as a necessary evil, the medicine that Britain needs. In the Conservative story, austerity is not a choice: it's the only sensible option. Just like medicine, austerity may be unpleasant but it will ultimately be good for us. And in order to paint the welfare state in a negative light, Conservatives frame welfare in terms of drug addiction; to receive support from the state is to be dependent on it. In line with Lakoff's theory, the more these frames have been repeated over the years, the more people have believed in the need for austerity, regardless of whether economic statistics suggest it is working.

Part of the reason for the success of the Conservative story about the economy is it connected with how British people were feeling after the economic crash. David Cameron and George Osborne's call for prudence and penance resonated with the public mood after 2008, which was pessimistic. The Conservative focus on welfare is also deliberate: British attitudes to welfare claimants have been steadily hardening over the last few decades. Twenty years ago, only a quarter of people responding to the British Social Attitudes survey agreed 'if benefits were less generous, people would stand on their own two feet'. Now over half the country think that statement is true. However, not all Conservative frames are connecting with their audience. Most British people think spending cuts are necessary, but do not buy into Conservative beliefs that we should permanently shrink the state. In fact, despite years of attacks on 'big government', the last British Social Attitudes survey found that the number of people willing to see an increase in their taxes to improve public service had risen slightly since 2010. Public satisfaction with the NHS remains high at 65 per cent; it has not really changed since 2009. British people have accepted the Conservative story about the economy, but not all Conservative ideas.

Conservatives have had a whole host of messengers telling their story about the economy. Coalition ministers from the Conservatives and Lib Dems made the case for austerity with incredible message discipline for five years. The result? Huge sections of the media accepted Conservative arguments for austerity (like the idea Britain has 'no money') as orthodoxy, meaning they effectively became messengers for Conservative ideas and frames. However, while the Conservatives may have had more messengers than progressives, that doesn't mean they are better messengers. When I conducted research into how journalists were covering the economy before the last election, many said the Conservatives' narrative was the dominant one because so few people articulated a clear alternative. Some media outlets and commentators are champions of Conservative ideas, but many others are just repeating the dominant story about the economy. And the two main messengers for austerity, David Cameron and George Osborne, are neither compelling nor fully credible advocates for it. Both are career politicians from wealthy families, unlikely to be the most trusted voices on the economy for most people in Britain.

HOW PROGRESSIVES ARE COMMUNICATING

The biggest problem with progressive communications about the economy is the absence of a single coherent story in the wake of the 2008 crash. Instead, the progressive community has told a range of stories about the economy, often with completely different starting points and conclusions. The result? Faced with the task of telling the progressive counterpart to the austerity story, many of us who consider ourselves progressives struggle. Agreeing on a common story about the economy across the progressive community may sound like a tall order, but it doesn't need to be. We don't need to tell identical stories, we just need to be pulling in the same direction. For example, a number of Conservative think tanks have criticised the government for not making deep enough spending cuts; meanwhile progressive parties have not agreed about whether cuts to public spending need to be made at all. The impact of Conservative arguments is greater because they are reinforcing the same story. If the broad strokes of our argument are the same we will be able to have more impact.

There have been three types of progressive story told about

the economy in the last few years. The first argues for some austerity measures but says the Conservative Party cannot be trusted to implement them fairly. For example: the Lib Dems under Nick Clegg, Labour under Ed Miliband's leadership. These stories make the mistake of accepting Conservative frames about the economy. By accepting the need for spending cuts we are communicating Conservative messages. A great example of this was the Labour slogan 'too far too fast' – it completely accepted the Conservative story about the economy as true. The second set of stories have denied the need for any cuts to public spending, instead calling for tax rises on the wealthy or a Keynesian stimulus of the economy (e.g. UK Uncut, most British trade unions, a number of Keynesian economists). These stories challenge arguments for austerity head-on, but in their own way by focusing mainly on why austerity is a bad idea, they frame debates about economic policy on Conservative terms. A third set of progressive stories argue the economic crash was not caused by a debt crisis but the failure to regulate the banking system and a sign of systemic problems in our economy like economic inequality or environmental unsustainability. These stories, currently told by the Green Party and the SNP, form the basis for alternative stories about the economy, but lack the coherence and striking imagery of their opponents' story at present. Which of these three types of story is best? At the moment, none of them. Each has its own strengths and weaknesses, but none currently offers a coherent world view to counterbalance the view of Conservatives. Many of the current stories we are telling could be fleshed out into a coherent alternative, but only if enough progressives start telling it.

There are two things we need to bear in mind about our audience when developing a new story about the economy. The first is that the best way to campaign against individual austerity measures is unlikely to be the best way to campaign against austerity as a whole. As long as Conservatives frame austerity as medicine, talking about how painful austerity is ultimately reinforces their economic frame. This is hard, because it can be effective in the short term to talk about how specific public sector cuts are hurting people in Britain, but ultimately as long as we focus our energies against specific cuts we are unable to make a general case against cuts. And we are not even attacking Conservatives who make it clear that austerity will be hard on people. The second is a much bigger challenge. As things stand, the majority (almost two-thirds) of people in Britain believe that spending cuts are necessary. Not only that, but this number has remained fairly constant for the last five years – even as perceptions of the economy and the government in power have changed. This viewpoint is incredibly resilient and well entrenched. We cannot tell a progressive story about the economy that ignores the fact that most people believe the case for austerity has been made, if we want it to appeal to the majority of people in Britain.

The good news is that, while we have had limited success developing a story about the economy, we have developed some frames that have resonated with British people. Progressive attacks on bankers and the financial sector's excess tend to connect well with people in the UK who still feel angry about the financial crisis. Ed Miliband's 'cost of living crisis' did not offer a coherent account of how progressives would fix the economy, but it did create an alternative way to reframe the debate away from paying off the public debt. And while it didn't emerge as a key message from the 2015 Autumn Statement, the Labour accusation that Conservatives had not only sold the family silver but were putting 'the family furniture, fixtures and fittings' up for sale was a smartly framed attack on a government who are usually just attacked for being 'nasty'.

Progressives have also seen the emergence of a set of compelling and credible messengers. The SNP's success at the 2015 election is testament to how powerful a story can be when it has the right messenger and a clear audience. The SNP's messages on the economy were not new, but their anti-Westminster rhetoric had more credibility with people in Scotland because they were not seen as a Westminster party. At a time when career politicians are not often trusted or liked, the voices of candidates like Mhairi Black were so compelling they helped to create an SNP landslide. In 2020, the SNP will struggle to tell this outsider story, as will most progressive parties, but their victory at the last election is a reminder that powerful progressive voices can challenge the pro-austerity narrative.

WHAT NEXT?

The challenges for progressives to collaborate and tell a compelling and true story about the economy are real. There are several progressive parties in Britain, all of which need to tell voters a story that will help them win elections, and often the strongest communications incentive is to attack one another.

But we also know that collaboration is possible. In 2012, the Welfare Reform Act introduced a spare room subsidy for people in social housing. Progressive politicians and campaigners successfully reframed this policy as the 'Bedroom Tax' as well as making it one of the least popular welfare reforms of the last government. At the height of the debate, government press officers were calling the

BBC, outraged that it had adopted the name 'Bedroom Tax', and frustrated that this framing meant they might be losing the debate.

More recently, the government was forced to back down on its plan to cut tax credits for working families after a concerted and effective campaign from progressives. This is a powerful example of how progressives can get it right: politicians from different parties, campaign groups and experts, worked together using the same framing and making an appeal that resonated with most people in Britain.

People in Britain voted the Conservatives into power in 2015, but they are not fully committed to Conservative ideology. When we tell the same story, and when we pull in the same direction, we have a chance to win.

Carys Afoko is director of communications at the consumer group SumOfUs. She was head of communications at the New Economics Foundation where she co-authored the research paper 'Framing the Economy: The Austerity Story'. She is a former adviser to Lisa Nandy and a member of the Labour Party.

FURTHER READING

Afoko, Carys and Dan Vockins, *Framing the Economy: The Austerity Story*, New Economics Foundation paper, September 2013.

Lakoff, George, *Don't think of an Elephant: Know Your Values and Frame the Debate*, White River Junction, VT: Chelsea Green Publishing Company, 2004.

Luntz, Frank, *Words That Work: It's Not What You Say, It's What People Hear*, New York: MJF Books, 2007.

Polletta, Francesca, *It Was Like a Fever: Storytelling in Protest and Politics*, Chicago: University of Chicago Press, 2006.

Sachs, Jonah, *Winning the Story Wars: Why Those Who Tell (and Live) the Best Stories Will Rule the Future*, Boston, MA: Harvard Business Review Press, 2012.

Westen, Drew, *The Political Brain*, New York: PublicAffairs, 2007.

Holmes, T., E. Blackmore, R. Hawkins and T. Wakeford, *The Common Cause Handbook*, (London: Public Interest Research Centre).

NatCen, *2015 British Social Attitudes Survey.*

CONCLUSION: THIS IS THE START OF SOMETHING BIG!

By Lisa Nandy, Caroline Lucas & Chris Bowers

We began this book by saying we're starting the process of the progressives working together, not because we have to but because we want to. We stress this again now – we profoundly believe political pluralism delivers better answers. That's why the theme running through this book is an optimistic one: a progressive alliance isn't a second-best option – it's a recognition that a negotiated future, drawing on the best of progressive political traditions, is more likely to point us to better results.

We believe there is an appetite for progressive politics. This is demonstrated by the number of people who have found alternative means of expression in recent years, whether through campaigning, community action, trade unions or other voices. The speed with which initiatives such as The Alternative in Denmark and Podemos in Spain have gained traction in their political systems suggests a longing for something different, and there are signs of this longing in initiatives closer to home, from the Make Poverty History campaign to the London Citizens, from the East Devon Alliance to the 'flatpack' democracy of Frome Town Council in Somerset. Whatever you think of these initiatives, the fact that significant numbers of people have been willing to vote for them confirms a willingness to engage in the political process, even where there is deep discontent with the traditional parties.

Many of those who choose to support these initiatives share a bafflement that if people can cooperate and seek common ground in domestic, social and professional situations to make the best decisions, then why shouldn't the same thing happen when we're making the decisions that will shape the future of our locality or country? They believe that politics has to be about more than the political classes 'doing' politics to the rest of the country – it's about all of us having a say in the decisions that affect us, not just politicians, but civil society groups and individuals, as part of the wider political environment. Some of these experiments deliver and others don't. But it tells us that if the progressives are to inspire the public, we need to offer an answer to the disenchantment that lies behind many of these initiatives, something more than just a tactical strategy to defeat the Conservatives.

A BASIC UNITY OF PURPOSE

What form this answer will take, how far cooperation among progressives will go in advance of the 2020 election, and whether it will involve a joint vision or programme for government, are still very much open to question. The range of possibilities extends from agreeing to make a common case to the electorate on areas where we agree to developing a progressive programme in the run-up to the election. Whatever approach is taken, one thing is certain: if we are asking for cooperation across the progressive spectrum, there has to be a basic unity of purpose across the progressive parties.

Such a unity of purpose would clearly have to focus on the areas where the parties can find common ground, the obvious ones being a commitment to a fairer, more sustainable economic policy that incorporates investment in affordable housing; the promotion of green energy and job creation; an approach to public services driven by public interest rather than profit; environmental priorities being given a central role in all government policy; and constitutional reform that at the very least ensures that the will of the public is genuinely represented, both locally and nationally.

The idea of an alliance that respects the identities and convictions of the progressive parties was explored in some detail by Stephen Moss in an article, 'Could you build a new party of the left?', published in *The Guardian* on 12 August 2015. As the headline suggests, Moss started out by considering the option of a new party, but came to the conclusion that the differences among progressives were too great to cram them into one unit of the kind we understand political parties to be. Instead, he proposed an alliance he called 'Platform'. This would be a grouping of four partners (he broke Labour down into two, to make for Socialist Labour, Social Democrats, Liberal Democrats and Greens) who first agree a set of common values, then settle on some basic policies they can all sign up to, and finally find the likeliest candidate to win in a given parliamentary seat; the candidate would then be either unopposed by the others or the others would just offer 'paper candidates'.

Moss even commissioned a design company to experiment with structures and draw up some provisional artwork that allowed each party to feature under the 'Platform' name, thus 'Socialist Platform', 'Green Platform', 'Liberal Platform' etc, all of them with their own colour. As a leading figure in this design company said, the idea of the 'Platform' alliance would allow for 'embracing the fragmentation rather than trying to fix it or pretending it doesn't exist … let's just support it and celebrate it and make it better'.

Moss's 'Platform' proposal is not the only option for a framework for cooperation. Another might be for the progressives to establish a 'progressive kite mark' to which candidates at the 2020 election (and even earlier elections) could sign up to demonstrate to their electorate a commitment to a core set of priorities, which would include red-line issues for all parties involved. This kind of pre-election identification could also help to prepare the ground for post-election cooperation without any formal agreement needing to happen before the election. And there are, no doubt, other options for cooperation.

WARNINGS FOR THE POLITICAL CLASSES

In our efforts to explore the scope for cooperation as an opportunity for the progressives, we are very mindful of the context. A bitterly fought EU referendum campaign has revealed the depths of people's anger and disillusion with both politics and politicians. Too often, when people look at politics they see self-interest and division, too much concern about issues that interest politicians and too little concern about issues that affect *them*. We know that politics can be better than this, and that most politicians enter politics to try to make a difference. By cooperating with others in common cause, we can show the public that we are more interested in their concerns than our own, win back confidence and change this country for the better.

The 2016 EU referendum was the latest and most important example of where the progressives have been failing – both by underestimating the extent of the anger over immigration and globalisation among their traditional supporters, and by focusing on arguments about what we stood to lose rather than appealing to a sense of ambition about what we stood to gain. There was a logic to this approach, but it simply didn't work for the millions of people whose denial of basic rights, decent housing, access to healthcare, secure jobs, wages and working conditions left them feeling they had nothing to lose and little to gain. The inability of many people to imagine politicians ever taking real action to ensure not only decent housing and public services, but decent opportunities too, along with the visible erosion of certainties resulting from the loss of traditional industries, cheap imports and the exploitation of migrant labour, led to a sense of anger and powerlessness that was all too easily capitalised on by the Leave campaign. Our justifiable belief in the need for transnational cooperation blinded some of us to the depth of this disenchantment with politics and systems of government.

We don't underestimate the difficulties in getting the progressives in British politics to work together. We cannot simply wipe out years of resentments dating from some keenly fought – and at times hostile – election campaigns and try to sweep residual tensions under the carpet. However, with the rules of British politics being rewritten in the aftermath of the Brexit vote, cooperation is badly needed, along with a sense that we are both listening to the public, and talking to them – and not just to each other. Perhaps one of the topics where the progressives most urgently need to end their unease is patriotism. Many people who voted to leave the EU did so on grounds of national pride. This follows a dramatic rise in the numbers of people in England who identify as English. Many among the progressives have been too slow to understand people's desire to celebrate and find rootedness in their own national identities, to preserve the best of what they have, and to gain much more control over the things that affect their lives. There is an important debate to be had about whether the UK – if it survives – might move towards a federal structure in which our political arrangements should mirror these loyalties. But, regardless of where this debate leads, there is clearly a pressing need for progressives to understand, respect and celebrate identity, and help make the case for a patriotism that is open, tolerant, outward-looking and draws on our best traditions of social justice.

A NEW POLITICAL CULTURE

In our everyday work, we meet numerous people who are desperate for something better from their government. Many are confronted daily with poverty, suffering, injustice, environmental degradation and fundamental disrespect for human dignity, and find themselves wondering how the fifth richest economy in the world can have lost its compassion and moral compass, and how the government can appear so indifferent to putting it right.

For this and other reasons, it is easy to believe there is a significant latent appetite for a compassionate government among people who do not identify as Labour, Liberal Democrat, Green, nationalist, or anything else. Many people who care about their country are not intrinsically party political at all, and are baffled by why the progressives in British politics don't work together more, why they seem to want to be defined more by what divides them than what unites them. Set against this longing for a government they can feel confident in – or even inspired by – it seems negligent to allow personal and political enmities to hinder cooperation. We have a responsibility to offer the electorate a caring but competent alternative to the Conservatives, to compromise in order to achieve it, and to unite around the things we have in common, rather than divide over our differences.

What motivated us to compile this set of essays is not simply the fact that a glance at modern-day British political reality suggests that, if the progressives don't work together, the next two decades are likely to be Conservative ones. It is also a sense that there has to be something better, and we have begun the process of articulating what it is. This could be the start of something big!

At one level, it's already happening. The EU referendum brought all sorts of people together across political divides, on both sides of the argument, in recognition of the fact that only by working together could they hope to achieve their aims. So, on an issue-by-issue basis, it's nothing new.

But we come back to our statement made at the beginning of this book: it won't be easy. We can rail against tribalism, but Duncan Brack's point, that tribalism among progressive parties can also be seen as loyalty to the cause to which one has given much time and energy to (page 202), is well made. Our desire to see greater cooperation among progressives should not gloss over the fact that there are conflicting loyalties and mutual suspicions among people of different parties who may share largely similar mindsets about what the world needs from its leaders. These have to be understood and dealt with if we are to avoid allowing simmering resentments to undermine the progressive project.

It has been done in much harder circumstances. In South Africa and Northern Ireland, many people put their differences aside in the name of peace, despite having lost friends and family in civilian atrocities, to create a new political culture. It would be wrong for us to imply that the suffering caused by the decades of apartheid and Protestant/Catholic Troubles is on the same level as the frustrations among those wanting a more compassionate Britain. But for that very reason, if people can show forgiveness for past atrocities that have devastated families and communities, surely the progressives can identify common ground and work for a common purpose, especially when a fundamentally shared mindset unites them?

We all enter politics out of a sense of trying to make the world a better place. We all have our ideas about how to do this, and they do sometimes differ from the ideas of people with fundamentally similar views. But we choose politics as the vehicle through which to make our contribution because we are more powerful as a group than we are on our own. The practical reality in British politics as we approach the 2020 election is such that we need to rethink our sense of who our group is. And if we can do that, then an awful lot becomes possible.

We may not have much time. With every Conservative government, the distance that has to be travelled by the progressives becomes greater: our public services become more run down, young people lose hope, and the environmental crisis deepens. It doesn't have to be like this. The progressives have an unprecedented opportunity to review our politics. We need to seize it!

ALSO AVAILABLE FROM BITEBACK PUBLISHING

144PP HARDBACK, £10

The best jobs in Britain today are overwhelmingly done by the children of the wealthy. Meanwhile, it is increasingly difficult for bright but poor kids to transcend their circumstances.

Hitherto, Labour and Conservative politicians alike have sought to deal with the problem by promoting the idea of 'equality of opportunity'. In politics, social mobility is the only game in town, and old socialist arguments emphasising economic equality are about as fashionable today as mullets and shell suits. Yet genuine equality of opportunity is impossible alongside levels of inequality last seen during the 1930s. In a grossly unequal society, the privileges of the parents unfailingly become the privileges of the children.

A vague commitment from our politicians to build a 'meritocracy' is not enough. Nor is it desirable: a perfectly stratified meritocracy, in which everyone knew their station based on 'merit', would be a deeply unpleasant place to live. Any genuine attempt to improve social mobility must start by reducing the gap between rich and poor.

— AVAILABLE FROM ALL GOOD BOOKSHOPS —

WWW.BITEBACKPUBLISHING.COM

ALSO AVAILABLE FROM BITEBACK PUBLISHING

368PP HARDBACK, £17.99

There is a lie at the heart of global capitalism. Politicians, financiers and global bureaucrats claim to believe in free competitive markets, but have constructed the most unfree market system ever. It is corrupt because income is channelled to the owners of property – financial, physical and intellectual – at the expense of society.

This book reveals how global capitalism is rigged in favour of rentiers to the detriment of all of us, especially the precariat. A plutocracy and elite enriches itself, not through production of goods and services, but through ownership of assets, including intellectual property, aided by subsidies, tax breaks, debt mechanisms, revolving doors between politics and business, and the privatisation of public services.

The Corruption of Capitalism argues that rentier capitalism is fostering revolt, and concludes by outlining a new income distribution system that would achieve the extinction of the rentier while promoting sustainable growth.

— AVAILABLE FROM ALL GOOD BOOKSHOPS —

WWW.BITEBACKPUBLISHING.COM

ALSO AVAILABLE FROM BITEBACK PUBLISHING

336PP PAPERBACK, £14.99

HAVE YOU EVER WONDERED…

… how people feel about sleeping with the political enemy?

… whether gambling markets are best at predicting political outcomes?

… who Santa Claus would vote for?

Then look no further. *More Sex, Lies and the Ballot Box* brings us another collection of concise chapters penned by leading political experts and delving into the fascinating field of electoral politics. Following on from the success of its bestselling predecessor, this illuminating book shines a light on how we vote in Britain and around the world.

You'll learn about the factors informing voter habits – from class, race and gender to the internet and the weather. You'll also learn which political party has the most sexually satisfied supporters.

Forget mind-numbing numbers and difficult demographics. This sharp and frequently hilarious volume is fizzing with accessible facts and figures that are more than just conversation starters – they're unexpected insights into the human condition.

— AVAILABLE FROM ALL GOOD BOOKSHOPS —

WWW.BITEBACKPUBLISHING.COM